LONDON'S BEST-KEPT SECRETS

Edited by David Hampshire

Survival Books • Bath • England

First published 2015

Survival Books Limited
Office 169, 3 Edgar Buildings
George Street, Bath BA1 2FJ, United Kingdom
+44 (0)1225-462135, info@survivalbooks.net
www.survivalbooks.net and www.londons-secrets.com

British Library Cataloguing in Publication Data
A CIP record for this book is available
from the British Library.

ISBN: 978-1-909282-74-2

Printed in China

Acknowledgements

We would like to thank all those who helped with research and provided information for this book, unfortunately too many to list here. Special thanks are due to Robbi Atilgan for additional editing; Peter Read for final editing and proof-reading; David Woodworth for final proof checking; John Marshall for DTP, photo selection and cover design; Jim Watson for the maps; and the editor's partner Alexandra for the continuous supply of tea, coffee and biscuits.

Last, but not least, a special thank you to the many photographers – the unsung heroes – whose beautiful images add colour and bring London to life.

Disabled Access

Many historic public and private buildings don't provide wheelchair access, or provide wheelchair access to the ground floor only. Wheelchairs are provided at some venues, although users may need assistance. Most museums, galleries and public buildings have a WC, although it may not be wheelchair accessible. Contact venues directly if you have specific requirements. The Disabled Go website (disabledgo.com) provides more in-depth access information for some destinations

Reader's Guide

The notes below refer to the general information provided for each entry:

♦ **Address:** The contact details include the telephone number and website address, where applicable. You can enter the postcode to display a map of the location on Google and other map websites (if you're driving you can enter the postcode into your satnav).

♦ **Opening hours:** These can change at short notice, therefore you should confirm by telephone or check the website before travelling, particularly over Christmas/New Year and on bank holidays, when many venues are closed. Note that the last entry to museums and galleries is usually at least 30 minutes before the closing time.

♦ **Cost:** Prices are liable to change and are intended only as a guide. Many venues – such as museums and galleries – offer free entry. Buildings owned or managed by the National Trust or English Heritage offer free entry to members, and some other places offer discounts to members of these organisations. Most, but by no means all, venues offer concessions for retirees, students and the unemployed (etc.), and many also offer family tickets.

♦ **Transport:** The nearest tube or rail station is listed, although in some cases it may involve a lengthy walk. You can also travel to most venues by bus and to some by river ferry. Venues outside central London are usually best reached by car, although parking can be difficult or impossible in some areas. Most venues don't provide parking, particularly in central London, and even parking nearby can be a problem (and very expensive). If you need to travel by car, check the parking facilities in advance.

Contents

3. EAST LONDON   109

4. NORTH LONDON   143

5. WEST LONDON   195

6. SOUTHWEST LONDON   227

London's Secrets:
PEACEFUL PLACES

ISBN: 978-1-907339-45-5, 256 pages, hardback, £11.95

David Hampshire

London is one of the world's most exciting cities, but it's also one of the noisiest; a bustling, chaotic, frenetic, over-crowded, manic metropolis of over 8 million people, where it can be difficult to find somewhere to grab a little peace and quiet. Nevertheless, if you know where to look London has a wealth of peaceful places: places to relax, chill out, contemplate, meditate, sit, reflect, browse, read, chat, nap, walk, think, study or even work (if you must) - where the city's volume is muted or even switched off completely.

LONDON FOR FOODIES, GOURMETS & GLUTTONS

ISBN: 978-1-908282-76-6, 288 pages, hardback, £11.95

David Hampshire & Graeme Chesters

London for Foodies, Gourmets & Gluttons is much more than simply a directory of cafés, markets, restaurants and food shops. It features many of the city's best artisan producers and purveyors, plus a wealth of classes where you can learn how to prepare and cook food like the experts, appreciate fine wines and brew coffee like a barista. And when you're too tired to cook or just want to treat yourself, we'll show you great places where you can enjoy everything from tea and cake to a tasty street snack; a pie and a pint to a glass of wine and tapas; and a quick working lunch to a full-blown gastronomic extravaganza.

see www.londons-secrets.com

Introduction

London is one of the world's leading tourist destinations, with a wealth of world-class attractions – more than any other city in the world – which draw millions of visitors a year, including amazing museums and galleries, beautiful parks and gardens, glorious churches and cathedrals, stunning palaces and grand houses, and much, much more. These are covered in numerous excellent tourist guides and need no introduction here. What aren't so well known are London's numerous smaller – but no less interesting – attractions, most of which are largely neglected by visitors and Londoners alike.

What our *London's Secrets* series of books does is take you off the beaten path – side-stepping the city's tourist-clogged major sights – to seek out its lesser-known, more off-beat and mysterious side. *London's Best-Kept Secrets* brings together the very best attractions – the 'greatest hits' – that we have discovered over the last five years. It includes some of the city's loveliest hidden gardens and parks, absorbing and poignant small museums, great art and architecture, beautiful ancient buildings, magnificent Victorian cemeteries, historic pubs, fascinating markets and much more.

Entries range from the enchanting Hill Garden to the magical canals of Little Venice, from the home of Britain's greatest naturalist to Dennis Severs' haunting home, from the moving Foundling Museum to the birthplace of Big Ben (and the Liberty Bell), the splendour of some of Wren's greatest churches to a lovely house designed by William Morris, and from the spectacular treasures of Syon House to atmospheric Kensal Green cemetery.

London's Best-Kept Secrets isn't intended as a walking guide, although many of the places covered are close to one another, particularly in central London and the City, where you can easily stroll between them, while some are situated in the suburbs. However, most are close to public transport links and relatively easy to get to. What's more the vast majority are free, so there's no excuse for not getting out there and exploring.

With a copy of *London's Best-Kept Secrets* to hand to inspire you, you need never be bored of London (or life). We hope you enjoy discovering the city's hidden secrets as much as we did.

David Hampshire

May 2015

CHAPTER 1

CENTRAL LONDON

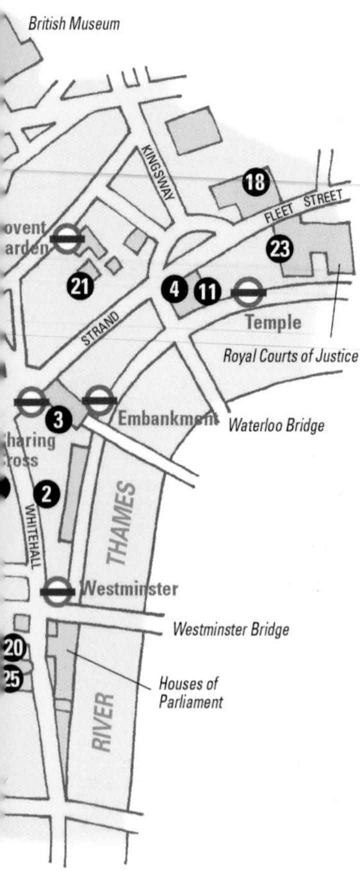

British Museum

KINGSWAY

FLEET STREET

Covent Garden

STRAND

Temple

Royal Courts of Justice

Embankment Waterloo Bridge

Charing Cross

WHITEHALL

THAMES

Westminster

Westminster Bridge

Houses of Parliament

RIVER

Address: **149 Piccadilly, Hyde Park Cnr, W1J 7NT (020-7499 5676, www. english-heritage.org.uk/daysout/properties/apsley-house).**

Opening hours: **Apr-Oct, Wed-Sun and bank holidays, 11am to 5pm. See website for 'winter' opening times.**

Cost: **£8.30 adults, £7.50 concessions, £5 children (5-15), £21.60 family (2 adults, 3 children). English Heritage members free.**

Transport: **Hyde Park Cnr tube.**

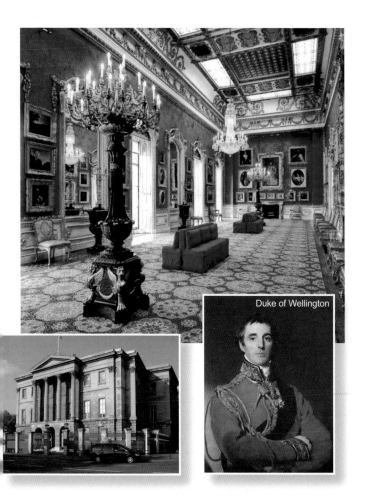

Duke of Wellington

APSLEY HOUSE

This Grade I listed building and residence of the Dukes of Wellington stands alone at Hyde Park Corner, on the southeast corner of Hyde Park. It's run by English Heritage as a museum and art gallery, although the current Duke of Wellington still uses part of the building as his London home.

Apsley House is sometimes known as Number One, London, as it was the first house seen by visitors after passing through the toll gates at Knightsbridge. Another nickname is the Wellington Museum. The house was originally built in red brick by Robert Adam (an influential Scottish neoclassical architect) between 1771 and 1778 for Lord Apsley, the Lord Chancellor. Some of Adam's interiors survive. It was acquired by the Duke of Wellington in 1817, who faced the house's brick walls with Bath stone, added the Corinthian portico and enlarged the property.

The interior has changed little since it was the home of the Iron Duke in the years following his victory over Napoleon at Waterloo. Many of the rooms were redesigned to reflect his growing status and influence (he was also a politician, becoming Prime Minister in 1828), and were a perfect setting for entertaining, including hosting an annual Waterloo Banquet to commemorate the famous victory, which continues to this day.

The 7th Duke gave the house and most of its contents to the nation in 1947, but the Duke retains the right to occupy just over half the property. The family's apartments are on the north side of the house, mainly on the second floor. The rest of the building is open to the public – the dazzling interiors are a magnificent example of Regency style – and there's a splendid collection of paintings and artworks that's one of the most intriguing in London and not nearly as well known as it should be.

There are over 200 paintings (some of them part of the Spanish Royal collection, which came into the Duke's possession after the Battle of Vitoria in 1813 – they'd been plundered from Spanish royal palaces by Napoleon Bonaparte's brother Joseph), including works by Brueghel the Elder, Goya, Landseer, Murillo, Rubens, Van Dyck and Velasquez.

On show are also the many gifts that the first Duke received from European rulers in gratitude for his military successes, including candelabras, porcelain, silver and gilt items, trophies, uniforms and weapons. A colossal (3.45m-high) nude marble statue of Napoleon by Canova stands in pride of place on the stairwell in the middle of the house.

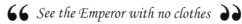

❝ *See the Emperor with no clothes* ❞

BANQUETING HOUSE

This is one of the hidden delights of Westminster, often overlooked by the many visitors who throng the streets around Whitehall. It's the only remaining part of the Palace of Whitehall, which was the main residence of English monarchs in London from 1530 until 1698, when all except Inigo Jones's 1622 Banqueting House was destroyed by fire. Before the fire, the palace had grown to become the largest in Europe, larger even than the Vatican and Versailles.

The Banqueting House is significant in the history of English architecture, being the first building to be built in the neo-classical style that would transform the country. It was designed by Jones in a style influenced by Palladio, an Italian Renaissance architect, himself influenced by Greek and Roman architecture. (Inigo Jones was a revolutionary architect and designer whose work shook up English building design in the early 17th century.)

The Banqueting House was controversially refaced with Portland stone in the 19th century, although the details of the original façade were carefully preserved. Today, the building is Grade I listed and cared for by the independent charity, Historic Royal Palaces. It's spread over three floors and the term 'Banqueting House' is something of a misnomer, as it's a hall that was used not just for banquets but also for ceremonies, royal receptions and the performance of masques (a cross between a ball, an amateur dramatic production, a play and a fancy dress party, which was an entertainment as well as a way of expressing ideas about royal authority, responsibility and privileges).

The building's major attraction is its richly-painted ceiling, a masterpiece by the Antwerp-based artist and diplomat Peter Paul Rubens, the only surviving in-situ ceiling painted by him. It was commissioned by Charles I and celebrates the benefits of wise rule and his father's flawed idea of the Divine Right of Kings. Therefore it's rather ironic that Charles I, as a result of his unwise rule, was beheaded on a scaffold erected outside the hall in 1649, after losing the Civil War (1642-49); an upstairs window was removed to allow Charles I to step straight out onto the scaffold. It's fortunate that the ceiling survived the short period of Puritan rule that followed: Cromwell took over the building as his hall of audience in 1654, but he died in 1658 and the monarchy was restored in 1660.

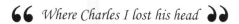

❝ *Where Charles I lost his head* **❞**

Address: 36 Craven St, WC2N 5NF (020-7925 1405, www. benjaminfranklinhouse.org).

Opening hours: The 'Historical Experience' show can be seen Wed-Sun at noon, 1pm, 2pm, 3.15pm and 4.15pm. There are also guided 'architectural tours' tours on Mon at the same times.

Cost: Historical experience: £7 adults, £5 seniors and students, under 16s free. Architectural tour: £3.50 adults, under 16s free.

Transport: Charing Cross tube/rail or Embankment tube.

Benjamin Franklin

BENJAMIN FRANKLIN HOUSE

While sympathetic to the view that visiting a museum dedicated to a man known for discoveries about electricity and for being a politician might be less than thrilling, we urge you to try this intriguing, well-conceived exhibit. The Grade I listed, architecturally-important house was built around 1730 and retains many original features, including the central staircase, lathing, panelling, stoves, windows, beams and more.

It's the world's only remaining home of Benjamin Franklin, which opened to the public on 17th January 2006 on the anniversary of his 300th birthday. Franklin (1706-1790) was born in Boston, Massachusetts to an American mother and a British father. He lived and worked in this house for 16 years, on the eve of the American Revolution, and it has a special place in Anglo-American history, being the first de facto US embassy.

Benjamin Franklin's work as a philosopher, printer and more contributed to the Age of Enlightenment, and his scientific work meant that he came to be regarded as the father of electricity. As if this wasn't enough for one person, he was also a key founder of the United States, the only statesman to sign all four documents that created the new nation.

This is an inventive museum, which offers a good flavour of Franklin's many achievements and of the times in which he lived. The 'Student Science Centre' allows the recreation of experiments from his time in London, while the 'Scholarship Centre' on the top floor is a centre for the study of the many subjects that Franklin was involved with.

The Historical Experience takes a 'museum as theatre' approach, an innovative, entertaining way of presenting history. You're 'accompanied' by an actress who plays Polly Hewson, Franklin's landlady's daughter, who became like a daughter to him. The live performance, along with lighting, sound and visual projections, brings the whole 18th-century experience to life.

To end on a grisly note, the remains of four adults and six children were found at the property when it was being restored. Franklin's landlady's daughter Polly married a surgeon, who ran an anatomy school here. There's a small exhibit in the basement about medical history, which displays some of the 'Craven Street bones'.

66 *An American genius in London* **99**

- 20 -

COURTAULD GALLERY

Although somewhat overshadowed by London's national galleries, The Courtauld Gallery contains a gem of an art collection, situated at the heart of The Courtauld Institute of Art, one of the world's leading centres for the study of art history and conservation. It's housed in Somerset House – designed by William Chambers (1723-1796) – a spectacular 18th-century building, once home to the Royal Academy of Art (1768). During summer months, 55 fountains dance in the courtyard, while in winter you can skate on London's favourite ice rink.

The gallery's celebrated collection of paintings ranges from the early Renaissance to modernist works of the 20th century, with a splendid array of Gothic and medieval paintings, plus Renaissance masterpieces by artists such as Cranach and Brueghel. Baroque highlights include a comprehensive display of iconic paintings by Rubens.

The art collection was begun by Samuel Courtauld (1876-1947), who donated an extensive collection of mainly French Impressionist and post-Impressionist paintings in 1932, enhanced by further gifts in the '30s and a bequest in 1948. In total, the gallery owns some 530 paintings and over 26,000 drawings and prints. The collection includes such masterworks as Manet's *A Bar at the Folies-Bergére* and a version of his *Déjeuner sur l'Herbe*; Renoir's *La Loge*; landscapes by Claude Monet and Camille Pissarro; a ballet scene by Edgar Degas and major works by Cézanne. Other paintings include van Gogh's *Self-Portrait with Bandaged Ear* (see left) and *Peach Blossoms in the Crau*; Gauguin's *Nevermore* and *Te Rerioa*; as well as important works by Seurat, Henri 'Douanier' Rousseau and Toulouse-Lautrec.

The collection extends into the 20th century with works by Modigliani, Matisse, Kandinsky and the Bloomsbury group, alongside masterpieces of German Expressionism and modern British art. The gallery also contains an outstanding collection of drawings and prints, and fine sculpture and decorative arts from Europe and the Middle East. Italian Renaissance wedding chests are displayed alongside marble reliefs and an outstanding collection of Renaissance *maiolica* (tin-glazed earthenware).

The Courtauld also houses an extensive collection of Iznik and Spanish lustreware ceramics, and superb items of Islamic metalwork, including pieces by the master craftsman Mahmud the Kurd. Furthermore, there's a priceless sculpture collection, with works by Henri Matisse, Auguste Rodin, César, Frank Dobson, Henry Moore, Barbara Hepworth, Antony Caro and Philip King.

❝ *A breathtaking art collection* ❞

FLEMING COLLECTION

The Fleming Collection is the finest assembly of Scottish art in private hands and the only dedicated museum granting public access to Scottish art all year round. The Collection was begun in 1968 by the Scottish banking firm Robert Fleming & Co, founded in Dundee. In 1968 the bank moved to a new building in Crosby Square in the City of London and it was decided to create a collection for the purpose of decorating the space.

This task was given to one of the bank's directors, David Donald. The only guideline was that the paintings should be by Scottish artists or Scottish scenes by any artists, to emphasise the bank's proud Scottish origins. Scottish art was largely unknown outside of Scotland until the '80s, making prices relatively low, enabling a large collection to be amassed in a short period.

The Collection comprises over 750 oils and watercolours from 1770 to the present day, including works by Raeburn, Ramsay, Wilkie, and the iconic paintings of the Highland Clearances, *The Last of the Clan* by Thomas Faed and *Lochaber No More* by John Watson Nicol. It's particularly noted for its works by William McTaggart, the Glasgow Boys, D.

> In March 2000, Flemings bank was sold to Chase Manhattan Bank, New York. To avoid the Collection being lost, the Fleming family funded a new charitable foundation, The Fleming-Wyfold Foundation, to purchase the Collection before the sale.

Y. Cameron, Anne Redpath and a superb group of paintings by the Colourists. It remains a living and growing collection through further acquisitions.

The Collection was moved to its current premises on Berkeley Street in 2002 as a revolving exhibition based on works from the Collection and a showcase for contemporary Scottish art in London. This meant that the exhibition programme has had to juggle between showing works from the permanent collection as well as loan exhibitions. However, in 2010 the opportunity arose to rent the floor directly above the gallery and create additional space. This opened in 2011 as Gallery Two, showing selected works from the permanent collection, while temporary exhibitions, drawn from both private and national collections, are held in the original 'Gallery One'.

The Fleming Collection continues to grow, the main thrust being directed towards buying the work of young Scottish artists, while opportunities are also taken to fill historical gaps. A unique collection well worth a visit.

66 *The 'embassy' for Scottish art* **99**

Address: Inner Circle, Regent's Pk, NW1 4NX (www.
londongardensonline.org.uk/gardens-online-record.asp?ID=WST108).

Opening hours: Daily, 7am to dusk.

Cost: Free.

Transport: Baker St or Regent's Pk tube.

GARDEN OF ST JOHN'S LODGE

The garden of St John's Lodge – built in 1817-19 by architect John Raffield for Charles Augustus Tulk, MP – is exquisite; it's the quintessential perfect English garden offering great views of the imposing lodge, which was the first house built on Regent's Park. In 1892, a new garden 'fit for meditation' was designed (for the third Marquess of Bute) with formal areas, a fountain pond, Doric temple, stone portico and partly sunken chapel, which reflected Arts and Crafts ideas and the revival of interest in the classical.

The garden has been open to the public since 1928 and is completely separate from the Lodge and maintained by the Royal Parks. It was renovated and redesigned in 1994 by Landscape Architects Colvin & Moggridge to reflect the original plan and honour the 3rd Marquess of Bute. A new entrance walk was created to the east of the gatehouse and bungalow, with double gates to provide privacy for the house. The east-west scalloped hedge was replanted in yew, but the '20s flower beds were renewed after public consultation, a variation from the original plan designed by architect, Robert Weir Schultz (1860-1951). New high-backed wooden benches were also commissioned. The new planting established quickly and today the gardens form a luxuriant oasis in the heart of the city.

> The Lodge remained in private hands until 1916 – past owners included Lord Wellesley (1st Duke of Wellington), Sir Isaac Goldsmid and the Marquesses of Bute. Today it's one of only two villas that remain within Regent's Park from John Nash's original conception and is now leased by Prince Jefri Bolkiah of Brunei.

A metal arbour, reflecting the original stone portico, and a wooden covered seat were created, along with the installation of a number of new statues and urns. Among the fine statues are the *Hylas* by Henry Pegram (central in a small round pond), a bronze of a nude man with a sensual mermaid seizing his legs to pull him to his doom, and a bronze by Charles L. Hartwell of a semi-draped shepherdess holding a lamb with the inscription 'To all protectors of the helpless.'

In order to enjoy this haven of calm and beauty, you first have to find it! From the Inner Circle, proceed anti-clockwise past Chester Road on your right, and some 200m further on you'll find the (hidden) entrance gate to St John's Lodge Gardens – if you pass the Lodge you've gone too far!

66 *A delightful, hidden garden* **99**

Address: Wellington Barracks, Birdcage Walk, SW1E 6HQ (020-7414 3428/3271, chapel 020-7414 3228, www.theguardsmuseum.com).

Opening hours: Daily, 10am to 4pm.

Cost: £6 adults, £3 senior citizens and students, children (16 and under) free.

Transport: St James's Pk tube.

GUARDS MUSEUM & CHAPEL

The Guards Museum is a captivating collection (housed in Wellington Barracks) that traces the history of the five regiments of Foot Guards – Grenadier, Coldstream, Scots, Irish and Welsh Guards – which together with the two regiments of Household Cavalry (the Life Guards and the Blues and Royals – who have their own museum – see page 31) make up Her Majesty's Household Division. Together they enjoy the privilege of guarding the Sovereign and the Royal Palaces.

The museum opened in 1988 and tells the story of the Guards' regiments from the 17th century to the present day. Displays include examples of different Guards' uniforms chronicling the evolving dress over 350 years, paintings, weapons, models, sculptures and artefacts such as mess silver, which paint a vivid portrait of the regiments' history and what being a soldier in the Guards is all about. The collection is primarily intended as an educational aid to help young Guardsmen learn about their regimental heritage and to show a wider audience the multi-faceted nature of the Guards' operational lives, both in combat and on ceremonial duties.

> Built in 1838, the chapel was damaged during the Blitz and in 1944 was totally destroyed by a V1 flying bomb during the morning service, which claimed 121 lives and injured 140. The chapel was rebuilt in the '60s in a modern style.

The Foot Guards are first and foremost professional soldiers, who perform dual combat and ceremonial roles. Many people are surprised to learn that the soldiers in the Household Division are primarily fighting soldiers at the forefront of Britain's commitment to the UN, NATO and the country's security. Over the centuries they have fought in most major British Army campaigns, which remains the case to this day. For example, in 2012 all five regiments of Foot Guards were either in, had just retuned from, or were training for operations in Afghanistan. Their high standard of training is recognised worldwide and their NCOs and Warrant Officers are called upon by many countries to train their own forces.

The Guards (or 'Royal Military') Chapel – situated a few hundred yards from the museum – is the religious home of the Household Division. Normal Sunday services are open to the public and are accompanied by a professional choir and the band of one of the regiments of the Household Division.

The engrossing Guards Museum also has a delightful shop, known as 'The Guards Toy Soldier Centre'.

66 *The Queen's Guards in all their glory* **99**

AT A GLANCE

Address: 25 Brook Street, Mayfair, W1K 4HB (020-7495 1685, www. handelhouse.org).

Opening hours: **Tue-Sat, 10am to 6pm (8pm Thu); Sun noon to 6pm. Closed Mons, including bank holidays.**

Cost: **£6.50 adults, £5.50 concessions, £2 children (5-16), under-5s free. Children free at weekends. National Trust members half price.**

Transport: **Bond St tube.**

George Frederic Handel

HANDEL HOUSE MUSEUM

This Grade I listed building was home to the noted baroque composer George Frederic Handel (1685-1759) from 1723 until his death. Handel was the first occupant of what was then a new house, and it's London's only museum to a composer. It's also where Handel composed some of his greatest music, including the Messiah, Zadok the Priest and Music for the Royal Fireworks.

The house has finely-restored Georgian interiors and is dedicated to celebrating Handel and his work; frequent music rehearsals, weekly concerts and special musical events in addition to regular displays and exhibitions bring Handel's world to life. There's also an impressive permanent display of Handel-related items. In 1998, the Handel House Collections acquired the Byrne Collection, a major Handel collection of several hundred objects, including books, letters, early editions of operas and oratorios, portraits, prints and sculpture. As can be seen from some of Handel's portraits, he was obviously a man with a healthy appetite. One of his early biographers, William Cox, put it succinctly, saying that he had 'a culpable indulgence in the sensual gratifications of the table'.

Handel was born in Halle, Germany, but became a British citizen in 1727. His Brook Street home was away from the artistic centres of Soho and Covent Garden but within easy walking distance of St James's Palace, where he conducted his official duties, and the King's Theatre, Haymarket, the focus of his Italian opera career at the time.

There must be something musical in the air in this expensive part of London, as the ground-breaking American rock guitarist Jimi Hendrix lived for a while with his English girlfriend next door in the top floor flat of 23 Brook Street, which is now the Handel House Museum's administrative office. In 2010 there was an exhibition at the museum, Hendrix in Britain. It's said that Hendrix was delighted to find himself living next door to Handel's old home and he bought a lot of the composer's music. Some people even claim to hear Handel's influence in some of Hendrix's later compositions!

Concerts are staged at the museum at 7.30pm on a few days a week (bookings, 020-7399 1953), with most tickets costing £9 (£5 students). Full programme details and information about temporary exhibitions are on the website.

❝ *Where Handel meets Hendrix* **❞**

Address: Horse Guards, Whitehall, SW1A 2AX (020-7930 3070, www. householdcavalrymuseum.co.uk).

Opening hours: **Daily, 10am to 6pm (Apr-Oct) and 10am to 5pm (Nov-Mar); closed 20th July and 24-26th Dec. Also private evening visits (1hr) for groups of 10 to 50 at 6.30 pm (Apr-Oct) and 5.30pm (Nov-Mar) – £15 (plus VAT) per head.**

Cost: **£7 adults, £5 children 5-16 and concessions, £18 families (max. 2 adults, 3 children).**

Transport: **Charing Cross or Embankment tube.**

HOUSEHOLD CAVALRY MUSEUM

The Household Cavalry Museum is a unique living museum – about real people doing a real job in a real place. Unlike other military museums, it offers a rare 'behind-the-scenes' look at the ceremonial and operational roles of the Household Cavalry Regiment (you can even see troopers working with horses in the original 18th-century stables via a large glazed partition). The experience is brought to life through personal stories, first-hand accounts of troopers' rigorous and demanding training, interactive displays and rare objects, many on public display for the first time.

The museum sits within Horse Guards in Whitehall in one of the city's most historic buildings dating from 1750 – the headquarters of the Household Division – where the Household Cavalry performs the daily 'changing of the guard' in a ceremony that has remained broadly unchanged for over 350 years.

The Household Cavalry was formed in 1661 by order of Charles II and consists of the two senior regiments of the British Army: the Life Guards and the Blues and Royals. The cavalry has two roles: as a mounted regiment (on horseback) that guards Her Majesty The Queen on ceremonial occasions in London and across the UK (and is a key part of royal pageantry); and as an operational regiment in the British Army serving around the world in armoured fighting vehicles (units were been deployed in both Iraq and Afghanistan).

Over the centuries the Household Cavalry has amassed an outstanding collection of rare and unique treasures from ceremonial uniforms, royal standards and gallantry awards, to musical instruments, horse furniture and silverware by Fabergé.

> **Each exhibit has its own story to tell, including two silver kettledrums given to the regiment in 1831 by William IV; the pistol ball that wounded Sir Robert Hill at Waterloo; and the cork leg which belonged to the first Marquess of Anglesey, who lost his real one at Waterloo.**

Modern additions to the collection include one of footballer Jacky Charlton's England caps (he did his national service with the regiment) and Sefton's bridle – the horse that was injured in the 1982 Hyde Park bombings.

Much of the collection has resulted from the close association between the Household Cavalry and royalty, whom the regiment has protected from rebels, rioters and assassins for 350 years. The Changing of the Queen's Life Guard takes place daily at 11am on Horse Guards Parade and the daily inspection at 4pm.

The museum shop sells a wide range of gifts and souvenirs.

 Real horses and troopers to swoon over

Address: The Mall, SW1Y 5AH (020-7930 3647, www.ica.org.uk).

Opening hours: Tue-Sun, 11am to 11pm. Exhibitions 11am to 6pm (Thu to 9pm). Closed Mon and 25th Dec to 1st Jan.

Cost: Most exhibitions are free (see website for films and other events).

Transport: Charing Cross tube/rail.

INSTITUTE OF CONTEMPORARY ARTS

The Institute of Contemporary Arts (ICA) is one of London's leading artistic and cultural centres, containing galleries, a theatre, two cinemas, a superb bookshop and a great bar. It's located within Nash House, part of Carlton House Terrace, a grand Regency period building on The Mall – a refreshing hidden gem in a totally unexpected neighbourhood.

The ICA was founded by a group of radical artists in 1946 to challenge the foundations of contemporary art. Its founders wished to establish a space where artists, writers and scientists could debate ideas outside the traditional confines of 'retrograde institutions' such as the Royal Academy. After occupying a variety of 'temporary' locations, the ICA moved to its present, splendid abode in 1968, which has become the home of British avant-garde. Originally conceived as a 'laboratory' or 'playground' for contemporary arts, the ICA continues to challenge traditional notions and boundaries of all forms of art.

In its early years, the Institute organised exhibitions of modern art, including Pablo Picasso and Jackson Pollock, and also launched Pop art, Op art, and British Brutalist art and architecture. Contributing to its history have been a who's who of artists and luminaries such as TS Eliot, Stravinsky, Elizabeth Lutyens, Ronnie Scott, Cartier-Bresson, Michael Foucault, Jeff Koons, Peter Blake, Yoko Ono, Don Letts, Wong Kar Wai, Lars von Trier, Takeshi Kitano, Jeff Wall, Vivienne Westwood, Malcolm McLaren, Ian McEwan, Philip Pullman and Zadie Smith – to name just a few. It has also played host to debut solo shows from some of today's highest profile artists including Damien Hirst, Jake & Dinos Chapman, Luc Tuymans and Steve McQueen.

> **The cinemas shows a brilliant selection of avant-garde and international films, classics and documentaries – perfect if you want to see something other than the usual blockbuster at your local Odeon.**

The ICA is also devoted to presenting a wide variety of musical acts and was one of the first venues to present The Clash in 1976 and the Stone Roses in 1989, and has seen debut London gigs from many bands that became household names. It also played host to the first iTunes Festival in 2007 with shows from the likes of Paul McCartney, Amy Winehouse and Kate Nash.

The ICA is never afraid of breaking the rules and doing something different, so be prepared to expect the unexpected – no-one who's serious about contemporary art can afford to ignore it.

66 *The hip, vibrant home of avant-garde art* **99**

AT A GLANCE

Address: **King's College, Strand, WC2R 2LS (020-7836 5454, www.kcl.ac.uk/aboutkings/principal/dean/chaplaincy/prayeratkings/strand/college-chapel.aspx).**

Opening hours: **During college hours and services (see website).**

Cost: **Free.**

Transport: **Temple tube.**

KING'S COLLEGE CHAPEL

The King's College Chapel (Grade I listed) is a magnificent example of Victorian architecture, designed by the eminent architect George Gilbert Scott (1811-1878) and completed in 1864. A century and a half later, the Chapel continues to provide a spiritual focus for King's community and a peaceful space at the heart of the college.

King's College was founded by King George IV and the Duke of Wellington in 1829 as a university college in the tradition of the Church of England, and became one of the two founding colleges of the University of London in 1836. Today, King's is a multi-faculty, research-led, teaching institution with over 16,000 students and 5,000 staff, catering for all faiths and beliefs.

When the original college building (Grade I listed) by Robert Smirke was completed in 1831 it included a chapel. However, it was considered too low church and plain, and in 1859 the council asked Sir Gilbert Scott to design a more impressive chapel, and his scheme – on the lines of an ancient Christian basilica – was accepted.

> The chapel was restored in 2000-01, when Scott's original decorative scheme was substantially reinstated, despite significant changes made in the '30s and the post-war period.

The beautiful Scott chapel is situated on the first floor directly above the Great Hall, reached by an impressive double staircase from the main entrance. Scott had to overcome a number of structural difficulties and used a lightweight construction system for the arcade and upper nave walls that concentrated the loading above the iron columns on the floor below. The wall is fabricated in iron with paired ornamental cast iron columns and an applied timber frame facing above.

Among the many highlights are the organ by Henry Willis, dating from the 1860s, reconstructed by his grandson in the '30s; the lovely angel designs on the largest pipes were only revealed during restoration. The lower walls of the chapel have a rich composition using a painted tile motif, also discovered during restoration work and faithfully recreated, while the west wall contains the original tile design. The chapel also houses a wealth of poignant memorials.

Regular services are held in the chapel representing many different traditions, all of which are open to the public. The chapel choir sing at the Wednesday communion service and choral evensong on Tuesdays at 5.30pm.

A wonderful, spiritual building, reflecting the college's motto: *Sancte et Sapienter* (with holiness and wisdom).

❝ *A 'secret' Gilbert Scott masterpiece* ❞

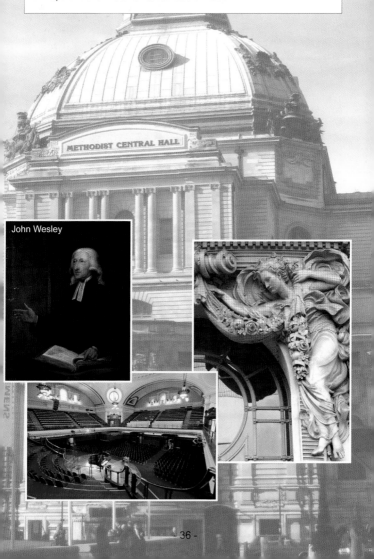

Address: Storey's Gate, SW1H 9NH (church, 020-7654 3809, events 020-7222 8010, www.methodist-central-hall.org.uk and www.c-h-w.com).

Opening hours: Daily, free guided tours between 9.30am and 5pm. Note that the Great Hall may be hired for private use, so it's advisable to check in advance.

Cost: Free.

Transport: Westminster or St James's Pk tube.

METHODIST CENTRAL HALL

John Wesley

METHODIST CENTRAL HALL WESTMINSTER

Methodist Central Hall – also called Westminster Central Hall – is a magnificent, richly-decorated Methodist church. It's a multi-purpose Edwardian building: Methodist church, conference and exhibition centre, concert hall, art gallery, office building, events venue and tourist attraction. The Hall was built in 1905-11 to mark the centenary of the death of John Wesley (the founder of Methodism) in 1791. It was funded by the 'Wesleyan Methodist Twentieth Century Fund' – or the 'Million Guinea Fund' as it became known – which raised one million guineas from one million Methodists.

It was designed by Edwin Alfred Rickards (1872-1920) of the firm Lanchester, Stewart and Rickards, in Viennese Baroque style with Romanesque decoration. It's an early example of the use of a reinforced concrete frame for a building in Britain – the domed ceiling of the Great Hall is a pioneering achievement in architectural engineering and the second-largest of its kind in the world. The vast scale of the self-supporting ferro-concrete structure reflects the original objective that Central Hall was intended to be 'an open-air meeting place with a roof on it'. The angels in the exterior spandrels were designed by Henry Poole RA.

> **The Football World Cup 'Jules Rimet trophy' was stolen from the Hall on 20th March 1966, but was recovered seven days later.**

The beautiful Great Hall seats up to 2,160 people and houses a splendid organ, containing 4,731 pipes. There's a long tradition of great music within the Central Hall, which is maintained through church services and regular free public organ recitals. In 1968 it hosted the first public performance of Andrew Lloyd Webber's *Joseph and the Amazing Technicolor Dreamcoat*, in a concert that also featured his father, organist William Lloyd Webber (who was Musical Director at Central Hall), his brother, cellist Julian Lloyd Webber, and pianist John Lill.

The Hall hosted the first meeting of the United Nations General Assembly in 1946. In return for the use of the Hall, the Assembly voted to fund the repainting of the walls of the church in light blue – which still remains. It has been regularly used for political rallies – speakers have included Winston Churchill – and has also welcomed members of the Royal Family and ambassadors from many countries: Mahatma Ghandi spoke in the Lecture Hall in autumn 1931 and General de Gaulle founded the Free French here in the early '40s.

" *A grand Edwardian building designed to inspire* "

Address: **South Audley Street, Mayfair, W1 (020-7641 2390, http://myparks.soario.com/parks/mount-street-gardens).**

Opening hours: **Daily, 8am to dusk.**

Cost: **Free.**

Transport: **Green Pk or Bond St tube.**

MOUNT STREET GARDENS

Mount Street Gardens are a secret oasis in Mayfair, and although well frequented by locals and Americans working at the nearby US embassy, are relatively unknown. They are situated on the site of an important early Georgian cemetery, built as a result of the 1711 'Fifty New Churches Act', which was acquired by the newly-formed church of St George's Hanover Square as a burial ground in 1723 (closed in 1854). Like many other urban cemeteries and former burial grounds in London, it was later converted into a public garden.

The gardens were laid out in 1889 with plants, paths and a small fountain, and have changed little since their inception, retaining their late 19th-century gate piers at the South Audley Street entrance.

> During the cold war the gardens were a favourite haunt of KGB spies, who left secret notes in the slats of the garden benches.

The bronze drinking fountain (restored in 2005), located at the east end of the gardens near the beautiful Farm Street Church, depicts a rearing horse and was designed by Sir Ernest George (1839-1922) and Harold Peto (1854-1933) in 1891 for Henry Lofts (a local estate agent). The church (built 1844-1849) is the scene of many society weddings and has a high altar by Augustus Pugin (the designer of the interior of the Palace of Westminster).

Planting in the gardens includes mature London plane trees and a variety of smaller trees, shrubs and ornamental flower beds. A microclimate (due to the protection afforded by the buildings which enclose much of the gardens) allows an Australian Mimosa, a Canary Islands Date Palm and three Dawn Redwoods to flourish. Around 90 sponsored benches line the paths, many of which were donated by Americans from the nearby US Embassy; inscriptions include 'An American who did not find a park like this in New York City.'

The gardens are designated a 'Site of Importance for Nature Conservation' and are home to various bird species (there's also a bird bath), depicted on a bird life interpretation panel. They won the London Gardens Society 'Public Large Squares Award' in 2002 and have been a Green Flag Award winner annually since 2007. The gardens were restored in 2005 through the efforts of local residents.

Mount Street Gardens are a haven of peace and quiet, and a lovely place to take a break and savour the magical atmosphere, cocooned from the noise and bustle of central London.

66 *Sanctuary for Mayfair birdlife – and spies!* **99**

AT A GLANCE

Address: 21 Stacey St, WC2H 8DG (020-7379 3187, www.thephoenixgarden.org).

Opening hours: Daily, 8.30am to dusk.

Cost: Free.

Transport: Tottenham Court Rd, Leicester Sq or Covent Gdn tube.

PHOENIX GARDEN

This little refuge is located next to the Phoenix Theatre and is the last remaining of Covent Garden's seven community gardens, and one of the West End's best kept secrets. Founded in 1984, it's maintained by volunteers and funded by donations, having risen, Phoenix-like, from the ashes. Built on the site of the old St Giles Leper Hospital (established by Queen Maud) which existed from 1117-1539, the award-winning garden has an fascinating history, having been the site of a charity school, a tragic WWII bombing and a car park.

The location's green-fingered connections date back to the 17th century, when a local gardener called Brown rented space in nearby St Giles-in-the-Fields churchyard, giving rise to Brown's Gardens (the name by which Stacey Street was originally known). Centuries later, its less than ideal growing conditions have proved no obstacle to the flourishing display of flowers, grasses, shrubs and trees (including rowan, willow, walnut, birch and ginkgo) that we see today. There's also a rockery and a small fish pond, benches (with quirky inscriptions) and a children's play area – this is very much a living garden with a real heart and soul.

Here innovation and environmentally-sound thinking go hand in hand, as the retaining walls made from recycled newspapers and its Gabion dry stone wall constructed from excavated bomb rubble demonstrate. The garden is maintained using sustainable techniques and an innovative approach to wildlife gardening, with plants that grow reliably in dry conditions, look good year round and are of maximum benefit to wildlife. It's become a haven for city wildlife, including five species of bee, butterflies and a variety of birds such as the blue and great tit, robin, wren, house sparrow, blackbird, greenfinch, sparrow hawk, woodpecker and kestrel. It's also home to the West End's only frogs, which inhabit its ponds along with colourful damselflies. Not surprisingly, the garden has won first prize many times for Best Environmental Garden in the Camden in Bloom contest.

In conjunction with St Giles-in-the-Fields, the garden plays host to regular community events such as an annual agricultural 'Country Show' which showcases locally grown plants and produce, Morris dancing and other traditional entertainments, including a Punch and Judy show and falconry displays.

So, when you're tired of tramping the West End streets and your batteries need recharging, make a beeline for this peaceful haven, relax, read a book, have a nap or eat your lunch, smell the roses or simply watch the clouds drift by.

 A little-known, magical garden in London's West End

Address: **16-18 Ramillies St, W1F 7LW (020-7087 9300, http://thephotographersgallery.org.uk).**

Opening hours: **Mon-Fri, 9.30am to 6pm (Thu until 8pm), Sat 10am to 6pm, Sun 11.30am to 6pm.**

Cost: **Free 10am to noon. Exhibitions £4.50 adults, £3.50 concessions.**

Transport: **Oxford Circus tube.**

PHOTOGRAPHERS' GALLERY

The Photographers' Gallery is the largest public gallery in London dedicated to photography. From the latest emerging talent, to historical archives and established artists, it's *The* place to see photography in all its forms. It was the first independent gallery in Britain devoted to photography, founded by Sue Davies in 1971 at 8 Great Newport Street in a converted Lyon's Tea Bar. Nine years later the gallery expanded to include an additional gallery space at 5 Great Newport Street, thus occupying two separate sites on the same street. In December 2008, the gallery moved to a nearby building on Ramillies Street, a former warehouse built in 1910, where a major redevelopment was undertaken in recent years.

Designed by award-winning Irish architects O'Donnell+Tuomey, the galley features three dedicated floors of gallery spaces. Situated at the heart of the building, between two of the exhibition floors, is the studio floor, which hosts a range of talks, events, workshops and courses, as well as a *camera obscura*, the study room, and Touchstone – a changing display of a single photographic work. Complementing the exhibition and education floors are a new bookshop, a print sales room and a café/bar, all at street level.

The Photographers' Gallery has been instrumental in establishing photography's important role in culture and society. It has provided a focus for the medium in London and was the first public gallery in the country to exhibit key names in international photography such as Juergen Teller (fashion), Robert Capa (photojournalism), Sebastião Salgado (documentary) and Taryn Simon (contemporary art), while also promoting the work of UK-based photographers such as Martin Parr, Zineb Sedira and Corinne Day.

One of Europe's foremost galleries dedicated to photography, The Photographers' Gallery awards the high-profile annual Deutsche Börse Photography Prize, worth £30,000 in 2014. Past prize winners include Andreas Gursky (1998), Shirana Shahbazi (2002), Robert Adams (2006), and Sophie Ristelhueber (2010).

The Photographers' Gallery occasionally displays work from unexpected sources, for example its exhibition of photographs from The London Fire Brigade archives and a presentation of studio portrait photography by Harry Jacobs, a high street studio photographer who worked for over 40 years in south London.

A wealth of inspiration for everyone from phone snappers to professionals.

66 *A picture perfect gallery for the 21st century* **99**

Address: Inner Circle, Regent's Pk, NW1 4NR (020-7486 7905, www.
londongardensonline.org.uk/gardens-online-record.asp?ID=WST094
and http://openairtheatre.com).

Opening hours: Daily, dawn to dusk; garden café, 8am to 4pm (open
later in summer).

Cost: Gardens are free. Theatre tickets from £25 to £60 (see website).

Transport: Baker St tube.

QUEEN MARY'S GARDENS & OPEN AIR THEATRE

Queen Mary's Gardens – tucked away in the Inner Circle of Regent's Park – contain London's largest and best formal rose garden, and are a honey-pot for garden lovers (and bees) in spring and summer, when tens of thousands of plants are in bloom. The gardens – named after the wife of George V – were laid out in 1932 on a site that had originally been used as a plant nursery and was later leased to the Royal Botanic Society. There are still some of the original pear trees in the gardens which supplied fruit to the London Market in the early 1800s. Queen Mary's Gardens are most famous for their beautiful rose garden, containing almost every species in existence.

The rose garden contains 400 different varieties of roses in separate and mixed beds, and a total of some 30,000 rose plants, plus around 30,000 other plants including the national collection of delphiniums and 9,000 begonias – a total of over 60,000 plants in landscaped beds surrounded by a ring of pillars covered in climbers and ramblers. The planting was renewed by landscape architects Colvin and Moggridge in the '90s, and is arranged in a design which is in harmony with the circular site and adds a 'sense of mystery'. Within the rose garden is a small lake filled with ornamental ducks and carp, in the centre of which is an island rockery.

> **The Inner Circle contains the beautiful Triton Fountain – at the northern end of the central walk – designed by William McMillan RA (1887-1977) and donated in 1950 in memory of Sigismund Goetze (1866-1939) by his wife.**

Queen Mary's Gardens plays host to the Open Air Theatre, a permanent venue (now in its 80th season) with a three- to four-month summer season. Each season typically consists of a production of *A Midsummer Night's Dream*, a second Shakespeare play, a musical and a children's show, performed in rotation. The theatre boasts one of the longest 'bars' in any theatre in London, stretching the entire length of the seating, which also serves full meals from an hour and a half before performances begin, as well as during the interval. A BBQ is also provided plus a picnic lawn with tables where the audience can enjoy their own food.

The park also contains the Garden Café, serving teas, coffees, lunch and summer suppers. The perfect spot to round off the perfect day.

66 *A fragrant theatrical experience* **99**

AT A GLANCE

Address: **Marylebone Rd, NW1 5HT (020-7873 7373, www.ram.ac.uk/ museum).**

Opening hours: **Mon-Fri, 11.30am to 5.30pm and Sat noon to 4pm. See website for schedule of public events.**

Cost: **Free.**

Transport: **Baker St or Regent's Pk tube.**

ROYAL ACADEMY OF MUSIC MUSEUM

This museum will delight anybody with an interest in music. The Royal Academy of Music was founded in 1822 by Lord Burghersh (1784-1859) and was granted its Royal Charter in 1830 by George IV. It moved to its current, custom-built premises in Marylebone Road in 1911. The museum is situated in the York Gate building, linked to the Academy's building via a basement, designed in 1822 by John Nash (1752-1835) as part of the main entrance to Regent's Park.

The Academy (as it's usually called) is Britain's oldest degree-granting music school and has been a college of the University of London since 1999. It's the country's leading specialist higher education institution and also number one for music, in addition to being Britain's leading conservatoire. Throughout its almost 200-year history it has trained thousands of accomplished musicians and has a student body of almost 700 (drawn from over 50 countries) in over 20 musical disciplines.

Many famous musicians – singers, players, conductors and composers – have studied at the Academy. Some have returned as teachers to stimulate new generations of musicians, while many have become leaders in their chosen musical fields and professions. Among the Academy's most distinguished living alumni are Sir Elton John, Annie Lennox, Michael Nyman, Sir Simon Rattle and Sir John Tavener, while those from previous generations include Sir John Barbirolli, Sir John Dankworth, Sir Arthur Sullivan and Sir Henry Wood (of Proms fame), to name just a few.

The museum displays material from the Academy's world-renowned collection of instruments, manuscripts, objects and images. An integral part of Academy life, it regularly hosts exhibitions and events, including daily piano demonstrations. Highlights of the collections include Cremonese stringed instruments from 1650 to 1740, English pianos from 1790 to 1850 from the famous Mobbs Collection, and original manuscripts by Purcell, Mendelssohn, Liszt, Brahms, Sullivan and Vaughan Williams. The galleries are a showcase for the work of performers, composers, instrument makers and scholars.

Since its foundation the Academy has acquired important collections of instruments, manuscripts, paintings, busts, drawings, teaching aids and artefacts, batons, furnishings, memorabilia and other objects, including many collections named after individuals such as composer Sir Arthur Sullivan, conductor Sir Henry Wood and the Foyle (Yehudi) Menuhin Archive. The Academy also has a shop, restaurant and a bar open in the evening for drinks and snacks.

 Where both pop and classical music flourish

Address: The Strand, WC2A 2LL (tours 07789-751248, www.justice.gov.uk/courts/rcj-rolls-building/rcj/tours).

Opening hours: Tours (2hrs) at 11am and 2pm on selected days.

Cost: Tours: £12 adults, £10 concessions (aged 60 and over), £5 children (under 14), £10 per head for groups (minimum 12 people).

Transport: Temple tube.

ROYAL COURTS OF JUSTICE

The Grade I listed Royal Courts of Justice (RCJ), commonly called the Law Courts, is a vast, imposing building housing the Courts of Appeal and the High Court of Justice of England and Wales. It's one of the last great wonders of Victorian neo-Gothic revival architecture, designed by George Edmund Street RA (1824-1881), a solicitor turned architect. Built in the 1870s, it was officially opened in December 1882 by Queen Victoria. The finished building contained 35 million Portland stone bricks, over 3.5mi (5.6km) of corridors and some 1,000 clocks, many of which had to be wound by hand.

Entering through the main gates in the Strand, you pass under two elaborately carved porches fitted with iron gates. The carvings over the outer porch consist of heads of the country's most eminent judges and lawyers. Over the highest point of the upper arch is a figure of Jesus, lower down (to the left and right) are figures of Solomon and Alfred the Great, while Moses is at the northern front of the building. Also at the northern front, over the Judges entrance, are a stone cat and dog representing litigants fighting in court!

The building is a Victorian interpretation of 13th-century Gothic architecture, with imposing Portland stonework, beautiful mosaic marble floors, stunning stained glass windows, elaborate carvings and oak wood panelling. The walls of the magnificent Great Hall – reminiscent of a cathedral – are

> The RCJ took over eight years to complete, due in part to a stonemasons' strike during which masons were brought from Germany to keep work going, and housed within the building to protect them from the wrath of their striking English counterparts. Supplies came in through a secret underground tunnel.

lined with portraits of past Lord Chancellors and keepers of the Great Seal. The building also houses the Costume Display Gallery which celebrates the evolution of legal costumes throughout history, as well as the Painted Room and Bear Garden, which Queen Victoria allegedly named as such because the crowds of litigants and lawyers here reminded her of a bear pit.

Public tours of the Royal Courts are available (see opposite) and visitors are also invited to watch civil trials (criminal trials take place at the Old Bailey down the road), although there may be restrictions depending on the particular cases being tried.

❝ *A marvel of Victorian Gothic architecture* **❞**

Address: 197 Piccadilly, W1J 9LL (020-7734 4511, www.sjp.org.uk and http://piccadilly-market.co.uk).

Opening hours: Daily, 8am to 6.30pm. The church grounds host a food market on Mon (11am to 5pm), antiques and collectables market on Tue (10am-6pm) and arts and crafts market Wed-Sat (10am-6pm).

Cost: Free.

Transport: Piccadilly Circus or Green Pk tube.

ST JAMES'S CHURCH

St James's is a majestic Anglican parish church on Piccadilly, designed by Sir Christopher Wren (commissioned in 1672) and consecrated in 1684. In many ways it's the finest of a group of four similar churches that Wren designed on large open sites (the others being St Anne's, Soho, the gloriously-named St Andrew's by the Wardrobe and St Andrew's, Holborn). Wren's own regard was such that he singled out St James's for description and commendation in his letter 'Upon the Building of National Churches.'

The church is built of red brick with Portland stone dressings, while the interior has galleries on three sides supported by square pillars and the nave has a barrel vault supported by Corinthian columns. The font, organ case and reredos are excellent examples of the work of Grinling Gibbons (born in Holland), widely regarded as the finest wood carver ever to work in England. The building was funded by the Earl of St Albans, whose beneficence was recorded by the carving of his arms on the keystone blocks over the doors and on the plaster enrichments of the ceiling (he died in 1684, before the church was consecrated).

The church has been associated with many famous people during its lifetime, including William Blake, who was baptised here in 1757; Leopold Stokowski, choirmaster from 1902 until 1905 (before he became internationally famous); and the poet Robert Graves, who was married here in 1918.

Like many central London churches surrounded by commercial buildings, St James's had a dwindling congregation in the '60s and '70s, and when (in 1980) Donald Reeves was offered the post of rector, the Bishop of London allegedly said: 'I don't mind what you do, just keep it open!' In the last few decades attendance and activity have grown, during which St James's has earned a reputation for being a progressive, liberal and campaigning church (it's also the city's most enterprising).

It has an impressive music programme, with free lunchtime recitals (1.10pm) on Mondays, Wednesdays and Fridays, as well as regular paid evening concerts to suit a range of musical tastes. The church's Southwood 'secret' Garden was created by Viscount Southwood after WWII (during which the church was badly damaged) as a garden of remembrance 'to commemorate the courage and fortitude of the people of London', and is a venue for outdoor sculpture exhibitions.

The church hosts various markets (see box opposite) from Monday to Saturday and also has a café.

❝ *A Wren masterpiece in bustling Piccadilly* **❞**

Address: St Margaret St, SW1P 3JX (020-7654 4840, www.westminster-abbey.org/st-margarets).

Opening hours: Mon-Fri, 9.30am to 3.30pm, Sat 9.30am to 1.30pm, Sun 2-4.30pm.

Cost: Free.

Transport: Westminster tube.

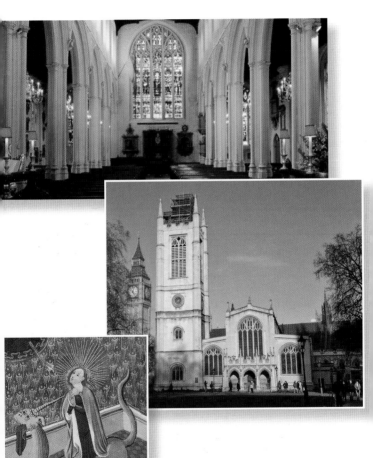

St Margaret of Antioch

ST MARGARET'S CHURCH

Standing between Westminster Abbey and the Houses of Parliament, it may seem surprising to find another large church. This came about when, in 1065 (just one year before the Norman conquest), Edward the Confessor gave orders for the consecration of the Collegiate Church of St Peter: Westminster Abbey. However, the Benedictine monks of the newly-founded monastery were constantly disturbed by the populace who came to hear mass, so they built a smaller church next to the Abbey where the local people could worship. The church was dedicated to the now little-known St Margaret of Antioch, one of the most popular saints among the laity in Medieval England.

The first church was Romanesque in style and survived until the reign of Edward III (1327-77), when the nave was replaced with one in the Perpendicular style. However, towards the end of the 15th century the church had fallen into disrepair and needed almost total reconstruction.

> It's thought that St Margaret's was built in the latter part of the 11th century, and until the Dissolution of the Monasteries by Henry VIII in 1540 the monks ministered to the spiritual needs of the people of Westminster. Thus was formed the close relationship between St Margaret's and Westminster Abbey, which has continued to this day.

Robert Stowell started to rebuild it in 1482, which continued until its consecration in 1523. Despite restorations in the 18th, 19th and 20th centuries, the structure is still essentially the same; the church's interior was restored and altered by Sir George Gilbert Scott in 1877, although many original Tudor features were retained.

Notable features include the east (Flemish stained glass) window of 1509, which commemorates the betrothal of Catherine of Aragon to Henry VIII. Other windows commemorate William Caxton (England's first printer), buried at the church in 1491; Sir Walter Raleigh, executed in Old Palace Yard and buried here in 1618; the blind poet John Milton (who married here and was a parishioner); and Admiral Robert Blake (responsible for England's naval supremacy). The church is a popular venue for 'society' weddings, including those of Samuel Pepys (1655) and Sir Winston Churchill (1908).

St Margaret's became the parish church of the Palace of Westminster in 1614, when the Puritans of the 17th century, unhappy with the highly liturgical Abbey, chose to hold Parliamentary services in the more 'suitable' St Margaret's. This practice continues to this day and has led St Margaret's to be dubbed 'the parish church of the House of Commons.'

 A 'hidden' gem in the shadow of Westminster Abbey

Address: 31 Bedford Street, Covent Gdn, WC2E 9ED (020-7836 5221, www.actorschurch.org).

Opening hours: Mon-Fri, 8.30am to 5pm, Sat varies depending on events, Sun 9am to 1pm (5pm when there's evensong).

Cost: Free.

Transport: Covent Gdn tube.

ST PAUL'S CHURCH, COVENT GARDEN

St Paul's Church, commonly known as 'The Actors' Church', is a beautiful parish church with an impressive Tuscan portico. It was designed by Inigo Jones in 1631 as part of a commission by Francis Russell, 4th Earl of Bedford, to create a square with 'houses and buildings fit for the habitations of gentlemen and men of ability'. The church was completed in 1633 but wasn't consecrated until 1638 due to a dispute.

The first known victims of the 1665 outbreak of the plague in London were buried in the churchyard on 12th April 1665: the start of the worst plague in London's history. In 1788, Thomas Hardwick began a major restoration, but the church was badly damaged by fire in 1795. Although much was destroyed, the parish records were saved, as was the pulpit by Grinling Gibbons. The church was restored again under the supervision of Thomas Hardwick and reconsecrated on 1st August 1798.

St Paul's connection with the theatre began as early as 1663 with the establishment of the Theatre Royal Drury Lane and was further assured in 1723 with the opening of Covent Garden Theatre, now the Royal Opera House.

On 9th May 1662, Samuel Pepys noted in his diary the performance of an 'Italian puppet play' under the portico – the first recorded 'Punch and Judy' show, now commemorated by the annual MayFayre service. The church contains a wealth of memorials dedicated to famous

> Among those buried at St Paul's are poet and satirist Samuel Butler, woodcarver Grinling Gibbons, painter Sir Peter Lely, Thomas Arne (composer of *Rule Britannia*) and the Australian conductor Sir Charles Mackerras. The ashes of Dame Ellen Terry and Dame Edith Evans also rest in St Paul's.

personalities, including Charlie Chaplin, Noel Coward, Gracie Fields, Stanley Holloway, Boris Karloff, Vivien Leigh and Ivor Novello. The artist JMW Turner and dramatist WS Gilbert (of Gilbert and Sullivan fame) were both baptised at St Paul's.

The church is famous for its concerts and has it own professional chamber orchestra, the Orchestra of St Paul's (OSP). In addition to a concert series in Covent Garden, the OSP gives regular performances throughout the UK. The church is also famous for its summer repertory season, when performances are given in the church's award-winning 'Inigo Jones Garden', which (when not being used as a theatre) provides a haven of calm amidst the bustle of central London.

66 *The other St Paul's, aka 'The Actors' Church'* **99**

Address: **27 St James's Pl, SW1A 1NR (020-7514 1958/7499 8620, www. spencerhouse.co.uk).**

Opening hours: **Sun (except Jan and Aug) 10.30am to 4.45pm. Access is by guided tour (ca. 1hr) only. Timed tickets on sale from 10.30am on the day (no bookings).**

Cost: **£12 adults, £10 concessions (students, seniors and under-16s). Children must be accompanied by an adult and be aged at least 10.**

Transport: **Green Pk tube.**

SPENCER HOUSE

According to its website, this is 'London's most magnificent private palace'. It's certainly one of the capital's best examples of a Palladian mansion, conceived as a showcase of classical design, and a visual treat for the visitor. Spencer House was built in 1756-66 for the Spencer family by the Palladian architect John Vardy, who was replaced in 1758 by James 'Athenian' Stuart, who did the interiors (the façades are Vardy's). The house thus became the first in London with accurate Greek interior detailing and one of the first (and finest) examples of the neo-classical style that was to sweep the country.

The house was conceived as a showcase of classical design but was also designed for pleasure, and a festive theme runs through the decoration of the many state rooms that were used for receptions and family gatherings. The first Earl Spencer (an ancestor of Diana, Princess of Wales) and his wife were prominent figures in London society, and the house often hosted lavish entertainments. Their descendants, notably the fourth and sixth Earls, both of whom served as Lord Chamberlain of the Royal Household, continued this tradition.

Spencer House is one of the last remaining of the many private palaces that once adorned central London. It's a great showcase of sophisticated, 18th-century aristocratic taste, lavishly furnished with elaborate period paintings (including some by Reynolds), objets d'art and furniture. A number of beautifully restored state rooms are open to the public.

There are magnificent views over Green Park and a spectacular garden, although it's only open to the public on a few days a year in spring or summer (see the website for details). The garden was designed by Henry Holland (the architect employed by the second Earl Spencer in the 1790s), possibly in collaboration with Lavinia, Countess Spencer; when it was planted in July 1798 it was one of the largest gardens in Piccadilly. It has recently been replanted with plants and shrubs appropriate to the late 18th and 19th centuries.

The Spencer family lived in the house until 1926, since when it has been let it to a variety of tenants. It's currently leased by Lord Rothschild for one of his companies, and he's extensively (and expensively) restored the building at a cost of many millions of pounds. Much of the work was done in the late '80s and it's thought by many to be one of the best examples of a building restoration and London's finest surviving 18th-century townhouse.

66 *Possibly London's best restoration* **99**

Address: Two Temple Pl, WC2R 3BD (020-7836 3715, www. twotempleplace.co.uk).

Opening hours: Annual exhibitions, Mon-Sat (except Tue), 10am to 4.30pm, Sun noon to 5pm (hours may vary – check website). Group tours are organised throughout the year by the Friends of Two Temple Place (020-7240 6044, www.twotempleplace.org/involved/friends).

Cost: Free.

Transport: Temple tube.

TWO TEMPLE PLACE

Two Temple Place, known for many years as 'Astor House', is a masterpiece of irreverent excess and fun – built in 1895 for William Waldorf Astor (1848-1919), later first Viscount Astor. It was built on reclaimed land following completion of the Victoria Embankment in 1870 and designed by John Loughborough Pearson (1817-1897) and his son Frank (1864-1947). Temple Place is both an architectural gem and a treasure house of exquisite works by the likes of William Silver Frith (1850-1924), Sir George Frampton RA (1860-1928), Nathaniel Hitch (1845-1938) and Thomas Nicholls (1825-1900).

The building has just two floors and a lower ground floor, and is broadly of Tudor design, built of Portland stone. It has splendid carvings on the exterior stonework by Nathaniel Hitch (1845-1938) and above the parapets is a superb gilded weathervane in beaten copper depicting Columbus' caravel *Santa Maria* by J. Starkie Gardner (1844-1930). The enchanting bronze lamp standards flanking the base of the balustraded entrance steps are a foretaste of the riches within.

> **Two Temple Place is postmodernism before its time, a Disney Gothic that's a thrill to visit – not to be missed!**

Palatial outside, inside it's a showcase of Britain's finest 19th-century craftsmen. Unfettered by the consideration of finance (it cost £250,000 to build in 1895, equivalent to £25m today!), emboldened by the freedom of expression granted to him, and with materials and craftsmen of the highest quality, Pearson was able to create a building worthy of its distinguished owner. From the splendid marble floor and imposing staircase in the grand hall and gallery (with its glorious stained glass and coved and panelled ceiling), to the great hall with its hammer beam ceiling, gilded carvings, silver gilt panels and huge stained glass windows, Temple Place is a masterpiece.

A widower, Lord Astor used it as his London home and as the Astor Estate Office until his death in 1919, when it was sold by the Astor family. Since then it has been owned by various companies and is now owned by the Bulldog (charitable) Trust, whose HQ it is. The Trust hosts annual exhibitions and tours and special events are also organised by the Friends of Two Temple Place (see the website for information).

❝ *A Gothic Revival extravaganza and treasure house* ❞

WALLACE COLLECTION

This is one of London's best art collections, but it doesn't pull in the crowds, which is a pity – except for those who visit, who get to enjoy the pictures and other treasures in rooms that are sometimes almost devoid of visitors. It's also located in an attractive house built in 1776, pleasantly situated in Manchester Square, one of central London's smaller but best-preserved Georgian squares (which is worth wandering around).

The Wallace Collection is a treasure trove of fine and decorative arts dating from the 15th to 19th centuries, spread over 25 galleries. It has many French 18th-century paintings, furniture (one of the finest collections of French furniture outside of France), Sèvres porcelain, arms and armour, and Old Master paintings.

It's mainly the collection of the first four Marquesses of Hertford, particularly the fourth, Richard Seymour-Conway (1800-1870), who left it and the house to his illegitimate son (although he never acknowledged his paternity) Sir Richard Wallace (1818-1890), who was also an important contributor to the collection and whose widow bequeathed it to the nation in 1897 (it opened to the public in 1900). A condition of the bequest was that no object should ever leave the collection, even for temporary exhibition elsewhere, and no works can be stored off-site.

The collection has around 5,500 objects and is split into six curatorial departments: Pictures and Miniatures; Ceramics and Glass; Sculpture and Works of Art; Arms and Armour; Sèvres Porcelain; and Gold Boxes and Furniture. The paintings collection includes work by such notables as Canaletto, Delacroix, Fragonard, Gainsborough, Hals (*The Laughing Cavalier,* shown far left), Landseer, Murillo, Poussin (*A Dance to the Music of Time*, left), Rembrandt, Reynolds, Rubens, Titian, Turner, Van Dyck and Velasquez. There's a fine collection of arms and armour – European and Oriental – plus bronzes, enamels, glass, majolica, miniatures and sculpture – something to appeal to almost everybody.

The detailed website has a useful facility for exploring the various collections and galleries, which is helpful when planning how to get the most from your visit. And when you're sated with culture and priceless treasures, the café and brasserie (operated by Peyton & Byrne) in the attractive, tranquil, glass-roofed courtyard is a great place for a drink or lunch.

 Ornate treasures in a lovely setting

Address: **20 Dean's Yd, SW1P 3PA (020-7222 5152, www.westminster-abbey.org).**

Opening hours: **Cloisters: daily 9.30am to 6pm. College Garden: Tue-Thu, 10am to 6pm (Apr-Sep) and 10am to 4pm (Oct-Mar). Café (Cellarium) 8am to 6pm.**

Cost: **Free.**

Transport: **Westminster tube.**

WESTMINSTER ABBEY CLOISTERS & COLLEGE GARDEN

Westminster Abbey Cloisters and College Garden are hidden, tranquil gems, accessed through Dean's Yard (south of Victoria Street), a handsome Westminster square. There are four gardens within Westminster Abbey: the three original gardens (the Garth, the Little Cloister and College Garden) and St Catherine's Garden, which lies in the area of the ruined monastery and was created more recently.

Each Garden had a separate function: the Garth with its square of turf, bounded by Cloisters, provided the monks with somewhere to rest their eyes and minds as they walked around it, while the Little Cloister Garden – small but charming, with borders of scented plants and a fountain – was reserved for recuperation after illness (its inner arcade is thought to date from the 17th century).

College Garden ('college' refers to the old meaning of the word: a community of clergy) is the largest and most important garden at the Abbey. A thousand years ago it was the infirmary garden of the monastery and is said to be the oldest garden in England under continuous cultivation, where a special medicinal herbarium was created in 1306. The infirmarer, a senior monk of the Abbey, took care of the sick and elderly members of the monastery, as well as administering a dispensary for local people. He would have directed the planting and cultivation of the various herbs needed for medicinal purposes in the infirmary, some of which are still grown today.

While the original garden was principally an area in which to grow herbs, fruit and vegetables, it also provided convalescing monks with a place for relaxation and gentle exercise. The oldest surviving features that can be seen today are the 14th-century stone precinct walls at the far end of the garden and running along the left-hand side as you stand at the entrance gate. The garden is dominated by five tall plane trees at its centre, planted in 1850; other trees of interest include quince, step-over apple trees at the entrance and a white mulberry near the fountain.

> **The Cloisters were the centre of monastic life, where the monks could enjoy some fresh air, sheltered from the rain and wind.**

Today, College Garden offers a tranquil space for everyone to enjoy and a retreat from the bustle of modern London just a step away. During July and August there are free lunchtime band concerts on

❝ *An ancient, secret oasis in bustling Westminster* **❞**

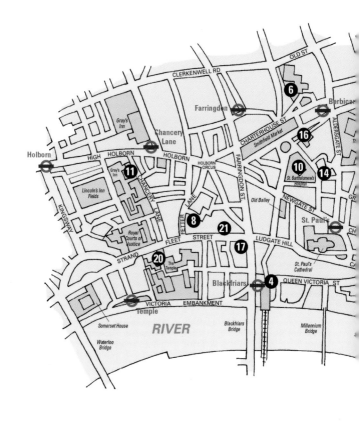

CHAPTER 2

CITY OF LONDON

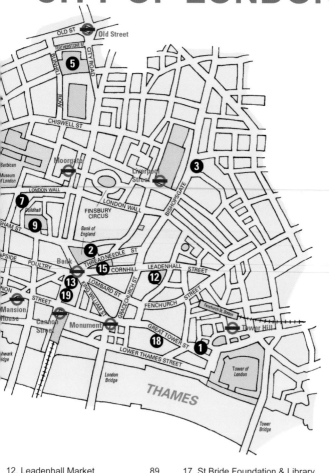

Address: Byward St, EC3R 5BJ (020-7481 2928, www.ahbtt.org.uk).

Opening hours: Usually **Mon-Fri, 8am to 5pm and Sat-Sun, 10am to 5pm (except during services). Free guided tours are available from Apr-Oct on most weekdays 2-4pm. Heritage group tours are available and can be booked through the church office.**

Cost: **Free. Heritage tours, £5 per person.**

Transport: **Tower Hill tube.**

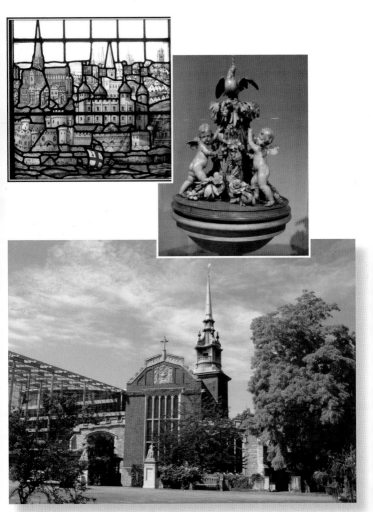

ALL HALLOWS BY THE TOWER

All Hallows by the Tower is an ancient, Grade I listed church overlooking the Tower of London. It's situated on an unpromising site between a busy road and a shopping precinct, which means that it's sometimes overlooked; a pity as it's positively dripping with history. It's London's oldest church, established in 675 by the Saxon Abbey at Barking and for many years it was (confusingly) named after the abbey, All Hallows Barking.

The site has been in use for much longer and the church was built on the site of a Roman building, of which there are traces in the crypt. All Hallows was expanded and rebuilt several times between the 11th and 15th centuries, and its location by the Tower saw the beheaded victims of executions (including Thomas More) buried here temporarily.

The church survived the Great Fire of 1666 (which began in Pudding Lane, only a few hundred yards away) thanks to the efforts of Admiral William Penn (the father of William Penn of Pennsylvania), who had the surrounding buildings demolished to create a firebreak. During the fire, Samuel Pepys famously climbed the church's spire to watch the progress of the conflagration.

It didn't fare so well during the Second World War, suffering extensive bomb damage necessitating major reconstruction. But many parts of the old church survived, the outer walls included, which are 15th-century with a 7th-century Saxon doorway from the original church. Three beautiful 15th- and 16th-century wooden statues of saints survive in the church, as does a lovely baptismal font cover carved in 1682 by Grinling Gibbons, widely regarded as one of London's finest carvings, if not the finest. There's also a fine collection of medieval brasses.

There's a museum – The Crypt Museum – which contains sections of a Roman pavement and artefacts discovered during excavations under the church. The church also hosts a wide variety of events, including regular organ recitals as well as concerts, plays and exhibitions (see website for details).

And last but by no means least, some claim that the heart of Richard I (the Lionheart) is buried in the northern part of the churchyard beneath a now-vanished chapel that Richard had built in the 12th century. Alas, this is untrue as it's now known that his heart was buried in Rouen.

There's also an excellent café, The Kitchen@Tower, where you can have a great breakfast or lunch.

 London's oldest church in its oldest district

Address: **Threadneedle St, EC2R 8AH (020-7601 5545, www. bankofengland.co.uk/education/pages/museum/visiting/default.aspx).**

Opening hours: **Mon-Fri, 10am to 5pm; closed weekends, bank holidays and 24-31 Dec.**

Cost: **Free.**

Transport: **Bank tube.**

BANK OF ENGLAND MUSEUM

At first glance, the prospect of visiting a display about the Bank of England (or the bank of anywhere) doesn't necessarily set the juices flowing, but it's a fascinating (and free) museum. It's of interest not simply to those who follow the world of finance but also to anyone with an interest in social history, politics and (strangely) classic children's literature.

Housed in a replica of the 18th-century bank designed by Sir John Soane (the current building is 20th century), the museum tells the story of the Bank of England from its foundation in 1694 to its current role as the UK's central bank, setting interest rates, controlling inflation, issuing banknotes and working to maintain a stable financial system. Audio and computer presentations explain the bank's modern responsibilities.

Displays include Roman and modern gold bars (you can test the weight of a gold bar – 28lbs, i.e. reassuringly heavy), and pikes and muskets once used to defend the bank. There are collections of banknotes and coins dating back to the 17th century (you'll learn, among many other things, that illustrations of the monarch didn't appear on banknotes until 1960); a wide range of books and documents; a small but interesting collection of furniture (some of it designed by Sir John Soane); pictures, cartoons and photographs; a small but historically significant silver collection, statues and a range of other artefacts, mostly associated with the business of banking.

There's also a permanent display about Kenneth Grahame (author of *The Wind in the Willows*), who worked at the bank for 30 years and rose to become its Secretary from 1898 to 1908. The display was opened in 2008 to mark the 100th anniversary of the publication of his famous book and includes his dramatic resignation letter, submitted four months before publication, citing mental pressures as the reason for his resignation. There are also letters from the bank's doctor, which give a rather different assessment of Grahame's mental health. The display includes details of how Grahame thwarted an attempted robbery in 1903 by an armed man who shot at him three times and who was later certified insane. Grahame managed to lock the man in the bank's waiting room.

Special exhibitions and events take place throughout the year at the museum, often including items that aren't usually on display. Free talks are also arranged, which must be booked (see website for details).

66 *Proof that finance can be interesting* **99**

Address: 230 Bishopsgate, EC2M 4QH (020-7392 9200, www. bishopsgate.org.uk).

Opening hours: Box Office: Mon-Fri, 9am to 6pm (see website for events); Library: Mon-Fri, 10am to 5.30pm (Wed until 8pm); Café: Mon-Fri, 7.30am to 9.30pm, Sat 10am to 9pm, Sun 10am to 4pm.

Cost: Use of the library and many events are free.

Transport: Liverpool St tube.

BISHOPSGATE INSTITUTE

The Bishopsgate Institute (Grade II* listed) is a celebrated cultural institute established in 1895 and housed in an historic 19th-century building. Described as a home for ideas and debate, learning and enquiry, and a place where independent thought is cherished, the Institute offers a cultural events programme, courses for adults, a historic library, archive collections and a community programme.

The Institute was the first of three major buildings designed by architect Charles Harrison Townsend (1851-1928), the others being the nearby Whitechapel Gallery and the Horniman Museum in south London. His work combined elements of Arts and Crafts and Art Nouveau styles, along with typical Victorian. The Great Hall of the Bishopsgate Institute was refurbished in 2011 and a new café-bar opened.

The original aims of the Institute were to provide a public library, public hall and meeting rooms for people living and working in the City. The Great Hall in particular was 'erected for the benefit of the public to promote lectures, exhibitions and otherwise the advancement of literature, science

> The Bishopsgate Institute was created largely through the vision and dedication of Reverend William Rogers (1819-1896), who persuaded the Charity Commissioners to allocate the vast funds – accumulated by St Botolph's church over 500 years – to build the Institute.

and fine arts'. The Institute's library is a free, independent library – open to all – which holds important historical collections about London, the labour movement, free thought and cooperative movements, as well as the history of protest and campaigning, dating from the early 19th century to the present day. The library's archives also contain a collection of over 20,000 images, including many of famous London landmarks (churches, statues, open spaces and buildings), plus social and cultural scenes from the early 20th century.

The Bishopsgate Institute hosts a range of cultural events throughout the year, including many inspired by Bishopsgate Library's historical and radical library and archive collections. These include a range of talks, walks and debates, as well as free lunch-time concerts in the Great Hall. The Institute also offers a full programme of adult courses that have been developed for complete beginners, with advanced classes in many subjects. Classes are held during lunch times, afternoons and evenings.

Whether you're visiting the Institute for the library, a course or a cultural event, or just wish to relax – you'll find the café (Bishopsgate Kitchen) a great place to unwind at any time of the day.

66 *An institution ahead of its time* **99**

Address: **174 Queen Victoria St, Blackfriars, EC4V 4EG (020-7236 5474, www.nicholsonspubs.co.uk/theblackfriarblackfriarslondon).**

Opening hours: **Mon-Sat, 10am to 11pm; Sun noon to 10.30pm.**

Cost: **Free.**

Transport: **Blackfriars tube/rail or Mansion House tube.**

THE BLACK FRIAR PUB

This narrow, wedge-shaped, Grade II listed pub is situated up against the railway line at Blackfriars, its shape resembling a slab of cheese or an iron. It wouldn't look so distinctive if all the buildings that used to surround it were still in place. The pub was built in 1875, near the site of a 13th-century Dominican Priory, which gives the area its name, and was the inspiration for the pub's design. In the '60s, John Betjeman (poet laureate, later Sir John) led a campaign to save the Black Friar from demolition, and thank goodness he did – no other London pub resembles it.

On the exterior, the pub's name is displayed in mosaic tiles and a statue of a large, laughing friar stands above the main door. It's an attractive, interesting façade, which was decorated by Henry Pool in 1903, but it's the interior of the pub that makes it truly extraordinary and well worth visiting (remodelled by H. Fuller Clark). It's decidedly ecclesiastical in design, resembling an ornate church or a mini cathedral, with a strong Art Nouveau character. Both Pool and Clark were strongly associated with the Arts and Crafts movement, and this building argues against the prevailing idea that the movement was all rather earnest.

Work on the interior began in 1904, with sculptors Nathaniel Hitch, Frederick T. Callcott and Henry Pool contributing. Every surface is decorated, in marble, mosaic, bas-reliefs and sculptures, often religiously-themed. The walls are decorated in cream, green or red marble, with illustrations of jolly monks; some sing and play instruments, some pick apples and grapes, others gather fish and eels for their meatless days, and one is about to boil an egg.

Various plaques on the walls carry words of so-called wisdom, such as 'Haste is Slow', 'Wisdom is Rare', 'Finery is Foolery', 'Industry is All' and 'Don't Advertise – Tell a Gossip'. The light fittings are carved wooden monks carrying yokes on their shoulders, from which the lights hang. There's a marble bar and, crowning it all, a vaulted mosaic ceiling.

As if all this wasn't enough, the pub also offers decent beer and food, with the pies especially recommended. However, it gets crowded during peak times, notably during the City lunch hour, although by 2.30pm the crowds dissipate and you have the time and space to inspect this extraordinary pub.

66 *London's most ornate pub* **99**

Address: 38 City Rd, EC1Y 1AU (020-7332 3505, www.cityoflondon.gov. uk/things-to-do/green-spaces/city-gardens/visitor-information/pages/ bunhill-fields.aspx).

Opening hours: Oct-Mar: weekdays 7.30am to 4pm; weekends and bank holidays, 9.30am to 4pm. Apr-Sep: weekdays 7.30am to 7pm; weekends and bank holidays, 9.30am to 7pm. Guided walks from Apr-Oct at 12.30pm on Wed from the attendant's hut.

Cost: Free. Guided walks £7.

Transport: Old St tube.

William Blake

BUNHILL FIELDS

Bunhill Fields is a tranquil, verdant cemetery in Islington, which is intriguingly out of step with its surroundings, sitting behind modern office blocks (meaning it's often missed by all except local office workers). It forms an oasis in central London and is a site of some historical and religious significance and interest. It has recently been granted Grade I status, while many of its monuments are Grade II listed.

The name comes from 'Bone Hill' and the area was associated with burials from Saxon times (perhaps much earlier). It was never consecrated ground and was therefore used for centuries to bury nonconformists (those who refused to conform to the rules of the established church), dissenters and others who weren't acceptable to or part of the Church of England.

The site was part of the ancient manor of Finsbury, dating back to 1104. Part of it became a burial ground in 1665, and by 1854 when it was closed it had become full, with around 120,000 interments. Today it covers 10 acres (it used to be much larger), around half of which is a park and the remainder a cemetery.

Like many London graveyards, by the mid-19th century it had become packed, with bodies piled on top of each other in graves until there was only a few inches of soil on the topmost corpse. This was cited as a major cause of London's frequent cholera outbreaks, and the 1852 Burials Act led to such graveyards being closed.

Many of the graves are packed closely together, giving a good idea of how inner London cemeteries used to look (as opposed to the more spacious ones created in the suburbs). Many of the old monuments remain, the earliest still visible dating from 1666. Of particular note are monuments to John Bunyan, author of *Pilgrim's Progress*, and Dr Isaac Watts, whose hymns are popular worldwide.

Other famous burials include William Blake, painter, poet and mystic; Daniel Defoe, author of *Robinson Crusoe*; Eleanor Coade, inventor of the artificial 'Coade' stone; George Fox, one of the founders of the Quaker movement; and Susanna Wesley, mother of John Wesley, the founder of Methodism. The spiked gate at the northeast corner of the cemetery was to deter body-snatchers (who presumably had an easy task, with bodies buried so close to the surface).

Bunhill also offers a refuge for nature in a built-up part of the city, with around 130 trees. During spring, there are beautiful swathes of crocuses, daffodils, hyacinths and snowdrops.

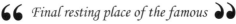 *Final resting place of the famous*

Address: Charterhouse, Sutton's Hospital, Charterhouse Sq, EC1M 6AN (020-7253 9503, www.thecharterhouse.org/tours).

Opening hours: Tours (usually at 2.15pm) take place on selected days (Tue-Thu) and every other Sat. There are also musical tours (see website).

Cost: Tour tickets £10 (must be pre-booked).

Transport: Barbican or Farringdon tube.

CHARTERHOUSE (SUTTON'S HOSPITAL)

Hidden away in Charterhouse Square is one of London's most beautiful and historic buildings, Charterhouse, formally known as Sutton's Hospital in Charterhouse. Located on the north side of the square, it was the location of London's largest plague pit, where around 50,000 victims of the Black Death were buried in 1348 when half the population died from plague. It's also the site of a former Carthusian monastery, founded in 1371 by Sir Walter de Manny and the Bishop of London. The order of monks were from La Grande Chartreuse near Grenoble in France, and the anglicising of their name led to 'Charterhouse' being applied to their English monasteries, which remained attached to the site in London. The monastery was dissolved by Henry VIII in 1537.

In 1545, the buildings were purchased by Sir Edward (later Lord) North (1496-1564), who transformed the complex into a luxurious Tudor mansion house. Following North's death the property was bought by Thomas Howard, 4th Duke of Norfolk, who was executed for treason in 1572 (the property passed to his son, Thomas Howard, 1st Earl of Suffolk).

Charterhouse was purchased in 1611 by Thomas Sutton (1532-1611), an Elizabethan merchant and adventurer, who endowed a hospital on the site. When Sutton died the greater part of his vast fortune was bequeathed to maintain a chapel, hospital – or almshouse, which it remains to this day – and school, much to the annoyance of his heirs, who fiercely contested the will (unsuccessfully). The hospital – a home for gentlemen pensioners – housed up to 80 men (now 40), and the school catered for 40 'poor' scholars who were the sons of doctors, lawyers and clergy, rather than the landed gentry.

Charterhouse established a reputation for excellence in hospital care and treatment, while the school developed beyond the original intentions of its founder, and now ranks among the most eminent public schools in England. The school remained on the site until 1872, when it moved to Surrey. Today, Charterhouse is part of the campus of Queen Mary, University of London, and lodgings are still provided for gentlemen who fall on hard times. The gorgeous Charterhouse buildings are well worth visiting: the tour takes in the Chapel, the Tudor Great Hall, the Old Library (sadly without books), the Norfolk Cloister, the Great Chamber, the Master's Cloister, Wash House Court and Preacher's Court.

66 *A medieval gem in the City* **99**

Address: 37 Wood St, EC2P 2NQ (020-7601 2328, www.cityoflondon. police.uk/about-us/history/museum/pages/default.aspx).

Opening hours: 9am to 4pm on selected weekdays. Closed at weekends and bank holidays. Visitors should confirm opening times (see website), which are liable to change at short notice. Groups larger than ten should make a booking.

Cost: Free.

Transport: St Paul's tube.

CITY OF LONDON POLICE MUSEUM

The City of London Police (COLP) Museum traces the history of the police force that has guarded the City of London since 1839. The COLP is responsible for law enforcement within the City of London – The Square Mile – including the Middle and Inner Temples, while the rest of Greater London is policed by the Metropolitan Police Service, a separate organisation. (For historic reasons, the City of London is administered separately from the rest of Greater London.) Nowadays the City is primarily a financial centre with a resident population of just 12,000, which is swelled by the daily influx of some 320,000 commuters who work within the City borders.

Policing in the City of London has existed since Roman times; Wood Street Police Station – the HQ of the City Police – is built on the site of a Roman fortress, which may have housed some of the first 'police' in the City. Before 1839 – when the COLP was formed – the responsibility for policing in the City was divided between the Day Police and Night Watch, primarily under two Sheriffs, which were merged into a single organisation.

There's a small collection related to the Jack the Ripper murders of 1888, including photographs of the victims and information about the police investigation, plus the Houndsditch Murders of 1910, which led to the infamous Siege of Sidney Street.

The City Police HQ on Wood Street houses a small but interesting museum dedicated to the history of crime and policing in the City. The museum offers a captivating insight into the deeds of criminals and villains, from Jack the Ripper to the enigmatic Latvian revolutionary criminal Peter the Painter, and takes a look at the lives of the men and women who have guarded the City since 1839. From the first police call box in London, via the history of the police uniform and Olympic glory (gold medals won by City policemen in 1908), to the grisly stories of the City's criminal past (murders, robberies, assassinations and gun battles), you'll discover the story of crime and policing in the City of London.

The unique collection charts the development of the UK police service, from the earliest days through to modern policing methods. Guided tours led by knowledgeable volunteers provide insights into crime in Victorian London, tell how social changes affect the work of the police force, and introduce you to the curious and eclectic museum collection.

66 *Meet Jack the Ripper and Peter the Painter* **99**

Address: 17 Gough Sq, EC4A 3DE (020-7353 3745, www.drjohnsonshouse.org).

Opening hours: **May-Sep, Mon-Sat 11am to 5.30pm; Oct-Apr, Mon-Sat 11am to 5pm. Closed Sun and bank holidays.**

Cost: **£4.50 adults, £3.50 concessions, £1.50 children (5-17), £10 family (2 adults and accompanying children), under 5s free.**

Transport: **Chancery Ln, Holborn or Temple tube.**

DR JOHNSON'S HOUSE

Samuel Johnson (1709-1784) was a biographer, editor, essayist, lexicographer, literary critic, moralist and poet (and obviously a splendid time manager). According to some he was the most distinguished man of letters in English history. He was also the subject of perhaps the world's most famous biography, by his friend James Boswell. So it's a surprise and a pity that this property is little visited.

The house was built around 1700 and is one of the few residential properties of its vintage surviving in the City of London (there are plenty in other parts of London). It was Johnson's home and workplace between 1748 and 1759, and it was here that he compiled the first comprehensive English Dictionary. Johnson first moved to London in 1737 with his friend David Garrick (the actor), and tried to earn a living as a journalist, writing for *The Gentleman's Magazine*. He was commissioned by a syndicate of booksellers to write the first comprehensive Dictionary of the English Language in 1746. He rented 17 Gough Square, and with the help of his six amanuenses, he compiled it in the garret and published it in 1755.

This elegant property has been restored to its original condition, with panelled rooms, a pine staircase, period furniture, and prints and portraits. Exhibits about Johnson's life and work provide an interesting insight into the man and place his work in context. The house's location adds to the atmosphere, in a maze of courtyards and passages to the north of Fleet Street, redolent of Georgian London.

And it tells the story of a fascinating, contradictory character. Johnson was a tall, robust man, yet prone to ill health throughout his life. He cut a shambling figure and was prey to a range of twitches and tics, which has led to the conclusion that he probably suffered from Tourette's Syndrome. Despite giving the impression from a distance that he might be an idiot, Johnson was very learned and eloquent. He was also a compassionate man, who supported a number of his poor friends in his house, even when struggling to support himself adequately.

After the death of Johnson's wife (who was over 20 years his senior), his Jamaican servant Francis Barber came to live with him in Gough Square, and many friends were entertained at the house, including Edward Burke, Charles Burney and Joshua Reynolds.

“ *A shambolic literary genius lived here* **”**

The Flight of Madeline and Porphyro, William Holman Hunt

GUILDHALL ART GALLERY & ROMAN AMPHITHEATRE

In 1988, the Museum of London made one of its most significant archaeological discoveries of recent years, when it unearthed the city's only Roman amphitheatre in Guildhall Yard. The City of London was keen to integrate the remains into its plans for a new art gallery (the original was destroyed during a 1941 air raid), so excavations and building work took place at the same time, over six years. It's a stone building in a semi-Gothic style planned to be sympathetic to the historic Guildhall, which is adjacent and to which it's connected internally.

The amphitheatre remains are now protected in a controlled environment within the gallery. Entry is included with entry to the Guildhall Art Gallery, which allows you to walk among visible Roman remains. It's an original, striking presentation and provides a good impression of the amphitheatre's scale, with the aid of digital technology, atmospheric lighting and sound effects. Outside, in Guildhall Yard, a curved line of dark stone bricks helpfully denote the edge of the old amphitheatre, which was around 100m wide and would have held up to 7,000 people (London's total population at the time was around 20,000).

The amphitheatre was built in AD70, from wood, and renovated in the 2nd century, with proper walls and tiled entrances. It was used for various public displays including gladiatorial contests, the execution of criminals and religious ceremonies. When the Romans abandoned Britain in the 4th century, the amphitheatre lay neglected for centuries, and the area was only reoccupied in the mid-11th century. In the early 12th century, the first Guildhall (London's old administrative centre) was built a few metres to the north.

The Guildhall Art Gallery houses the collection of the City of London and displays around 250 works of art at any one time (from a total collection of some 4,500), which have been collected since the 17th century. The Gallery was established in 1886 as 'a collection of art treasures worthy of the capital city'. It contains works dating from 1670 to the present, including 17th-century portraits, pre-Raphaelite masterpieces and a fascinating collection of paintings documenting London's dramatic history. Artists represented include Constable, Rossetti, Landseer and Millais, among others; the centrepiece of the largest gallery is John Singleton Copley's huge painting 'The Defeat of the Floating Batteries of Gibraltar'.

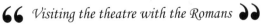

66 *Visiting the theatre with the Romans* **99**

Address: **St Barts Hospital, West Smithfield, EC1A 7BE (020-3465 5798, www.spitalfieldslife.com/2010/10/20/hogarth-at-st-bartholomews-hospital).**

Opening hours: **The paintings are visible from St Barts Hospital museum, open Tue-Fri, 10am to 4pm. Closed on bank holidays. To see them in more detail, you'll need to take a guided 'historic' tour (Fri 2pm), which meets at the Henry VIII gate.**

Cost: **The museum is free. Guided tours are £7 adults, £6 concessions, accompanied children free.**

Transport: **Chancery Ln or St Paul's tube.**

HOGARTH MURALS AT BARTS

When the governors of St Bartholomew's Hospital (widely known simply as Barts) wanted a spectacular display for the entrance hall to the north wing of their new hospital building in 1734, the renowned painter William Hogarth (1697-1764) – a local boy (born in Bartholomew Close next to the hospital – offered his services free of charge.

He was already famous for his paintings and engravings, which usually had a moral message, but it's thought that he was insecure about his social position and wanted to make a grand gesture. He also wished to be generous to the hospital and to demonstrate that an English artist could paint in the grand historical style (the hospital's governors were planning to approach the Venetian artist, Jocopo Amigoni, before Hogarth made his offer to work for free).

The two huge paintings (one is 30 feet wide) that now adorn the walls were completed by Hogarth between 1734 and 1737. One is of Christ healing the lame man at the Pool of Bethesda, the other is of The Good Samaritan. Hence both reflect the spirit of the hospital in caring for the injured and sick.

The Bethesda painting was done first, in a studio in Covent Garden. It was put in place on the staircase in 1736 and the people depicted in the painting 'Jesus at the Pool of Bethesda' are said to have been modelled on real patients. The 'Good Samaritan' work was painted in situ on the staircase (via scaffolding) to ensure that it would tone in with the other painting.

The paintings caused quite a stir at the time, with their 'figures seven feet high' and they still create a dramatic impression today. Some people, however, don't regard them as Hogarth's best work and find them kitschy, bizarre even, and not quite working. They argue that Hogarth's strengths were his humanity and carefully observed recording of the grubby life of 18th-century London, showing his sympathy with those living at the margins of life – critics don't think that trying to paint in the grand historical style suits this, although others disagree.

Barts is also well worth a visit for its history (it was founded in 1123 by Raherus), architecture and museum; it has existed on the same site for almost 900 years, surviving both the Great Fire and the Blitz. The Henry VIII entrance to the hospital remains the main public entrance and the statue of Henry VIII is the only public one of him in London.

66 *Hogarth at the hospital* **99**

Address: Four self-contained precincts, in a zig-zag from Holborn through Chancery Lane to Blackfriars and the Embankment. The four are at Lincoln's Inn Fields, WC2, Gray's Inn Rd, WC1, King's Bench Walk, EC4, and Middle Temple Ln, EC4 (http//barcouncil.org.uk/about-the-bar/what-is-the-bar/inns-of-court).

Opening hours: Unrestricted access to the exterior much of the time, but most gates into the precincts are closed at weekends. Tours of the interiors must be booked, although the chapels are often open to the public, 11am to noon and 1-4pm.

Cost: Free.

Transport: Temple or Chancery Ln tube.

Gray's Inn

Middle Temple Hall

Middle Temple Gatehouse

Combined Arms, Inns of Court

INNS OF COURT

Few locals realise that the four Inns of Court (Lincoln's Inn, Inner Temple, Middle Temple and Gray's Inn) are open to the public. This is understandable, as why would institutions that assist and regulate the country's barristers be open or of interest to the average person? However, they're an unexpected delight and drenched in history, with quadrangles, lawns, plane trees and Grade I listed medieval chapels, bringing an air of scholarly peace and tranquillity to the centre of London.

According to the Bar Council, their function is to 'provide support for barristers through a range of educational activities, lunching and dining facilities, access to common rooms and gardens, and provision of various grants and scholarships'. They also have supervisory and disciplinary roles over their members, and anyone wishing to train for the Bar must join one of the Inns.

They have a long history and the term 'Inns' comes from their origins as hostelries for law students. Lawyers took over the Inner and Middle Temples in the mid-14th century from the Knights Templar (who had occupied the site since the 12th century). Lincoln's Inn and Gray's Inn grew from associations with Henry de Lacy, Earl of Lincoln, and the de Gray family, respectively.

Each Inn is a large complex, with a great hall, libraries, a chapel, chambers and gardens, and resemble Oxbridge colleges in their layout and cover several acres. They're very rewarding to wander around and it's a treat to watch their gas lamps being lit at dusk. Middle Temple Hall (which has a striking double hammer-beam roof) dates from the 1560s, and is the only surviving building from Shakespeare's time where it's known that one of his plays had its première: *Twelfth Night* on 2nd February 1602. (You can even have lunch in Middle Temple Hall – bookings, 020-7427 4820 or banqueting@middletemple.org.uk).

You can enter the Middle and Inner Temples by several lanes off Fleet Street, but the most atmospheric way is through a stone gateway leading to Inner Temple Lane, which pre-dates the Great Fire and is surmounted by the City's only complete remaining timber-framed Jacobean townhouse.

The Inns of Courts' great character and atmosphere have attracted many film makers over the years and they've been used as backdrops many times, including in *Harry Potter and the Order of the Phoenix*. See also Temple Church on page 105.

❝ *Unexpected legal splendour* **❞**

Address: 1a Leadenhall Market, Gracechurch St, EC3V 1LR (020-7332 1523, www.leadenhallmarket.co.uk).

Opening hours: Stalls and shops are open Mon-Fri, 10am to 5-6pm. Public areas are usually open 24 hours a day.

Cost: Free.

Transport: Bank tube.

LEADENHALL MARKET

Leadenhall Market is an ornate, restored Victorian covered market selling traditional game, poultry, fish, meat and 'designer' items, standing on the site of 1st-century Londinium's Roman basilica. In 1411, the site was acquired by Richard 'Dick' Whittington, the Mayor of London and grew in importance as a granary and chapel were built. In 1463, the beam for the tronage (toll or duty) and weighing of wool was fixed at Leadenhall Market, signifying its importance as a centre for commerce. In 1488 leather was sold exclusively from Leadenhall and cutlery was added in 1622. The market was largely destroyed in the Great Fire (1666) and was rebuilt as a covered structure, when it was divided into a Beef Market, Green Yard and Herb Market. Somewhat surprisingly, in the mid-18th century the porters were women.

The 17th-century building was demolished in 1881 and redesigned by Sir Horace Jones (architect of Billingsgate and Smithfield Markets), when the beautiful ornate wrought iron and glass building (painted green, maroon and cream) you see today was erected (Grade II listed). In 1990-91 it received a dramatic redecoration which transformed its appearance, enhancing the architectural character and detail. The main double height entrance is on Gracechurch Street, flanked by tall, narrow, gabled red brick and Portland stone blocks in a Dutch 17th-century style. The adjacent buildings to the south have a continuous retail frontage, punctuated by narrow entrances to pedestrian ways into the market. (It has featured in a number of films – in 2001 it featured as Diagon Alley in *Harry Potter and the Philosopher's Stone*.)

> A celebrated 'character' in Leadenhall during the 18th century was 'Old Tom', a goose which managed to escape execution even though it's recorded that 34,000 geese were slaughtered here in two days. He became a great favourite in the market and was fed at local inns. After his death in 1835 at the age of 38, he lay in state in the market and was buried there.

Leadenhall Market sells some of the finest food in the City, including fresh meat and cheese and delicacies from around the world, and has a variety of other vendors including a florist, a chocolate shop, a pen shop and fashion shops, plus a number of restaurants, pubs (try the Lamb Tavern) and wine bars. Leadenhall isn't just a scenic market place but also a lovely place to stroll around; a varied programme of events means the area is always bustling.

 An elegant Victorian market on a Roman site

Address: Walbrook, EC4N 8BH (020-7626 2500, www.cityoflondon.gov.
uk/about-the-city/history-and-heritage/mansion-house/pages/default.
aspx).

Opening hours: Guided tours (1 hour) are held on most Tue at 2pm,
meeting at the A-board near the porch entrance to Mansion House in
Walbrook (exit 8 from Bank tube station). Tours cannot be booked in
advance. Group tours can also be arranged (£50, maximum 40 people)
and tours of the art collection (£90, maximum 20 people).

Cost: Scheduled city guide tours, £7 adults, £5 concessions.

Transport: Bank tube.

MANSION HOUSE

The Mansion House is a City gem – a rare surviving grand Georgian town palace – which you can visit! It's the official residence of the Lord Mayor of the City of London and the Lord Mayor's private office (a department of the City of London Corporation), and provides a centre for business meetings, conferences, banquets and entertaining. (The Lord Mayor is elected for one year, the position being unpaid and apolitical, not to be confused with the Mayor of London, which is a paid, elected, political position with a four-year term.)

> The cellars once held prisoners' cells, due to the building's former use as the Lord Mayor's Court. The suffragette, Emmeline Pankhurst, famous campaigner for women's rights, was once held here.

Mansion House has magnificent interiors and elegant furniture, and is used for a number of the City's grandest official functions, including an annual dinner hosted by the Lord Mayor, at which the Chancellor of the Exchequer gives his 'Mansion House Speech' about the state of the British economy. It was built between 1739 and 1752 by the architect and Clerk of the City's Works, George Dance the Elder; the site had formerly been occupied by St Mary Woolchurch Haw church, which was destroyed in the Great Fire (1666).

Mansion House's design is a classical Palladian style with ornate gold trim Corinthian columns and a grand Egyptian Hall (seating 350) on the first floor. The hall isn't, however, Egyptian in style, but is based on designs by the classical Roman architect Vitruvius of Roman buildings in Egypt, with giant columns supporting a narrower attic area. The second floor contains a ballroom and the private apartments of the Lord Mayor. The building has played host to many momentous occasions of global importance over the last two and a half centuries.

Mansion House is home to a magnificent collection of gold and silver plate – one of the best in the world and still in use on ceremonial occasions – a collection of sculptures, and one of the finest art collections outside London's public art galleries. It includes the Harold Samuel Art Collection of eighty-four 17th-century Dutch and Flemish paintings by masters such as Frans Hals, Nicolaes Maes, Jacob Ruisdael and Jan Steen (bequeathed to the City in 1987). It's probably the best collection of Dutch art in Britain and adds further splendour to the Mansion House's interior.

66 *A palace fit for a Lord Mayor* **99**

Address: **Saint Martin's Le-Grand, EC1A (020-7374 4127, www. cityoflondon.gov.uk > things to do > green spaces > city gardens).**

Opening hours: **8am to 7pm or dusk.**

Cost: **Free.**

Transport: **St Paul's tube.**

POSTMAN'S PARK

A short distance north of St Paul's Cathedral is one of the City of London's largest parks (although still small), best known as the site of the poignant Memorial to Heroic Self Sacrifice. The park stands on the old burial ground of St Botolph's Aldersgate and is a peaceful refuge in the City. It's quite a lot higher than the surrounding streets, as a result of the rather grisly history of many of central London's burial grounds: lack of space meant that corpses were often piled on top of one another, with only a thin layer of soil separating them (and the top one from the ground surface), so the burial area quickly grew higher than the surrounding land.

The name Postman's Park reflects the park's popularity with (and use by) workers from the nearby Post Office headquarters. In 1900 it became the site of the Memorial to Heroic Self Sacrifice, which was the brainchild of George Frederic Watts, a popular Victorian painter, sculptor and philanthropist. He'd noticed that memorials were invariably to the good and the great, and he wanted to commemorate ordinary people who died saving others and who might otherwise be forgotten.

The memorial is in the form of a series of plaques (ceramic memorial tablets) on a long wall underneath a loggia (similar to an arcade or a single side of a cloister). Parts of it are Grade II listed and the plaques are attractive, William Morris-style, with Arts and Crafts lettering, some with lovely Art Nouveau borders. They're hand-lettered and on Royal Doulton tiles.

The original idea was to have 120 plaques eventually, but just four had been installed by the time of the opening ceremony (which Watts was too ill to attend). Another nine were added in 1902 and 11 more in 1905. Watts died in 1904 and his wife Mary took over the management of the project, although she later became frustrated by problems with the tile manufacturers and the costs involved.

By 1938 (when Mary Watts died) there were 52 plaques and in 2009 a 54th was added (by the Diocese of London), the first addition for many decades. It's hoped that there will be more in the future. The park received a boost and increased public attention in 2004 with the release of the film *Closer*, in which a key plot element revolves around the park.

It's well worth taking the time to wander around the park, soak up its tranquil atmosphere and read the plaques (there are only a few lines on each) telling their tales of selfless sacrifice; an inspiring and humbling experience.

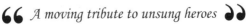

66 *A moving tribute to unsung heroes* **99**

ROYAL EXCHANGE

The Grade I listed Royal Exchange (RE) is a building steeped in history, although often overlooked in favour of its more illustrious neighbours; from its proud beginnings in 1565 to its latest incarnation as a luxury shopping centre, the RE has always stood for trade. Today, flanked by the Mansion House, the Bank of England and close to the Lloyd's building, the Royal Exchange stands at the heart of London's commercial hub.

Early 16th-century London was fuelled by commerce, with merchants coming from throughout Europe to trade their wares, negotiating in shops, homes, taverns and even in the streets. Meanwhile in the great port of Antwerp, merchants had a base within which to trade – a Bourse – where trade was regulated and controlled, and credit could be guaranteed and loans raised. Richard Gresham, a London cloth merchant (who supplied the tapestries for Henry VIII's Hampton Court), realised the trading centre's importance and urged the establishment of a similar centre in London. However, it was to fall to his son, Thomas, to realise his father's vision.

The first Royal Exchange was established in 1565 but wasn't officially opened (by Elizabeth I) until 1571. The resulting building, adorned with the Gresham family crest of a grasshopper (which can still be seen on the weathervane), was to survive until 1666, when it was destroyed in the Great Fire. A second exchange was designed by Edward Jarman and opened in 1669, but was also gutted by fire (in 1838).

The third Royal Exchange building, which we see today, was designed by Sir William Tite and opened by Queen Victoria in 1844. It adheres to the original layout of a four-sided structure surrounding a central courtyard, where merchants and tradesmen could do business. In 1892, 24 large panel paintings were installed on the walls of the ambulatory and can be viewed today. The first, showing Phoenicians trading with ancient Britons on the coast of Cornwall, is by Sir Frederick Leighton (1830-1896); together the paintings constitute a colourful history of British trade from its earliest times.

The Royal Exchange survived WWII and was used variously by a theatre company, the Guardian Royal Exchange (GRE) and (in 1982) by the London International Financial Futures Exchange (LIFFE). It was restored in the '80s, when 20 new Corinthian capitals were installed. In 2001, it was refurbished again and became a luxury shopping centre and a showplace for many of Britain's and the world's finest merchants (it's also home to a number of excellent restaurants).

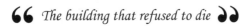

66 *The building that refused to die* **99**

Address: West Smithfield, EC1A 9DS (020-7606 5171, www. greatstbarts.com).

Opening hours: Mon-Fri, 8.30am to 5pm (4pm between 11th Nov and 13th Feb); Sat 10.30am to 4pm; Sun 8.30am to 8pm (except during services). Individual and group tours are available by appointment and tours are also conducted after the 11am service on Sun.

Cost: £4 adults, £3.50 concessions, £3.50 pre-booked groups, £10 family ticket (2 adults and up to 3 children), £1 photography. Or you can attend a service for free!

Transport: Barbican, Farringdon or St Paul's tube.

ST BARTHOLOMEW THE GREAT

St Bartholomew's (one of the 12 Apostles) is one of London's oldest churches, with a rich history and interesting architecture and interior features, but it's rather ignored and little known. A priory church was first established here in 1123 as part of a monastery of Augustinian canons and the site has been in continuous use as a place of worship since at least 1143.

It was founded by Rahere (who was of Frankish origin), a courtier, jester and favourite of Henry I, supposedly in gratitude after recovering from an illness he suffered on a pilgrimage to Rome. As he was returning to England, he apparently saw a vision of St Bartholomew, who told him to found a church in Smithfield (an admirably precise instruction). Rahere's tomb lies in the church, although it's actually 16th-century (he died in 1145).

The priory was dissolved in 1539 and the nave of the church was demolished. It was briefly a Dominican friary and reverted to being a parish church under Elizabeth I. It survived the Great Fire and the Second World War, and there was some restoration in the 19th century, although it remains London's most significant Norman interior, with massive pillars, Romanesque arches and zig-zag moulding.

The entrance to the church from Smithfield is accessed via a lovely medieval gate surmounted by a half-timbered Tudor building, which displays impressive craftsmanship. St Bartholomew's has a number of different styles of architecture, which some people regard as jumbled, others as interesting, but it's definitely atmospheric and has a range of notable features, including lots of interesting Tudor and Jacobean memorials.

Grade I listed, many City Livery Companies have close associations with the church. And it's no stranger to the world of cinema, having featured in several films, including *Elizabeth: The Golden Age*, *Four Weddings and a Funeral*, *Shakespeare in Love* and *The Other Boleyn Girl*.

The atmospheric and peaceful Cloister Café is open daily, except Saturdays, in the church's 15th-century cloister; among the many treats are superb home-made cakes, fresh mint tea and monastic beer!

❝ *A mix-and-match delight* **❞**

Address: Bride Lane, Fleet St, EC4Y 8EQ (020-7353 3331/4660, www. stbride.org and http://stbridefoundation.org).

Opening hours: Library: Tue noon to 5.30pm, Wed noon to 9pm and Thu noon to 5.30pm. Lunchbox Theatre: performances (45 mins), Mon-Fri at 1pm. Bridewell Theatre: see website for performances.

Cost: Library is free.

Transport: Blackfriars tube.

ST BRIDE FOUNDATION & LIBRARY

The St Bride Foundation – named after nearby St Bride's Church – is a stimulating cultural centre and library in the City. It was established in 1891 (as the St Bride Institute) to meet the educational, cultural and social needs of a community working within the burgeoning print industry of the Victorian era; it housed both a technical library and printing school, providing tuition for local printers and students. Today, the Foundation brings together exhibition spaces, a theatre, an educational centre and a library – one of the most significant collections of typography and historical printed reference books and documents in the world.

> **Opened in 1895 as a technical library for the printing school and printing trades, the library's collections cover printing and related subjects, including paper and binding, graphic design and typography, typefaces and calligraphy, illustration and printmaking, publishing and book-selling.**

St Bride lies in the heart of Fleet Street, synonymous with the British press and former home to many of London's newspaper publishing houses. Though the presses have moved away (mostly to Canary Wharf), there continues to be a working community here. In the spirit of its philanthropic originators, the Foundation continues to provide a stimulating community environment that creates a focal point for encouraging and developing everyone's potential through a broad range of activities. The processes and techniques explored at St Bride Printing School years ago are again thriving as letterpress undergoes something of a renaissance in the UK. The Foundation keeps the traditions and heritage of printing alive through a wide range of workshops, lectures, conferences and exhibitions.

The Foundation has long recognised the importance of dramatic arts in the development of the community and has produced theatrical entertainments as part of its remit for over 100 years. Visitors can take in a free lunchtime show at the Lunchbox Theatre (1pm daily) – including everything from classics to brand new pieces by up and coming writers – or attend an evening performance in the Bridewell Theatre (one of London's few off-West End theatres). From classics to contemporary, the Bridewell plays host to a variety of companies including the Guildhall School of Music and Drama and the Artelier Dance Company. There's also the Bridewell Bar, which hosts live music and special events.

Note that in early 2015 the library was closed for redevelopment (see website for the latest information).

 A unique cultural centre and font of inspiration

AT A GLANCE

Address: St Dunstan's Hill, EC3 (020-7332 3505, www.cityoflondon.gov.uk > things to do > green spaces > city gardens).

Opening hours: Unrestricted access.

Cost: Free.

Transport: Monument or Tower Hill tube.

ST DUNSTAN-IN-THE-EAST GARDEN

This beautiful garden was one of the authors' most delightful discoveries. There's been a church here from ancient times and a large churchyard from the 12th century. In 1366, St Dunstan-in-the-East required rebuilding (when the Archbishop forced parishioners to contribute to the cost!) and in 1417 it closed temporarily after a fatal brawl. It was severely damaged in the Great Fire of 1666, but rather than being completely rebuilt it was patched up and a tower and steeple added in 1695-1701 by Sir Christopher Wren. It was built in a Gothic style sympathetic to the main body of the church, although with heavy string courses of a kind unknown in the Middle Ages. The restored church had wooden carvings by Grinling Gibbons and an organ by Father Smith (moved to the abbey at St Albans in 1818 when the church was rebuilt).

St Dunstan's was largely destroyed in the Blitz of 1941 – only the north and south walls remained – although Wren's tower and steeple survived intact. The spire was reconstructed in 1953 and the tower restored in 1970-1, but it was decided not to rebuild the church.

The Corporation of London acquired the Grade I listed ruins (the walls, gates and railings are from the Wren period) in 1967, which along with the former churchyard were incorporated into a garden, opened in 1971. It includes a lawn, a circular cobbled area and a low fountain in the middle (what was the nave), with unusual trees, shrubs, flowers and climbers growing among the ruined arches and tracery.

Today, St Dunstan's is one of the City's most beautiful gardens and a welcome retreat from the surrounding bustle. Visitors can enjoy a huge variety of plants wending their way around the ruins; the walls and majestic windows have been draped and decorated with Virginia creeper and ornamental vine, which turn crimson in the autumn. Exotic plants such as pineapple-scented Moroccan broom and New Zealand flax thrive in the sheltered conditions, while in the lower garden is winter's bark (with leaves that are high in vitamin C, once eaten to prevent scurvy), and a Japanese Snowball by the fountain that displays breathtaking blossom in late spring.

The tower and adjoining All Hallows House are used as a complementary medicine centre and form part of the parish of All Hallows by the Tower. Occasional services are held in the garden, such as on Palm Sunday before a procession to All Hallows along St Dunstan's Hill and Great Tower Street.

66 *The loveliest public garden in the City* **99**

Address: 39 Walbrook, EC4N 8BN (020-7626 9000, www. ststephenwalbrook.net).

Opening hours: Weekdays, 10am to 4pm. It's usually closed at weekends except for significant festivals. See website for concerts and recitals.

Cost: Free.

Transport: Bank or Monument tube.

ST STEPHENS WALBROOK

Walbrook in the City of London has a long history, dating back at least to the time of the Romans, probably much longer. In the 2nd century AD, a temple of Mithras stood on the bank of the River Walbrook, a stream running across London from the City Wall near Moorfields to the Thames. Its foundations are preserved to this day.

There's been a church here since some time between 700AD and 980AD, when a Saxon church stood on the west bank of the Walbrook. It was common to build churches on what had previously been pagan sites in order to hallow them. The church was rebuilt in 1439 on the eastern side of the Walbrook and lost in the Great Fire of London in 1666 (which destroyed around three quarters of the City). The current church was built by Sir Christopher Wren between 1672 and 1680.

It's thought by many to be one of Wren's finest church interiors – if not the finest – and the influential German-born British scholar of art and architecture Sir Nikolaus Pevsner went as far as to declare it one of England's ten most important buildings, so it certainly merits attention.

As you approach the church, you might find Sir Nikolaus's claim to be rather overblown, but it's the interior rather than the exterior that's stunning. Some commentators maintain that it's Wren's masterpiece, and there's something of a Byzantine feel to the interior. It's rich and cream-coloured, yet calm and understated, with Britain's first and best Roman dome, the prototype for St Paul's. The dome is 63ft high and is centred over a square of 12 columns.

The church suffered slight bomb damage during the Second World War but was later restored. It's Grade I listed and also has some interesting modern features, including a controversial, massive white stone altar by the renowned sculptor Henry Moore. Unusually, it sits in the centre of the church, a block of pale travertine stone, not so much sculpted as subtly rounded by Moore. Some people love it, but its critics have rather cleverly labelled it the 'camembert'.

The church also displays a telephone in a glass box, which is a tribute to the fact that the Samaritans was founded here (by the rector of the church) in 1953. The counselling helpline charity began with this actual telephone, in a crypt beneath the church.

 A Wren masterpiece and Henry Moore's camembert

Address: Temple, EC4Y 7BB (020-7353 3470, www.templechurch.com).

Opening hours: The church is usually open to visitors Mon-Fri 10am to 4pm (but check on the website as opening times vary). It's closed Sat and open only for services on Sun.

Cost: £5 adults, £3 concessions, 18s and under free.

Transport: Temple or Chancery Ln tube.

TEMPLE CHURCH

At the heart of legal London sits The Temple Church, a mysterious, spiritual space with wonderful acoustics, where you can hear some of the City's finest church music. It's also one of London's most striking and historic churches, with 800 years of unbroken history. From the Crusaders in the 12th century, through the turmoil of the Reformation, the Civil War, the Great Fire and WWII bombs – it has survived virtually intact.

The church is in two parts: the rare circular 'Round' from 1185 and the Chancel (the 'Oblong'), dating from 1240. The Round Church

> The church was featured in the controversial novel, *The Da Vinci Code*, by Dan Brown, and was also used as a location in the film of the book.

(made of Caen stone) is one of only four Norman round churches remaining in England. Designed to emulate the holiest place in the Crusaders' world, the Church of the Holy Sepulchre in Jerusalem, it was consecrated by Heraclius, Crusader Patriarch of Jerusalem. Its choir is said to be perfection, with stunning stained glass windows, an impressive organ and a handsome wooden altar by Sir Christopher Wren. Inside the Round Church are nine knightly effigies, which were believed to be tombs until restoration revealed no bodies.

The church was built by the Knights Templar or Red Knights (after the red crosses they wore), the order of crusading monks founded to protect pilgrims going to and from Jerusalem in the 12th century. It was originally part of a centre that included residences, military training facilities, and recreational grounds for the military brethren and novices, forbidden to go into the City without permission from the Master of the Temple. The order of the Knights Templar was very powerful in England during this early period – unanswerable even to kings – when the Master of the Temple sat in parliament as *primus baro* (the first baron of the realm). After the downfall of the Knights Templar, which begain in 1307, Edward II took control of the church as a crown possession, and it was later given to the Knights Hospitaller (or Knights of Malta).

The church was rented to two colleges of lawyers which evolved into the Inner and Middle Temples, two of the four Inns of Court (see page 87). Today, the Temple Church is held in common by both Inns and is the main chapel of those who work in the Temple, but don't let that deter you from visiting this Gothic-Romanesque masterpiece.

 Famous long before the Da Vinci Code!

Address: Wine Office Court, 145 Fleet St, EC4A 2BU (020-7353 6170, http://en.wikipedia.org/wiki/ye_olde_cheshire_cheese).

Opening hours: **Mon-Sat, 11am to 11pm. Closed Sun.**

Cost: **Free.**

Transport: **Chancery Ln or Temple tube.**

YE OLDE CHESHIRE CHEESE

Ye Olde Cheshire Cheese is one of the oldest pubs in the City, dating to 1667 during the reign of Charles II, the previous one having been destroyed in the Great Fire in 1666, although there's been a pub on this site since at least 1538, when the Horn Tavern is recorded. It's one of the City's most atmospheric pubs, thanks to its lack of natural lighting, (possibly original) wood panelling and cellar-like rooms. The vaulted cellars are thought to have belonged to a 13th-century Carmelite Monastery which once occupied the site.

The unassuming entrance in a narrow alleyway belies the ample space and number of bars and rooms within, while in winter there's an open fire to provide warmth and atmosphere.

In the bar room are posted plaques showing famous people who were regulars or visitors – from the 1850s the

> By 1900, the Cheese had a resident who was to become almost as famous as the pub itself – Polly the eccentric parrot. Polly was famous far and wide for her antics, intelligence and ability to mime – and her rudeness to patrons! When she died in 1926, she was thought to be over 40 and her obituary appeared in over 200 newspapers!

Cheese was on the itinerary of many visitors to London – and over the centuries has attracted many distinguished drinkers, including such literary alumni as Oliver Goldsmith, Alfred Tennyson, Mark Twain, Sir Arthur Conan Doyle, G. K. Chesterton, Ben Jonson, Edward Gibbon, Thomas Carlyle, James Boswell and Dr Samuel Johnson (who lived in Gough Square nearby). Charles Dickens was known to frequent the Cheese and may well have modelled some of his characters on regulars here (the pub is alluded to in *A Tale of Two Cities*). The Rhymers' Club, a group of London-based poets, founded in 1890 by W. B. Yeats and Ernest Rhys, also used to meet here.

Approached through a narrow alleyway (Wine Office Court), the Cheese beckons you into a bygone age; by the entrance a notice board lists the reigning monarchs during its almost 350-year existence. Today the pub is operated by Yorkshire's Samuel Smith brewery, which has a reputation for excellent 'real' ales. The atmosphere is warm and friendly (if dark), with a multitude of rooms, stairs, nooks and crannies. There's a chophouse and restaurant on the ground floor, so you can enjoy both the surroundings and good traditional food – without the distractions of muzak, widescreen TV (footy) or pinball machines.

66 *Drink in the history in this Tardis-like pub* **99**

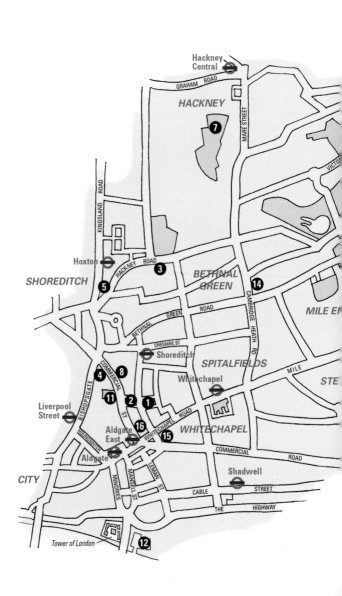

CHAPTER 3

EAST LONDON

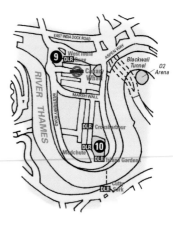

Address: Shoreditch, E1 6QL (www.visitbricklane.org and www.trumanbrewery.com).

Opening hours: Unrestricted access. Sat market 11am to 6pm; Sun market 10am to 5pm.

Cost: Free.

Transport: Aldgate E or Shoreditch High St tube.

BRICK LANE & MARKETS

Brick Lane is a street in Tower Hamlets which runs from Swanfield Street in Bethnal Green to Whitechapel High Street in the south via the short stretch of Osborn Street. Today, it's the heart of the Bangladeshi-Sylheti community – known to some as *Banglatown* – noted for its numerous curry houses, although this is only one of its many claims to fame.

It derives its name from former brick and tile manufacturers dating to the 15th century. From the 17th century it was home to successive waves of immigrants, beginning with Huguenot refugees spreading from Spitalfields, followed by Irish,

> After you've had your fill of shopping, enjoy a coffee and bagels (we love Beigel Bake at number 159) or an inexpensive lunch in one of the many authentic Bangladeshi restaurants.

Ashkenazi Jews and, in the last century, Bangladeshis. The area became a centre for weaving, tailoring and the clothing industry, due to the abundance of semi- and unskilled immigrant labour. It continues to be a microcosm of London's shifting ethnic patterns and was once associated with poor slums and the notorious Jack the Ripper murders in 1888.

Brewing came to Brick Lane in the 17th century with Joseph Truman, first recorded in 1683. His family, particularly Benjamin Truman (1699-1780), established the Black Eagle Brewery (Grade II listed) at 91 Brick Lane, the largest in London, covering 11 acres (4.5ha). The brewery closed in 1988 and is now a vibrant arts and events centre, housing over 250 businesses, ranging from cultural venues and art galleries to bars, restaurants and shops. Since the late '90s, the Brewery has also been the site of several of the East End's best night clubs. It's also home to two indoor weekly markets: the Backyard (Saturday/Sunday) and the Sunday UpMarket.

Brick Lane Market is a chaotic, colourful, artistic hub, attracting hordes of young people in search of second-hand furniture, unusual clothes, jewellery, arts and crafts, bric-a-brac and food. Go on a Sunday to catch it at its best. The joy is that you never know what you'll find; anything from cheap leather and vintage clothes to old magazines and kitsch collectibles, stunning silks to period furniture. Street performers enhance the vibrant, lively atmosphere, while Brick Lane is also famous for its graffiti, featuring artists such as Banksy, D'Face and Ben Eine.

 One of London's most colourful streets

Address: Commercial St, E1 6LY (020-7377 6793, www. christchurchspitalfields.org and www.ccspitalfields.org).

Opening hours: Mon-Fri, 10am to 4pm (if not booked) and Sun 1-4pm. Tours (50 mins) for ten or more people may be booked in advance (see www.spitalfieldsvenue.org/node/14).

Cost: Free, except for tours, £6 adults, £5 concessions.

Transport: Aldgate E or Shoreditch High St tube.

CHRIST CHURCH SPITALFIELDS

The lovely 18th-century Christ Church Spitalfields is off the usual tourist track, although its locale of Spitalfields is becoming more popular with the discerning visitor. The church was designed by Nicholas Hawksmoor (1661-1736), a pupil of Sir Christopher Wren and one of England's foremost architects. It was built between 1714 and 1729 as part of the church building programme initiated by the Fifty New Churches act of 1711 (only 12 of which were completed, six by Hawksmoor), to cater for the 'godless thousands' outside the City of London who had no adequate church provision.

Noted for the eloquence of its beautiful stonework and pleasing geometry, Christ Church is the size of a small cathedral and inside is the height of Exeter Cathedral, with a volume half that of the nave of St Paul's. Its architectural composition demonstrates Hawksmoor's usual abruptness: the plain rectangular box of the nave is surmounted at its west end by a broad tower of three stages, topped by a steeple more Gothic than classical (the magnificent porch was a later addition).

Inside, large glass-paned doors lead from the vestibule into the nave, an oak-panelled hall with a Purbeck stone floor and a ceiling of flowers, each one unique. Lit by chandeliers, this grand space has been lovingly restored to retain its authentic 18th-century charm. Hawksmoor's bold symmetrical design complements the ornate ceiling perfectly, while the huge columns provide natural divisions, giving the room a unique versatility. Above the nave on either side are galleries.

The church has seen at least two large-scale renovations, the first in 1866 (directed by the architect Ewen Christian), which 'savagely' changed the entire look of the interior, and the second which began in the '60s when the church was derelict. The latter restoration – to its original state, following the ill-advised changes wrought by Christian – was only completed in 2004 at a cost of £10m (the estimate was £1m!). The restoration is a revelation and has revealed one of the most complex and sumptuous of Hawksmoor's interiors.

Just as Christ Church is the masterpiece of its architect, the organ installed in 1735 was the masterpiece of the greatest organ builder in Georgian England, Richard Bridge (d 1758). It's the only remaining Bridge organ and bears witness to the vibrant and rich musical life of Georgian London. Free lunchtime recitals on the first Friday of the month (see website).

 Nicholas Hawksmoor's Baroque masterpiece

Address: Columbia Rd, E2 (www.columbiaroad.info).

Opening hours: Sun, 8am to 3pm.

Cost: Free.

Transport: Hoxton rail and 26, 48 and 55 buses.

COLUMBIA ROAD FLOWER MARKET & SHOPS

Columbia Road Flower Market is a colourful street market in East London and the city's only dedicated flower market. On Sundays the street is transformed into an oasis of foliage and flowers – everything from bedding plants to 10-foot banana trees. The market was established as a covered food market in 1869 by the heiress and philanthropist Angela Burdett-Coutts (1814-1906); Columbia Road was named in her honour after she instituted a Bishopric in British Columbia (Canada). The food market closed in 1886 after which the buildings were used as warehouses and small workshops, and were finally demolished in 1958.

The Flower Market began as a Saturday trading market, but as the local Jewish population grew a Sunday market was established and the Saturday market lapsed, which also (conveniently) provided the opportunity for Covent Garden and Spitalfields' traders to sell their stock left over from Saturday. The demand for cut flowers and plants among East Enders was created by Huguenot immigrants, together with a fascination for caged song birds, a reminder of which is the pub at the end of the market – The Birdcage.

The market went into a long decline during WWII, when a civilian shelter beneath the market suffered a direct hit during the Blitz. From the '60s, new rules forced traders to attend regularly, although the whole area deteriorated in the '70s and faced demolition. The market enjoyed a resurgence in the '80s with the increasing popularity of television gardening programmes, and today a wide range of plants, bedding plants, shrubs, bulbs and freshly cut flowers is available at competitive prices (even lower near closing time). Many traders are also growers and are second or third generation.

The area offers much more than a flower market and encompasses over 50 independent, mostly Victorian, shops, making it one of London's most interesting shopping streets. Outlets include tiny art galleries, cup cake vendors, perfumers, vintage clothing boutiques, homeware retailers, English and Italian delis, garden accessory sellers, jewellery makers and antique dealers, plus more unusual wares such as hand-made soap, candlesticks and Buddhist artefacts. There's also a wealth of great pubs, cafés and restaurants. Not surprisingly, the market is popular with photographers and television companies, who regularly film there.

 London's most colourful and fragrant market

Address: 18 Folgate St, Spitalfields, E1 6BX (020-7247 4013, www.dennissevershouse.co.uk).

Opening hours: Sun, noon to 4pm; selected Mon, noon to 2pm (no booking required). Mon and Wed evening 'silent night' tours between 5 and 9pm (45 mins, booking necessary). There are also exclusive silent night tours and private group visits (see website), plus extended opening hours over Christmas for the Annual Christmas Installation, which is a special time to visit the house (book early!).

Cost: £10 (£5 concessions) Mon lunchtime and Sun, £15 Mon and Wed evening tours.

Transport: Liverpool St tube/rail.

DENNIS SEVERS' HOUSE

This is one of London's most singular, intriguing attractions, in one of its most magical settings. It's really a work of fantasy, designed to create an atmosphere redolent of the 18th century and paint a picture of what life was like then. It's the brainchild of an American artist, Dennis Severs, who purchased the house in the '70s when the old Huguenot district of Spitalfields was rundown and little valued. Today parts of it have been gentrified and it's home to artistic luminaries such as Tracey Emin and Gilbert and George.

Severs began to live life in the house as he imagined its original inhabitants would have done in the 18th century, and he spent time in (and slept in) each room in order to 'harvest the atmosphere' of each one. As a result, he gradually gave life to an invented family, whose imagined lives became a detailed 'still life drama' for visitors to experience. They're a family of Huguenot silk weavers – the Jervis family – invisible and invented.

Severs filled the house with period fittings and furniture as well as authentic smells and sounds, to create a genuine atmosphere. Each of the house's ten rooms reflects a different era of the house's past, a snapshot of the life of the families who 'lived' here between 1724 and 1914. Dennis Severs died in 1999, but the house has been preserved and is open for tours, which last for around 45 minutes, including a short introduction.

You're 'instructed' to remain quiet and use your imagination during the tour, and it isn't recommended for children, all of which some people find a little bossy or precious on the part of those running the house. Others disagree and find this attitude healthy in our noisy era, when people seem incapable of keeping quiet or concentrating for more than 17 seconds.

The atmosphere of a bygone age is best maintained if you refrain from looking out of the windows – which allow the 21st century to intrude – and the night-time, candlelit (and most expensive) tours are the most atmospheric.

66 *Spend some time with 18th-century*
Spitalfields silk weavers 99

Address: **Kingsland Rd, Hackney, E2 8EA (020-7739 9893, www.geffrye-museum.org.uk).**

Opening hours: **Museum: Tue-Sat 10am to 5pm; Sun and bank holiday Mon, 10am to 5pm. Closed Mon (except for bank holidays), Good Fri, 24-26th Dec and 1st Jan. The rear 'period' gardens are open during museum hours from around 1st Apr to 31st Oct (there's free access to the front gardens all year round). A restored almshouse is open on selected days (see website for dates).**

Cost: **Museum and gardens free; £3 adults for almshouse guided tour (free for children under 16).**

Transport: **Hoxton rail.**

GEFFRYE MUSEUM

The Geffrye Museum and its tranquil gardens are something of a haven in the busy, scruffy clutter of this part of Hackney, with its heavy traffic, Turkish shops and Vietnamese eateries. This isn't a part of the borough that's been gentrified, so it's ironic that the museum is devoted to the history of British middle class interior design, furniture, decorative arts, paintings and textiles, and traces the changing style of domestic interiors from 1600 to the present day.

The museum is named after Sir Robert Geffrye (1613 to 1703), former Lord Mayor of London and Master of the Ironmongers' Company. Under his bequest, 14 almshouses were built in 1715, mainly for widows of ironmongers. These beautiful Grade I listed almshouses now house the museum, adding greatly to its appeal. A modern extension was opened in 1998, including a restaurant.

Eleven period rooms (see box) are on display, all showing remarkable attention to detail.

Music and readings from the relevant period add to the atmosphere. In addition, there are regular exhibitions about subjects relating to the museum's displays, as well as seminars, workshops, drama and music. See the website for the current programme of events. Some are seasonal – for example an exhibition of Christmas Past, detailing 400 years of seasonal traditions in English homes.

The museum also has four period gardens, depicting garden design, layout and planting from the 17th to 20th centuries, and a walled herb garden with over 170 types of herb. The gardens are designed to reflect the key features of middle class town gardens over the centuries.

The museum's comprehensive website allows a brief virtual tour of each of the eleven rooms and five gardens, allowing you to do your homework before you visit.

Room Displays

1. hall, 1630
2. parlour, 1695
3. parlour, 1745
4. parlour, 1790
5. drawing room, 1830
6. drawing room, 1870
7. drawing room, 1890
8. drawing room, 1910
9. living room, 1935
10. living room, 1965
11. loft-style apartment, 1998

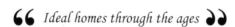

❝ *Ideal homes through the ages* **❞**

Address: Three Mill Ln, Bromley-by-Bow, E3 3DU (020-8980 4626, www.housemill.org.uk).

Opening hours: Sun May-Oct, 11am to 4pm and the first Sun in Mar, Apr and Dec. Guided tours around 45 mins (last tour 3.30pm). Café: Mon-Fri 10am to 3pm and when the mill is open for tours.

Cost: £3 adults, £1.50 concessions, accompanied children free.

Transport: Bromley-by-Bow tube.

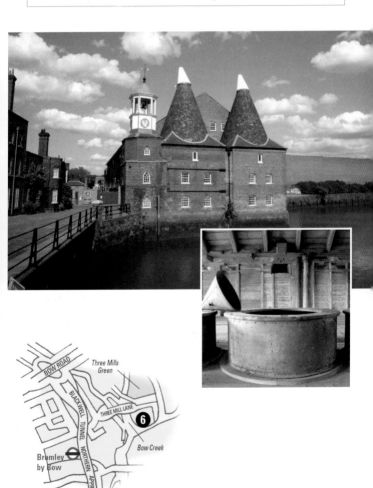

HOUSE MILL MUSEUM

The House Mill is a Grade I listed, 18th-century tidal mill set in a beautiful riverside location in the heart of London's East End – believed to be the largest tidal mill still in existence in the world. The mill was built in 1776 by Daniel Bisson on the site of an earlier mill, between two houses occupied by the miller and his family, hence its name. It's a timber framed building clad in brick on three sides.

In addition to flour-making, the mill also prepared grain for a (gin) distillery next door on Three Mills Island. Built across the River Lea, the mill trapped the sea and river water at high tide to turn the water wheels on the ebb. The outflowing water turned four large wheels driving twelve pairs of millstones, all of which survive together with other historic machinery (though it isn't currently operational). The mill ceased operation in 1941 after the area was bombed during WWII.

In medieval times the site was known as Three Mills and provided flour for the bakers of Stratford-atte-Bow, who in turn supplied bread to the City of London. In 1728, Three Mills was purchased by Peter Lefevre, a Huguenot, who entered into partnership with Daniel Bisson and several others. The mills co-operated with a distillery and the company had its own carpenters and coopers, and also operated a large piggery fed on the mills' waste products.

In the mid-'70s, House Mill was threatened with demolition and was saved by the intervention of the governors of the Passmore Edwards Museum (Newham). In 1989 work began on the House Mill, the fabric of which has been fully restored. The Miller's House was rebuilt in 1995 with a modern interior but retaining the original façade, and now contains a visitor, information and education centre and a small café.

> The *Domesday Book* (1086) recorded eight mills in this area – among the earliest known tide mills in England – and as windmills came later these must have been tidal water mills on the River Lea.

Nowadays, the mill is owned by The River Lea Tidal Mill Trust, which plans to reinstate the water wheels and other machinery in order to demonstrate grinding, and together with modern turbines (installed at the rear of the building), the wheels will also be used for hydro power generation.

A fascinating historic mill well worth visiting.

❝ *A rare surviving 18th-century mill* **❞**

Address: London Fields Westside, E8 3EU (020-7254 9038, www.hackney.gov.uk/cp-londonfields.htm, www.hackney.gov.uk/c-londonfields-lido.htm and www.londonfieldsusergroup.org.uk).

Opening hours: Park: unrestricted access. Lido: daily, 6.30am to 9pm (see website for bank holiday periods).

Cost: Park: unrestricted access. Lido: £3.45 members (£2.05 juniors 15 and under); £4.80 non-members (£2.90 juniors).

Transport: London Fields rail.

LONDON FIELDS & LIDO

London Fields (31 acres/12.5ha) is one of East London's most popular green spaces and also the name of an area of Hackney with many interesting shops. Due to its proximity to the City of London, Hackney was a favourite of wealthy Londoners from the Middle Ages until the 19th century, and became increasingly attractive following the Great Plague in 1665 and the Great Fire in 1666. Wealthy residents who wished to be close to the court, entertainment and London's financial centre, but also enjoyed country living, built large houses here. Though it seems hardly credible today, in 1756 Hackney was declared to exceed all other villages in the kingdom in the opulence of its inhabitants.

London Field (as it was then called) was first recorded in 1540, at which time it was common ground extending to around 100 acres (40ha), used by drovers to pasture their livestock before taking them to market in London. It's uncertain how the name London Field came into being, but it was probably due to the field's position on what had for centuries been the main footpath from the village of Hackney (and beyond the River Lea, from Essex) to the City of London. When travellers crossed this field they were only two miles from the City gate.

> A much-used cycle path runs from the Pub on the Park – a popular local watering hole – to Broadway Market (www.broadwaymarket.co.uk), a mouth-watering food market on Saturdays from 9am to 5pm.

London Fields has a lido (see below), a popular cricket pitch, soccer pitches, a BMX track, two tennis courts, a table tennis table and two children's play areas with a paddling pool (open May to September).

London Fields lido first opened in 1932 but closed in 1988, only re-opening in 2006 following a determined local campaign after being neglected for 18 years. It has been rebuilt to modern standards and is the only heated outdoor 50-metre Olympic-size swimming pool in London. One of only ten survivors from the original 68 lidos in the Greater London area, it's open year round and supervised by lifeguards. There's a café which also caters for park visitors.

London Fields is a beautiful green space with extensive grassy areas and many beautiful trees (notably plane trees), and has won a number of Green Flag awards. It's a great place to play sports, swim, enjoy a picnic or just chill out.

66 *London's best all-round park?* 99

AT A GLANCE

Address: **19 Princelet St, E1 6QH (020-7247 5352, www.19princeletstreet.org.uk).**

Opening hours: **Group visits (1-2hrs) by appointment. Also usually open during London Open House weekend (www.londonopenhouse. org).**

Cost: **No set fee, but most groups (maximum of 30-40 people) are expected to make a 'donation' of at least £5 per person or a minimum of £100 per group.**

Transport: **Shoreditch High St tube.**

MUSEUM OF IMMIGRATION AND DIVERSITY

The Museum of Immigration and Diversity is a unique museum – Europe's only cultural institution devoted to the movement of people in search of a better life – in one of East London's prettiest streets. It's situated in Spitalfields, which has been home to waves of dispossessed immigrants from Ireland, Europe and beyond, from the 17th century to the present day; nowadays it's home to Bangladeshi, Bengali and Somali communities.

The Museum is housed is an unrestored (Grade II* listed) house built in 1719, which was home to a Huguenot silk merchant, Peter Abraham Ogier, fleeing religious persecution in France. With the decline of the British silk weaving industry as the Industrial Revolution gathered pace, the Huguenots moved on and were replaced by Irish immigrants escaping the potato famine that swept Ireland in the mid-19th century. The Irish provided local industries with a vast supply of cheap labour for East London's docks and factories.

Between 1870 and 1914, thousands of Jewish settlers arrived from Eastern Europe, fleeing appalling conditions, growing anti-Semitism and Tsarist pogroms in Russia. By the '30s, the Jewish community was well established in East London, many working in cabinet making, the fur trade and tailoring. Houses like this one, where Huguenots once wove silk, later became workplaces and homes for

> In keeping with the house's multicultural past, it's now owned by a charity established to preserve the building, and to remember and celebrate the lives of those who lived, worked and worshipped here over the centuries.

Jewish families. Life was hard for new arrivals and a Jewish self-help group called the Loyal United Friends leased rooms at number 19, which they converted into a synagogue with a meeting place in the basement. The synagogue remained in use until the '70s, when the congregation dwindled.

The moment you step through the door of 19 Princelet Street you realise that you're entering a rare and remarkable building, made all the more poignant by its fragile state and air of decay. There's a touching exhibition entitled 'Suitcases and Sanctuary', exploring the history of the waves of immigrants who shaped Spitalfields, seen through the eyes of today's children. The building is in desperate need of restoration – which is why it's only open infrequently – and the charity hopes to restore it and create a permanent exhibition. One hopes that its unique atmosphere won't be lost in the process.

❝ *A unique and poignant museum and house* **❞**

AT A GLANCE

Address: **West India Quay, Canary Wharf, E14 4AL** (020-7001 9844, www.museumoflondon.org.uk/docklands).

Opening hours: **Daily, 10am to 6pm. Closed 24-26th Dec.**

Cost: **Free.**

Transport: **Canary Wharf tube or West India Quay DLR.**

MUSEUM OF LONDON DOCKLANDS

Sitting on the Isle of Dogs (a former island in East London, now bounded on three sides – east, south and west – by one of the largest meanders in the River Thames), this used to be called the Museum in Docklands. This is appropriate, as the museum is housed in a Grade I listed Georgian 'low' sugar warehouse, built in 1802; the Isle of Dogs was at the heart of London's docks, being the site of the West India Docks, East India Docks and Millwall Dock.

The three dock systems were unified in 1909 when the Port of London Authority took control of them. (With the docks stretching from east to west, and with locks at either end, the Isle of Dogs was once again almost a genuine island). The heart of the Museum of London Docklands collection is the museum and archives of the Port of London Authority.

The museum covers the period from the first port of London in Roman times to the closure of the docks in the '70s, and the area's subsequent redevelopment as a residential and financial area. It shows how the Thames became an international gateway, bringing invaders, merchants and immigrants to one of the world's longest serving ports.

The Museum of London Docklands is the best place in the city to get a sense of how crucial the Thames has been to the growth and rise to power of London. It explores the social and economic significance of the port of London, which for a time was the world's busiest. And it doesn't pull its punches by avoiding difficult subjects, for example London's part in the transatlantic slave trade; there's a permanent exhibition called London, Sugar and Slavery.

It's a large museum, with 12 galleries, including a children's gallery, and is modern and contemporary in its approach, using all the latest presentation techniques, including videos presented by (Sir) Tony Robinson (a former comedy actor and the slightly excitable host of a long-running archaeological television programme on Channel 4, *Time Team*). There are lots of historical objects, models and pictures, with impressive displays and exhibits, including a walk-through of a working quay and a local back alley.

The museum also regularly hosts talks, temporary exhibitions and events related to the river and the docks. There's also a shop and restaurant. Somewhat overshadowed by its better-known big brother, the Museum of London (one of the world's largest urban history museums), the exhibit in Docklands is well worth visiting.

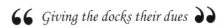

“ *Giving the docks their dues* **”**

Address: Pier St, Isle of Dogs, E14 3HP (020-7515 5901, www. mudchute.org).

Opening hours: Park: dawn to dusk. Farm: Daily, 9am to 5pm. Café: Tue-Fri, 9.30am to 3pm, Sat-Sun, 9.30am to 5pm.

Cost: Free, but you're invited to make a donation.

Transport: Crossharbour, Mudchute or Island Gardens DLR.

MUDCHUTE PARK & FARM

Mudchute Park and Farm is a slice of country life in the heart of East London. Not only is it London's largest city farm (extending to 32 acres) but it's one of Europe's largest inner city farms, with over 200 animals and fowl. It sits just to the south of Canary Wharf, whose towers form an impressive, contrasting backdrop. Most people don't know it exists, which is perhaps understandable, as it's incongruous to find a working farm in the shadow of one of the capital's financial hubs.

Mudchute is an area of the Isle of Dogs, its inelegant name deriving from the fact that it was the site of the dumping of spoil from the Millwall Dock excavations. Silt from the channels and waterways was deposited here using a conveyor system, which sounds unfortunate but actually created an area of fertile, hilly land.

In 1974 the site was earmarked for the building of a high rise estate, having remained an untouched natural wilderness of flora and fauna for decades. However, there was a backlash from locals which led to the formation of the Mudchute Association in 1977 to preserve and develop the area. Farm animals and horses were introduced and plants and trees were planted.

The farm now has an impressive range of animals of various breeds, including cows (the Irish Moiled, a hornless breed), pigs (Gloucestershire Old Spot and Tamworth), sheep (Oxford Down and White Faced Woodland), goats (Anglo-Nubian and Pygmy), donkeys and llamas, while there are also small animals in Pets Corner such as ferrets, giant rabbits and guinea pigs.

Aviary birds include budgies, canaries, Chinese painted quail, diamond doves, golden pheasant, Java sparrows and zebra finches, while chicken breeds include Brahma, Light Sussex, Rhode Island Red and White-crested Black Polish. There's also a variety of ducks (including Call, Indian Runner and Muscovy), geese (Chinese and Greylag) and turkeys (Pied), plus an Equestrian Centre with some 25 horses and ponies.

The farm is an idyllic, verdant spot close to the centre of London, which allows visitors to relax and reconnect with nature. It's a genuine piece of countryside in a heavily urban environment and offers free access to a wide variety of animals and birds, while also providing a realistic impression of a working farm.

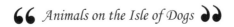

66 *Animals on the Isle of Dogs* **99**

OLD SPITALFIELDS MARKET

Old Spitalfields Market is one of London's finest surviving Victorian market halls, located just outside the City in Spitalfields. The area is something of a hidden gem, famous not only for its handful of cobbled streets of Georgian houses, but also for its contemporary apartments, many converted from soup kitchens, Victorian baths and old tannery warehouses.

There's been a market on the site since 1638, when Charles I granted a licence for 'flesh, fowl and roots' to be sold on Spittle Fields, then a rural area on the outskirts of London. The current buildings were erected in 1887 to service a wholesale fruit and vegetable market, which moved to Leyton in 1991 (the New Spitalfields Market). The original Victorian market buildings and the market hall and roof were restored – now resplendent under a Fosters & Partners-designed glass canopy – and offer a fusion of Victorian splendour and cutting-edge contemporary architecture.

Nestled in the shadow of Christ Church (see page 113), the market is the perfect antidote to out-of-town shopping malls, and hosts popular themed markets seven days a week. Escape from the cloned high streets and discover lost treasures from fashion and arts to interiors and antiques, as you wander through an area steeped in history, now a centre of creativity and style. Spitalfields market is surrounded by independent shops, cafés, bars and awarding-winning restaurants such as Jamie Oliver's Canteen, Carluccio's, Michelin-starred La Chapelle and the popular family chain, Giraffe.

Although the market is open seven days a week, the busiest days are Thursdays to Sundays (particularly when the Arts Market is held), with Sundays the most popular. From Mondays to Fridays and Sundays there's a general Traders Market, where stalls include contemporary and vintage fashion, music, bespoke children's toys, jewellery and accessories, and home interiors. On selected Thursdays to Sundays (see website for dates) there's an Arts Market offering a wide choice of original artworks, from paintings to photography. On Saturdays there's the Style Market, where you'll find original clothing, accessories, homewares and ethical goods from independent designers. There's also the Kerb Street Food Market on Wednesdays (noon to 2.30pm).

The market also offers regular free events, including lunchtime concerts, festivals, tango classes, fashion shows and much more.

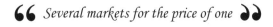

Several markets for the price of one

Address: **50 St Katharine's Way, E1W 1LA (020-7264 5312, www. skdocks.co.uk).**

Opening hours: **Unrestricted access.**

Cost: **Free.**

Transport: **Tower Hill tube, Tower Gateway DLR or boat.**

ST KATHARINE DOCKS

St Katharine Docks were one of the commercial docks that formed the Port of London, situated just east of the Tower of London and Tower Bridge. The foundations of today's buildings can be traced back to the 10th century, when King Edgar gave 13 acres (5.3ha) of land to 13 knights to use for trade. There's evidence of there having been a dock at St Katharine's since 1125, and it has also housed a hospital and monastery; in fact the Docks took their name from the former hospital of St Katharine by the Tower, established in the 12th century.

The first use of the name St Katharine Docks can be traced to Elizabethan times, when the area around the hospital was thriving with busy wharves. By the end of the 18th century St Katharine's was a prosperous settlement with its own court, school and

> **The Docks have their own pier serving boats to Westminster and Greenwich, while boats to other destinations call at nearby Tower Millennium Pier (see www.tfl.gov. uk/river).**

almshouses, and along with the hospital was home to some 3,000 people. However, when the government wanted to expand the Docks the area was earmarked for redevelopment; construction commenced in 1827 with the demolition of 1,250 slum houses and the medieval hospital of St Katharine.

The scheme was designed by celebrated engineer Thomas Telford (1757-1834) – his only major project in London – with the Docks' warehouses (designed by Philip Hardwick) built on the quayside so that goods could be unloaded directly into them. The Docks opened in 1828 and although well used, they weren't a huge commercial success, being unable to accommodate large ships. However, they gained a reputation for handling valuable cargoes and as late as the '30s were described as a focal point for the world's greatest concentration of portable wealth. They were badly damaged in WWII and never fully recovered, and were among the first London docks to be closed in 1968. Most of the original warehouses were demolished when the docks were redeveloped in the '70s,

Today, St Katharine Docks features offices, luxury warehouse apartments, a large hotel, shops, a Friday street food market (10am to 4pm), bars, restaurants, cafés and a pub (The Dickens Inn, a former brewery dating to the 18th century), a yacht marina and other recreational facilities. It's a great place for a family day out in the city.

 From bustling docks to tranquil yachting haven

Address: Southern Grove, E3 4PX (020-8983 1277, www.towerhamlets. gov.uk/lgnl/leisure_and_culture/parks_and_open_spaces/cemetery_ park.aspx).

Opening hours: Daily, dawn to dusk. There are usually guided tours (2hrs) at 2pm on the third Sun of the month organised by the friends (see www.fothcp.org).

Cost: Free.

Transport: Mile End or Bow Rd tube.

TOWER HAMLETS CEMETERY PARK

Tower Hamlets Cemetery Park (known locally as Bow Cemetery) is a historic cemetery opened in 1841 – the last and least known of London's Magnificent Seven Cemeteries created in the 1830s and 1840s to solve the city's chronic shortage of burial grounds. The other six were Abney Park (see page 147), Brompton, Highgate, Kensal Green (see page 207), Nunhead (see page 297) and West Norwood. It was the most working class of the cemeteries and during its first two years 60 per cent of burials were in public graves for those who couldn't afford a plot and funeral (which increased to 80 per cent by 1851).

The cemetery became neglected, which led to it being purchased by the Greater London Council in 1966 and closed to burials in order to create a public park in the heart of this intensively built-up area. In 1986, ownership was passed to the borough of Tower Hamlets, and in 1990 the Friends of the Tower Hamlets Cemetery Park was created. The cemetery became Tower Hamlets' first local nature reserve in 2001 and is managed and maintained by the Friends.

The park covers an area of 33 acres (13.4ha) of mature broadleaf woodland and meadow, with an outstanding variety of wild plants, flowers and animals. Wildlife includes over 20 butterfly species and around 40 bird species, which can be heard on the annual International Dawn Chorus Day walk (usually 1st May). Parts of the park are managed wilderness, while others, such as the pond areas, are used as an outdoor classroom to teach environmental science to local school children.

In 2002, the Cantrell Road Maze was created in scrap yard meadows – the name indicates its former use – where Friends and local volunteers made a chalk maze based on a classical

> **People entirely unrelated to each other would be buried in the same grave within the space of a few weeks, and there were stories of some graves being 40 feet deep and containing up to 30 bodies.**

design. A green corridor link – the Ackroyd Drive Greenlink – has also been created between the Cemetery Park and Mile End Park.

The high brick walls surrounding the cemetery are Grade II listed, as are 16 individual grave memorials – there are some fascinating memorial stones, particularly of angels. Today the park is a wonderful, if slightly spooky, green space, and has been designated a conservation area, a Local Nature Reserve and a site of Metropolitan Importance for Nature Conservation. It's a wonderful place to relax and forget the stresses of the modern world.

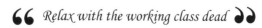

❝ *Relax with the working class dead* **❞**

Address: Cambridge Heath Rd, Bethnal Grn, E2 9PA (020-8983 5200, www.vam.ac.uk/moc).

Opening hours: Daily, 10am to 5.45pm. Closed 24-26th Dec and 1st Jan.

Cost: Free.

Transport: Bethnal Grn tube.

VICTORIA & ALBERT MUSEUM OF CHILDHOOD

Somewhat overshadowed by its parent in Kensington and often ignored, possibly due to its location away from London's main tourist centres to the west, this free attraction is well worth visiting; nostalgic adults usually enjoy the museum as much as children.

Housed in an iron-framed building resembling a Victorian train station (or shed, if you're feeling less generous), it has lots of glass and natural light to help show off its many varied exhibits. And if these don't compensate for being in such an inevitably child-heavy environment, the café is licensed to help calm the nerves and raise the mood of stressed and bored adults.

The museum houses the Victoria and Albert Museum's collection of childhood-related objects, covering the period from the 17th century to the present. It includes toys (dolls, dolls' houses, puppets, teddy bears and much more), clothes, games, art, furniture and photographs. There's also a regular programme of temporary exhibitions, as well as activities, events and workshops. The museum's stated aim is to encourage people 'to explore the themes of childhood past and present'.

The permanent displays are arranged in three main galleries: Moving Toys, Creativity and Childhood. Moving Toys is itself divided into four (self-explanatory) sections: Pushes and Pulls; Springs and Cogs; Circuits and Motors; and Look See. Creativity is about the ability to challenge, question and explore, and features toys related to the development of creativity and imagination (in maths and science as well as in art). It's also divided into four sections: Imagine, Be Inspired, Explore and Make it Happen. In Childhood, the displays tell the social story of childhood and are organised into the following themes: Babies, Home, What We Wear, Who Will I Be? How We Learn, Good Times and Families.

The website contains comprehensive information about these various categories and sub-categories, allowing visitors to identify what they most want to see and plan their trip accordingly. Children seem fascinated by most of the exhibits, while adults are especially drawn to those that remind them of their own childhoods and also to the 18th-century dolls' houses, some of which are more than mere toys, being veritable works of art.

66 *The original 'Toys R Us'* 99

Address: 32-34 Whitechapel Rd, Whitechapel, E1 1DY (020-7247 2599, www.whitechapelbellfoundry.co.uk).

Opening hours: Pre-booked tours (1½hrs, minimum age 14) on selected Sat at 10am, 1.15pm and 4pm (see website for dates). You're advised to wear robust clothing and shoes, and nothing smart, as foundries are mucky places. The museum display and shop are open Mon-Fri, 9am to 5pm.

Cost: Tours £14 per head, payable on booking.

Transport: Aldgate E or Whitechapel tube.

WHITECHAPEL BELL FOUNDRY

Whitechapel Bell Foundry is listed in the *Guinness Book of Records* as the oldest manufacturing company in Britain, and is full of history and interest. The company dates back to at least 1570, and there's a link to an Aldgate bell foundry in 1420, so it may be even older. The present premises on Whitechapel Road date from 1670 and used to be a coaching inn, quaintly named 'The Artichoke'.

Whitechapel Bell Foundry's business has always been, and still is, the manufacture of bells and their associated fittings. These include large bells for change ringing peals in church towers, single tolling bells, carillon bells, and their complete range of accessories such as framework, wheels and clappers. The company also makes handbells for tune and change ringing, and other small bells of many shapes and sizes.

It has produced many famous bells, including Big Ben, the Liberty Bell (see box), the Great Bell of Montreal Cathedral, Great Tom of Lincoln Cathedral and the Clock Bells of St Paul's Cathedral. Westminster Abbey is one of its oldest customers, with the two bells calling people to services dating from the reign of Elizabeth I.

Big Ben (the nickname of the great bell in the clock tower of the Palace of Westminster) was cast here in 1858. At 13.5 tons, 7.5ft tall and 9ft in diameter, it's the largest bell ever cast at the foundry, comprising 10.5 tons of molten copper and three tons of tin, which took 20 hours to cool. Visitors to the foundry pass through a full-sized profile of the bell that frames the main entrance to the building.

If you cannot take one of the (relatively infrequent) tours, the museum display provides a flavour of this obscure, interesting industry, while the shop has a wide range of bell-related souvenirs.

The Liberty Bell

The Liberty Bell, weighing around 2,000lb (907kg), was cast in 1752 and shipped to America. Formerly installed in the steeple of the Pennsylvania State House (now renamed Independence Hall), the bell was cast with the lettering (part of Leviticus 25:10) 'Proclaim LIBERTY throughout all the land unto all the inhabitants thereof.' It cracked when first rung after its arrival in Pennsylvania, but was repaired and the large crack that can now be seen occurred sometime in the 19th century. The Liberty Bell became widely famous as it was thought to be one of the bells rung to mark the reading of the United States Declaration of Independence on July 4th, 1776.

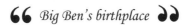

" *Big Ben's birthplace* "

Address: 77-82 Whitechapel High St, Whitechapel, E1 7QX (020-7522 7888, www.whitechapelgallery.org).

Opening hours: Tue-Sun, 11am to 6pm (Thu 9pm). Closed Mon.

Cost: Usually free to the gallery and exhibitions.

Transport: Aldgate E tube.

WHITECHAPEL GALLERY

Whitechapel is associated in many minds with grisly crimes rather than art – it was the setting for Jack the Ripper's murders (at least five and possibly more) and the Kray Brothers' murder of George Cornell at The Blind Beggar pub on Whitechapel Road. But it's also the home of one of Britain's most forward-thinking and influential art galleries, which is sometimes under-appreciated and ignored by those outside the world of contemporary art, being sited away from London's hub of large, famous galleries in the West End.

The gallery is located on the north side of Whitechapel High Street in a striking building with a distinctive façade designed by Charles Harrison Townsend (who also designed the Horniman Museum – see page 293). Both museums are usually referred to as Art Nouveau or Arts and Crafts in style, although Townsend was an original architect and his style is difficult to pigeonhole.

Founded in 1901 to 'bring great art to the people of the East End of London', the Whitechapel Gallery exhibits the work of contemporary artists and is noted for its temporary exhibitions. It has a long-standing reputation for premiering the work of international artists, as well as supporting local causes and promoting artists who live and work in the East End.

It exhibited Picasso's painting *Guernica* in 1938 as part of a touring exhibition organised by the English artist and collector Roland Penrose to protest against the Spanish Civil War and, among many others, it hosted exhibitions that brought Pop Art to the general public and highlighted artists, designers and photographers who defined the 'Swinging Sixties'. The Whitechapel also premiered international painters such as Frida Kahlo, Jackson Pollock and Mark Rothko, and showcased British artists including Lucian Freud, Gilbert and George, David Hockney and Mark Wallinger. It has also exhibited art from Africa, India and Latin America.

In the later '60s and '70s the gallery became less significant and cutting-edge, as newer venues such as the Hayward Gallery at the Southbank Centre displaced it, but it bloomed again in the '80s under the directorship of the noted British art curator Nicholas Serota (he took the bold step of closing it for over a year for extensive refurbishment) and is well worth visiting regularly.

In addition to its exhibitions (see website for details), the recently expanded gallery offers historic archives, educational resources, art courses, a bookshop and a well-regarded café/bar (which alone makes a visit worthwhile) – see website for opening times.

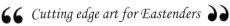

66 *Cutting edge art for Eastenders* **99**

CHAPTER 4

NORTH LONDON

See next page for more maps

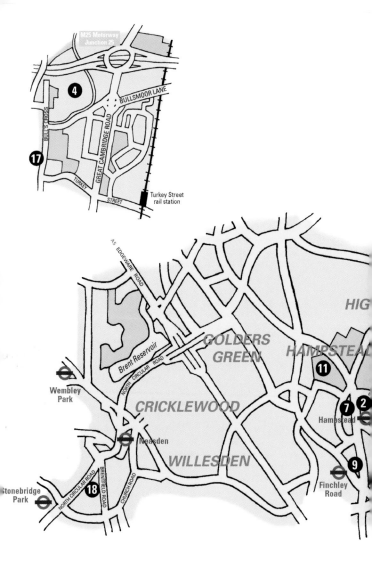

See previous page for key

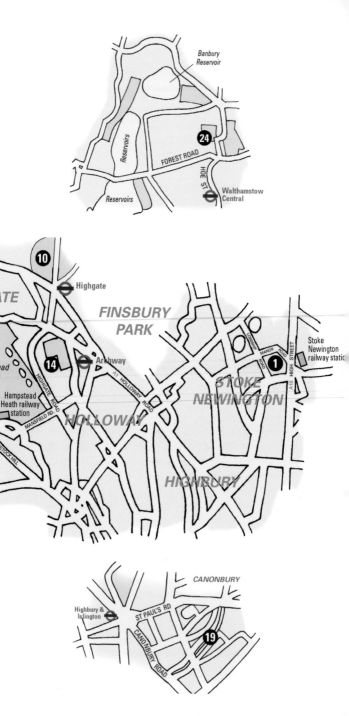

ABNEY PARK CEMETERY

Now a memorial park and woodland nature reserve run by Abney Park Trust, Abney Park Cemetery was one of London's 'Magnificent Seven' garden cemeteries, built between 1832 and 1841 by the Victorians to cope with London's rapid population increase. The other six were Brompton, Highgate, Kensal Green (see page 207), Nunhead (page 297), Tower Hamlets (page 135) and West Norwood.

Abney Park was originally laid out in the early 18th century on the instructions of Lady Mary Abney and others. In 1840 it became a non-denominational garden cemetery, but also a semi-public arboretum and educational institute. It was set out in an entirely different way from the other Magnificent Seven and had a wider purpose that was rather ahead of its time. The first wholly non-denominational garden cemetery in Europe, it was specifically designed using motifs not associated with contemporary religion. It has an impressive entrance in the then-popular Egyptian revival style, designed by William Hosking, the first professor of architecture at Kings College, London, who also designed the Grade II listed Abney Park Chapel.

The park's arboretum was originally designed as a labelled tree collection for educational walks, and much enhanced the wooded character of the park, which already had several exotic trees from various far flung places, some planted in the 1690s. The planting of the original 2,500 arboretum trees and shrubs was designed to be botanical and naturalistic, rather than purely aesthetic, which led Abney Park to become regarded as the most impressively landscaped garden cemetery of its time.

Burial rights in the park ceased in 1978, and it's now dedicated to a wide range of projects in the fields of arts, education, nature conservation and recreation. However, ashes can be scattered at certain locations and there's still the occasional discretionary or courtesy burial.

Today, the park is a romantic wilderness and bolthole in a grittily urban part of London, every bit as atmospheric and interesting as the much better-known Highgate Cemetery (another of the Magnificent Seven). Its wild and crumbling state adds to its charm and interest, with some magnificent urns, inscriptions, plinths, ivy-clad statues and sculptures – many in a terrible state – leaning, tumbling and falling over, and merging with the planting. The most famous 'resident' is William Booth, founder of the Salvation Army, who lies beneath a huge, striking headstone. The park is full of atmospheric walks and picnic spots, and rich in wildlife.

 London's most impressive landscaped garden cemetery

Address: New End Sq, Hampstead, NW3 1LT (020-7431 0144, www. burghhouse.org.uk).

Opening hours: House and museum: Wed-Fri and Sun, noon to 5pm. Buttery café: Wed-Fri, 11am to 5pm and Sat-Sun, 9.30am to 5.30pm.

Cost: Free.

Transport: Hampstead tube.

BURGH HOUSE & HAMPSTEAD MUSEUM

Leafy, upmarket Hampstead in north London is one of the capital's most desirable residential areas, much favoured by wealthy media executives and successful actors, writers, rock stars and other creative types. It's one of those districts that merits simply wandering around, soaking up the atmosphere, admiring the architecture and realising that you couldn't afford to rent a garage here, let alone buy a house.

It's eminently civilised, as is Burgh House, nestled in the heart of old Hampstead and home to the area's local museum. It wouldn't claim to be one of the capital's great collections, but it's varied and interesting, and, like so many of London's local displays, often passes under the radar – of local residents as well as visitors.

Burgh House is Grade I listed and was built in 1704 in the time of Queen Anne. It's a handsome building and one of the oldest houses in Hampstead, with original panelled rooms and staircase. It's named after a certain Reverend Allatson Burgh, a notably unpopular cleric, who bought it in 1822. Among its many tenants over the years was Rudyard Kipling's daughter, Elsie Bambridge, in the '30s.

The property is now used for a variety of purposes: as a local history museum, art gallery, classical music venue, shop and café. The museum's permanent display comprises over 3,000 objects, many relating to social history, fine art and notable Hampstead residents (and the area has played host to many). There's a display dedicated to the painter John Constable, who spent time in Hampstead (and is buried in St John-at-Hampstead graveyard), and to the poet John Keats, who lived in the area for a short time (see Keats House on page 171).

The museum traces Hampstead's long history, from prehistoric times to the present day. Hampstead Heath (around 800 acres of heathland, meadows and woodland, and one of the highest points in London) contains traces of Hampstead's earliest known inhabitants, Mesolithic hunters from around 7,000 BC, plus evidence of Bronze Age settlement.

Burgh House's Buttery Café attracts many locals who've probably never thought of visiting the museum. As well as a cosy indoor space, there are tables in the pretty garden which is full of nooks and crannies; a lovely place to sit with a coffee or a glass of wine in this most civilised part of London.

 The story of north London's most desirable area

Address: Camden Passage, Angel, Islington, N1 8EA (www.camdenpassageislington.co.uk).

Opening hours: The market days are Wed and Sat (9am to 6pm), Fri (10am to 6pm) and Sun (11am to 6pm).

Cost: Free.

Transport: Angel tube.

CAMDEN PASSAGE ANTIQUES MARKET

Camden Passage is a pedestrian thoroughfare built as an alley along the backs of houses on Upper Street, then Islington High Street, in the mid-18th century. Hidden down a cobblestoned Angel backstreet, visiting the Passage is like stepping back in time. Here you'll find a multitude of stalls selling an eclectic mix of antiques and collectibles – vintage clothes, handbags, jewellery, silver, porcelain, glass and assorted bric-a-brac – intermingled with a range of elegant Georgian antiques shops, pubs, cafés and restaurants.

Whether you're a dealer, interior designer, collector or just a curious browser, you'll find Camden Passage intriguing. Most of the traders are specialists who know their stuff, so just chatting to them can be an education and very rewarding, but you'll need to arrive early to pick over the stalls or haggle hard to get a bargain.

The Passage's current incarnation dates back to the early '60s, when local businessman John Payton had a vision that it would make a great antiques' market. With the assistance of local shopkeepers, antiques' centres were created from bomb sites and arcades of small shops built. Antiques' dealers soon flocked to the area creating a unique antiques' village, which at its peak boasted some 350 dealers.

Nowadays the market is smaller, but what it lacks in quantity it more than makes up for in quality, with a unique collection of traders of all types and levels. Today's specialist dealers include Vincent Freeman (no. 1), music boxes, singing birds and automata; Kevin Page's Oriental Art (nos. 2-6), one of London's leading dealers in Chinese and Japanese antiques; Mike Weedon (no. 7), Art Deco, Art Nouveau and European ceramics; and Piers Rankin (no. 14), silver and Sheffield plate. The camaraderie of the traders has ensured that the Passage has survived where other antiques areas have failed. Standards have remained consistently high and the wide range of quality goods on offer has ensured its enduring success as a centre of excellence.

Camden Passage Antiques Market (not to be confused with the much larger Camden Markets in Camden Town) is open on Wednesdays and Friday to Sunday, although the larger antique shops also open on other days or by appointment. There's also a farmers' market on Sundays. After you've had your fill of antiques, you can enjoy an excellent lunch in one of the local eateries.

66 *A mecca for antiques enthusiasts and the peckish* **99**

Address: Bullsmoor Ln, Enfield, EN1 4RQ (08456-122 122, www. capelmanorgardens.co.uk).

Opening hours: **Nov-Feb: Mon-Fri, 10am to 5pm. Mar-Oct: daily, 10am to 5.30pm. Closed 25th Dec to 1st Jan.**

Cost: **Adults £5.50, concessions £4.50, children £2.50 (5 and under free), family £13.50 (2 adults and up to 3 children). See website for special musical and theatrical events.**

Transport: **Turkey St rail (20 minutes walk) or by car.**

CAPEL MANOR GARDENS

Capel Manor Gardens is a stunning 30-acre (12.1ha) estate surrounding a Georgian manor house and Victorian stables. The Gardens feature a variety of richly-planted themed areas, including historical gardens, an Italianate maze, a Japanese garden, Kim Wilde's Jungle Gym Garden and many others. They also contains the *Gardening Which?* magazine demonstration and trial gardens and the National Gardening Centre, which includes specially designed gardens such as Sunflower Street – seven front and back gardens designed by former students. There's

> **Enjoy the stunning scenery, picnic by the lake or have lunch in the Terrace restaurant – a perfect day out for budding horticulturalists.**

also the gold-medal-winning Australian Garden from the 2011 RHS Chelsea Flower Show.

The history of Capel Manor dates back to 1275 when the land, then known as 'Honeylands and Pentriches', was held by Ellis of Honeyland. There's evidence of a manor house at this time but the one you see today was built in the 1750s. In 1486, Sir William Capel became the owner of the house here, which remained in his family (later Lords of Essex) until the 16th century, when Sir Giles, Sir Henry and Edward Capel surrendered it to the crown.

The estate then passed through a succession of owners until, in 1932, Lt Col Sydney Medcalf occupied it and remained here until his death in 1958. The last private owner of Capel, Colonel Medcalf had a passion for horticulture but is best remembered for his association with the breeding of Clydesdale horses, having established a stud farm at Capel House. Capel Manor became a National Centre for Clydesdale horse breeding and the Medcalf cup is still awarded today. Colonel Medcalf left the house to the Incorporated Society of Accountants and in 1965 the contents were sold at auction.

Today, Capel Manor is a college of horticulture and London's only specialist centre for land-based studies. Capel Manor College is a working estate where students and staff gain 'hands-on' experience in all aspects of land-based studies, including horticulture, arboriculture (tree surgery), garden design, floristry, animal care, saddlery and environmental conservation.

The Animal Corner has Kune Kune pigs, goats, poultry, rabbits, pygmy goats and guinea pigs, plus Clydesdale horses exercising and working in the grounds. There's also a varied programme of shows and events throughout the year, while the Hessayon (visitors) Centre contains a garden gift shop with plant sales in summer.

 A year-round inspiration for gardeners

Address: **48 Doughty St, WC1N 2LX (020-7405 2127, www. dickensmuseum.com)**

Opening hours: **Daily, 10am to 5pm. There are also costumed tours and walks. The café is open Mon-Sun (10am to 4m).**

Cost: **£8 adults, £6 concessions, £4 children (6-16), under-6s free. Admission to the café, garden and gift shop is free.**

Transport: **Chancery Ln, Holborn or Russell Sq tube.**

Charles Dickens

CHARLES DICKENS MUSEUM

Charles Dickens's novels have done much to inform people's view of London, and the term 'Dickensian' is still used to describe certain parts of the city. Therefore it's surprising that not only is the museum not on the front page of the average 'to visit' list, but probably isn't on it at all.

It's spread over four floors of a typical Georgian terraced house, although the rooms have a traditional Victorian appearance. Dickens lived here for over two years, from March 1837 (a year after his marriage) until December 1839, and it's the only surviving house he occupied in London. He and his wife Catherine lived here with the eldest three of their ten children, and the older two of Dickens's daughters were born in the house. He had a three-year lease on the property at £80 per year, subsequently moving to a larger home as his family grew and his wealth increased.

This was a productive time for the author: he completed *The Pickwick Papers*, wrote *Oliver Twist* and *Nicholas Nickleby*, and worked on *Barnaby Rudge* in this property. So it's appropriate that it houses the world's most important Dickens' collection, with over 100,000 items, including manuscripts, rare editions, paintings, personal items and a research library. The photographic collection has over 5,000 photographs, 2,000 magic lantern slides, 1,000 35mm slides and a large number of colour transparencies. There are also over 500 portraits of Dickens, many interesting views of 19th-century London, illustrations from his novels, and cartoons and caricatures.

The most famous exhibit is probably the portrait of Dickens known as *Dickens' Dream* by R. W. Buss, an original illustrator of *The Pickwick Papers*. This unfinished picture shows Dickens in his study at Gads Hill Place in Kent, surrounded by many of the characters from his books.

You can see a 25-minute film about Charles Dickens' life in London, and the museum has permanent displays and exhibitions about his life and work. There are also a range of resources for teachers, students and researchers, and workshops for school groups. See website for dates and details.

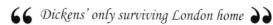

❝ *Dickens' only surviving London home* ❞

Address: 39a Canonbury Sq, Islington, N1 2AN (020-7704 9522, www. estorickcollection.com).

Opening hours: Wed-Sat, 11am to 6pm; Sun noon to 5pm (open until 9pm on the first Thu of each month). Closed Mon-Tue, Easter Sun and over Christmas and New Year (check website for exact dates).

Cost: £5 adults, £3.50 concessions, free for schoolchildren and students. Free entry to the café and shop.

Transport: Highbury & Islington tube/rail.

Crouching Nude, Emilio Greco

Metaphysical man: Il Trovatore, Georgio de Chirico

ESTORICK COLLECTION

Little-known (or even heard of outside the local area), this is a hidden London gem, not just Britain's only gallery devoted to modern Italian art, but one of the world's best collections of early 20th-century Italian art. It's a favourite with locals for its peaceful setting in a beautiful, early 19th-century house and its garden café, which is a great spot for an alfresco summer lunch.

The collection is named after Eric Estorick (1913-1993), an American sociologist, writer and art collector who later became a full-time art dealer. He was very successful and his clients included a number of Hollywood stars, among them Lauren Bacall, Burt Lancaster and Billy Wilder. He set up the Eric and Salome Estorick foundation, to which he left his Italian collection, and 39a Canonbury Square was purchased to house it.

The Estorick collection has six galleries, an art library, café and bookshop, and regularly stages temporary exhibitions, well-regarded talks and educational events (see website for details). The permanent collection is internationally regarded, particularly for its Futurist works.

Futurism was founded in 1909 by the poet F. T. Marinetti and was Italy's most significant contribution to 20th-century European culture. It sought to move beyond Italy's old, conservative cultural heritage and develop a new aesthetic, based on modern ideas drawing inspiration from machines, speed and technology. Several painters were eager to extend Marinetti's ideas to the visual arts. Estorick developed a passion for their works on his honeymoon in 1947, during which he bought 'hundreds and hundreds of drawings and as many paintings as I could get into my Packard Convertible Roadster', and his collection grew from there throughout the '50s.

Other artists represented in the Estorick Collection include Amedeo Modigliani, noted for his elegant, elongated portraits, and Giorgio de Chirico, whose dream-like works with illogical juxtapositions of objects were a great influence on the Surrealists. As well as paintings, the collection contains sculpture and figurative art, including work by Medardo Rosso, who, on the death of Rodin, was called 'the greatest living sculptor' by the French writer and critic Apollinaire. There are also sculptures by Giacomo Manzu and Marino Marini, hailed as bringing about the rebirth of Italian sculpture in the 20th century.

66 *Some of the best Italian art in London* **99**

Address: Hampstead Grove, Hampstead, NW3 6SP (020-7434 3471, www.nationaltrust.org.uk/fenton-house).

Opening hours: Mar-Oct: Wed-Sun, 11am to 5pm (see website for exact dates) plus selected days in Nov-Dec. Closed Jan-Feb.

Cost: £6.50 adults, £3 children, £16 family. National Trust members free.

Transport: Hampstead tube.

FENTON HOUSE

Affluent, leafy Hampstead is full of sizeable, attractive properties and this is one of the earliest, largest and most architecturally important – a charming 17th-century merchant's house. It was built around 1686 and has been virtually unaltered over 300 years of continuous occupation. The large garden is also remarkably unchanged.

Country Life magazine described it as 'London's most enchanting country house' and it's now owned by the National Trust. The Fentons, who bought the house in 1793, gave it the name and made some Regency alterations that gave the house its current appearance.

The house is in a classic, almost idealised, Queen Anne style, of a type that has been copied by generations of dolls' house makers ever since. It stands back from the street, which gives it an air of tranquillity, and is built from elegant, deep brown brickwork, with red-rubbed brick for the dressings and an absence of carved stone. There are Doric pilasters around the door and a boldly carved wooden cornice under the eaves. The ground plan of the house is a perfect square cut into quarters by a cross. Two arms contain the staircases, the other two the hall and landings.

Fenton House is home to a collection of early keyboard instruments assembled by the many-named Major George Henry Benton Fletcher (1866-1944). He had a varied career as a soldier, social worker and archaeologist (who dug with the famous Flinders Petrie), and was also a perhaps unlikely instrument collector. One of them is sometimes played for visitors during opening hours.

The house also boasts collections of paintings (notably some fine portraits – artists represented in the collection including Jan Bruegel, Albrecht Durer, John Russell, Francis Sartorius and G. F. Watts), porcelain (there are world-class collections of English, European and Oriental porcelain), 17th-century needlework pictures and Georgian furniture (of the decorative and delicate sort).

The garden is laid out on the side of a hill and divided into upper and lower levels. It's an almost rural haven in a heavily populated part of London, noted for its sunken walled section, with a glasshouse, vegetable beds, culinary herb border and flower beds. There's also a 300-year-old orchard of agreeably gnarled apple trees, producing over 30 different varieties.

 *Lovely Queen Anne architecture in north London*

Address: 40 Brunswick Sq, WC1N 1AZ (020-7841 3600, www.
foundlingmuseum.org.uk).

Opening hours: Tue-Sat, 10am to 5pm; Sun 11am to 5pm. Closed Mon
and some bank holidays (see website for details).

Cost: £8.25 adults, £5.50 concessions, under-16s free. National Trust
members half price.

Transport: Russell Sq tube.

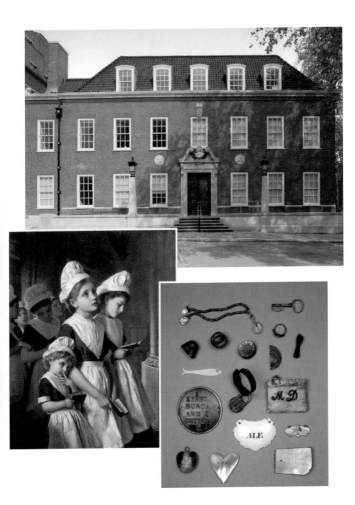

FOUNDLING MUSEUM

The Foundling Museum's location in a leafy Bloomsbury cul-de-sac is certainly attractive, but has contributed to it being off the main tourist radar. This is a pity because, according to the British broadsheet newspaper, *The Daily Telegraph*, it's 'one of London's most intriguing collections'. The website calls it 'Britain's original home for abandoned children and London's first ever public art gallery'.

It tells the story of the Foundling Hospital, London's first home for abandoned children, which involves three major figures in British history: the philanthropist Sir Thomas Coram (1668-1751, who founded the hospital), the artist William Hogarth and the composer George Frederic Handel. The hospital is said to be the world's first incorporated charity, which Coram established after being appalled by the number of abandoned, homeless children living on London's streets.

The museum's collection charts the history of the Foundling Hospital between its foundation in 1739 and closure in 1954. It's a fascinating blend of art, period interiors and social history, housed in a restored building adjacent to the hospital's original home, which was demolished in 1928. The museum has two principal collections.

The Foundling Collection relates to the hospital itself and the story of the 27,000 children who passed through its doors during its 215-year history. Especially poignant is the collection of tokens mothers left with their babies, allowing the hospital to match a mother with her child should she ever come back to claim it, which, sadly, didn't happen in the vast majority of cases.

The Gerald Coke Handel Collection relates to the life and work of the composer G. F. Handel, who was a governor and benefactor of the hospital. It's an internationally significant collection, the largest privately-held collection of Handel material, including books, engravings, libretti, manuscripts, memorabilia, paintings and more, and was collected by Gerald Coke (a banker and patron of the arts) over a period of around 60 years.

William Hogarth (who was childless) had a long association with the Foundling Hospital and was a founding governor. He designed the children's uniforms and the coat of arms, and he and his wife fostered foundling children. He also set up a permanent art exhibition here and encouraged other artists to produce work for the hospital. In this way, it became Britain's first public art gallery. There are paintings and sculptures by Thomas Gainsborough, Hogarth himself, Joshua Reynolds and many others.

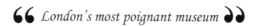

66 *London's most poignant museum* **99**

Address: 20 Maresfield Gardens, Hampstead, NW3 5SX (020-7435 2002, www.freud.org.uk).

Opening hours: Wed-Sun, noon to 5pm. See website for holiday opening times.

Cost: £7 adults, £5 senior citizens, £4 concessions (students, children 12-16, etc.), under-12s free.

Transport: Finchley Rd tube.

Sigmund Freud

FREUD MUSEUM

The address says Hampstead, but this is the western reaches of that leafy district, hence the nearest tube. As a result, it's slightly 'off the map' and sometimes ignored. But it's an interesting, atmospheric museum, housed in what was the home of Sigmund Freud (1886-1939) and his family when they fled the Nazi annexation of Austria in 1938. Built in 1920 in Queen Anne style, it's a large, red-brick house, striking and handsome as befits this upmarket part of London.

It remained the Freud family home until 1982, when Anna Freud, Sigmund's youngest daughter (he had six children), died. Sigmund Freud himself didn't have the chance to live in the house for very long, dying a few weeks after the Second World War broke out in September 1939.

In view of the chaos of the late '30s, the Freuds were lucky to be able to bring their furniture and household effects to London, including lovely Biedermeier chests, tables and cupboards, and a collection of 18th- and 19th-century Austrian painted country furniture. Their possessions include a drawing of Freud by Salvador Dali (the Surrealists were strongly influenced by his writings).

The museum's centrepiece is Freud's study, preserved as it was during his lifetime, and exactly as it had been in Vienna: Freud wrote down the position of everything so that it could be faithfully recreated. The most famous exhibit is his psychoanalytic couch, on which all his patients reclined. It's covered with a richly coloured Iranian rug with chenille cushions piled on top.

The study also displays his impressive collection of antiquities (Egyptian, Greek, Roman and Oriental), totalling almost 2,000 items. Freud stated that his passion for collecting was second only to his addiction to cigars, and he sometimes used archaeology as a metaphor for psychoanalysis. The walls of the study are lined with shelves containing his large library of books.

The house also contains much from the life and works of Anna Freud, who lived here for 44 years and continued her father's psychoanalytic work, notably with children. Both she and Sigmund loved the garden (he was particularly fond of flowers), which is beautifully maintained, much as Freud would have known it. There's also a shop, selling many things Freud-related, and the museum hosts a series of courses, films and lectures about subjects relevant to Freud and to psychoanalysis in general.

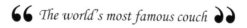

❝ *The world's most famous couch* **❞**

HIGHGATE & QUEEN'S WOODS

Highgate Wood and Queen's Wood (separated by Muswell Hill Road) are two stunning preserved segments of the ancient Forest of Middlesex, which covered much of London and was mentioned in the *Domesday Book*. Both woods are wildlife oases and local nature reserves, designated Sites of Metropolitan Importance for Nature Conservation.

Highgate Wood – owned and managed by the City of London Corporation – covers an area of 70 acres (28ha) rich in oak, holly and hornbeam trees, plus the rare wild service tree, the presence of which commonly indicates an ancient woodland. The wood is home to over 50 other tree and shrub species and is rich in wildlife, including five species of bat, foxes, grey squirrels, over 70 bird species and more than 250 species of moths.

Excavations show that Romano-Britons were producing pottery from local materials here between AD 50-100, and there are ancient earthworks that may have formed part of an enclosure for deer during the medieval period, when the Bishop of London owned the wood. Between the 16th and 18th centuries the wood, then known as 'Brewer's Fell', was leased to various tenants who managed (coppiced) the wood and produced timber (particularly oak) for the Crown to construct ships and for church buildings. In 1886, the City of London Corporation acquired the wood, then known as Gravelpit Wood, for public use and renamed it Highgate Wood.

Queen's Wood is owned and managed by the borough of Haringey. It covers an area of 51 acres (21ha) and was known as Churchyard Bottom Wood (possibly due to the discovery of human

> In addition to football and cricket pitches, Highgate Wood also has a children's playground, a café and an information centre, while Queen's Wood has a café and an organic community garden.

bones, thought to be a burial pit for victims of the bubonic plague in 1665) until being purchased by Hornsey Council in 1898, when it was renamed Queen's Wood in honour of Queen Victoria. Like Highgate Wood, it's ancient woodland, featuring English oak and the occasional beech, which provide a canopy above cherry, field maple, hazel, holly, hornbeam, midland hawthorn, mountain ash, lowland birch and the rare wild service tree. Queen's Wood reputedly has a greater diversity of flora and fauna than Highgate Wood, as it's wilder and has greater structural diversity and a denser shrub layer.

Visit Highgate and Queen's Woods and prepare to be enchanted.

 A captivating glimpse of London's ancient forests

Address: Inverforth Cl, off North End Way, NW3 7EX (www.hampsteadheath.net/introduction-2.html and www.londongardensonline.org.uk/gardens-online-record.asp?ID=CAM055).

Opening hours: Daily, dawn to dusk.

Cost: Free.

Transport: Golders Grn or Hampstead tube.

HILL GARDEN & PERGOLA

Charming Hill Garden and its beautiful pergola (Grade II listed) – 800ft (244m) in length – are among the hidden delights of Hampstead Heath. This formal Arts and Crafts garden was created between 1906 and 1925 by celebrated landscape architect Thomas Mawson (1861-1933) for the soap magnate Lord Leverhulme (1851-1925). It's situated at the rear of Inverforth House, formerly The Hill, which Leverhulme purchased in 1904 as his London residence. He subsequently acquired some adjoining land, which led to the creation of the pergola. The first part of the project was completed in 1906 and extended in 1911, but it wasn't finally completed until 1925, shortly before Lord Leverhulme died. The Hill was then purchased by Baron Inverforth (and renamed Inverforth House), who lived here until his death in 1955.

Mawson brought architectural treatment and formality to garden design, and the pergola and gardens were destined to become

> **A favourite haunt of local artists, the pergola and Hill Garden are a delightful sanctuary and a perfect antidote to the stresses of modern life.**

the best surviving examples of his work. He overcame the difficulty of the public right of way between the two parts of the structure by building a fine stone bridge. The pergola was a magnificent Edwardian extravagance and became the setting for garden parties and summer evening strolls. The pergola walk, linking the formal gardens of the main house and the more gentle lawns of the lower garden, was a master stroke, enhanced by the dramatic contrast between the towering trees of West Heath and the exotic plants climbing the graceful pergola.

WWII and subsequent years weren't kind to the pergola and gardens, which were purchased by the London County Council in 1960, when they were in an appalling state. The area was restored and opened to the public in 1963 as the Hill Garden. Since 1989 it has been owned and managed by the City of London Corporation, which restored the pergola in 1995.

In late spring and early summer the raised, covered pergola is festooned with fragrant flowers, including jasmine, buddleia, sage, honeysuckle, vines, clematis, kiwi, potato vine, lavender and wisteria. Visit during the early evening and you may even see roosting long-eared bats. In contrast to the wild decadence of the pergola, Hill Garden is beautifully manicured and designed and a slice of paradise, offering panoramic views of London.

66 *A secret, magical, gem of a garden* **99**

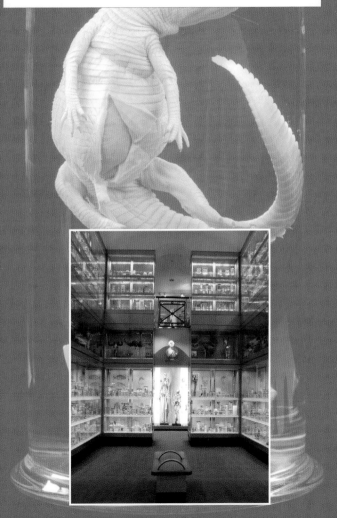

HUNTERIAN MUSEUM

This museum might not be suitable for those of a sensitive or squeamish disposition, but nevertheless it's fascinating. As might be expected from its setting in the building of the Royal College of Surgeons, this is very much a medical exhibit, undoubtedly one of the world's greatest museum collections of comparative anatomy, pathology, osteology and natural history.

The museum is named after the noted Scottish surgeon and keen collector John Hunter (1728-1793), whose collection of around 15,000 items was purchased by the government in 1799 and given to the Company (later the Royal College) of Surgeons. (John Hunter's brother's collection forms the basis for Glasgow's Hunterian Museum.)

Today's museum contains around 3,500 items from Hunter's original collection, with another 2,500 or so objects acquired after 1799, including an odontological (tooth) collection and natural history collections. The many objects that cannot be displayed are held in the Royal College's reserve collection, which is available for research and teaching (see the website for details).

The Hunterian's collections are rather grisly for some tastes – notably the large selection of preserved human and animal remains, with rows of jars of organs – but they're varied and fascinating, and show just how far medicine has (thankfully!) progressed in the last few centuries. The museum also stages regular temporary exhibitions.

Among the many permanent items on display are a mummified hand, old wax models of dissections, diseased bones, Winston Churchill's dentures, photographs of pioneering plastic surgery, videos of modern operations and the skeleton of an Irish giant who was 7ft 7in tall, called Charles Byrne, sometimes referred to by his stage name Charles O'Brien.

The Royal College of Surgeons dates from the 14th century (believed to be 1368) with the foundation of the 'Guild of Surgeons Within the City of London'. There was an ongoing dispute between the surgeons and the barber surgeons until an agreement was signed in 1493, giving the fellowship of surgeons the power of incorporation. This union was formalised further in 1540 by Henry VIII between the Worshipful Company of Barbers (incorporated 1462) and the Guild of Surgeons, to form the Company of Barber-Surgeons. In 1745, the surgeons broke away to form the Company of Surgeons, which in 1800 was granted a royal charter to become the Royal College of Surgeons in London. A further charter in 1843 granted it the present title of the Royal College of Surgeons of England.

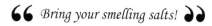

❝ *Bring your smelling salts!* **❞**

Address: Keats Grove, Hampstead, NW3 2RR (020-7332 3868, www. cityoflondon.gov.uk/things-to-do/attractions-around-london/keats-house/pages/default.aspx).

Opening hours: **Nov-Feb (winter): Fri-Sun, 1-5pm, Tue-Thu, pre-booked groups only. Mar-Oct (summer): Tue-Sun, 1-5pm. Also open on bank holiday Mon and Good Fri. Tours (45 mins) at 3pm.**

Cost: **£5.50 adults, £3.50 concessions, under 17s free. The garden can be visited free of charge and is a popular spot for summer picnics.**

Transport: **Hampstead Heath rail or Hampstead tube.**

John Keats

KEATS HOUSE

This Grade I listed building is a shrine to one of the leading poets of the English Romantic movement (along with Lord Byron and Percy Bysshe Shelley), in a part of London long favoured by literary and creative types. John Keats (1795-1821) lived here for a mere 17 months, from 1818, before travelling to Italy where he died of tuberculosis, aged just 25.

The house was built between 1814 and 1816, and was originally two separate properties, a pair of semi-detached houses with a shared garden called Wentworth Place. In 1838, the actress and one-time favourite of King George IV, Eliza Jane Chester, bought the property and created one house.

John Keats lodged in one of the two properties with his friend Charles Brown, from December 1818 to September 1820, which although only a short period was perhaps his most productive. *Ode to a Nightingale* was allegedly written under a plum tree in the garden. He also found love here (appropriate for a member of the Romantic movement), in the form of Fanny Brawne, who lived with her family in the adjacent house.

Keats House has a large variety of Keats-related material, including books, paintings and household items. There are letters by Keats, books in which he wrote some of his poetry, the engagement ring that he gave to Fanny Brawne (he died before they could be married), busts and portraits of Keats, and three locks of his brown hair.

Various rooms in the house have been faithfully recreated as they would have been when lived in by Keats, Brown, the Brawnes and Eliza Chester. The attention to detail is impressive; for example, paint analysis has been used to determine the exact colours originally used on the walls.

The museum holds regular literary and poetry events (related not just to Keats's work, but to poetry in general), as well as regular talks and exhibitions about various aspects of life in Regency London, e.g. architecture, fashion and garden design. See website for details.

❝ *Poetic inspiration in north London* ❞

Address: Lauderdale House, Waterlow Park, Highgate Hill, N6 5HG (house 020-8348 8716, park 020-7974 8810, www.lauderdalehouse.co.uk and www.waterlowpark.org.uk).

Opening hours: Park: dawn to dusk. House: Exhibitions Tue-Fri, 11am to 4pm, Sun 10am to 5pm. Restaurant: daily, 9.30am to 4pm.

Cost: Free.

Transport: Archway or Highgate tube.

LAUDERDALE HOUSE & WATERLOW PARK

Lauderdale House was built in 1582 for Sir Richard Martin (d 1617), the Master of the Mint and three-time Lord Mayor of London, and has a rich and interesting history. Over the next 60 years it had a number of occupants, until Mary, Dowager Countess of Home, bequeathed it to her daughter Anne, wife of the Scottish Royalist John Maitland, the notorious Earl of Lauderdale (1616-1682), thus beginning the connection with the name. Charles II's mistress Nell Gwynn lived here for a brief period with their infant son, the Duke of St Albans. Over the next century or so the House changed hands many times and was described by John Wesley, who preached here in 1782, as 'one of the most elegant boarding houses in England.'

Lauderdale's last private owner was Sir Sidney Waterlow (1822-1906), after whom the park is named, who leased the house for a period to St Bartholomew's Hospital as a convalescent home. By 1883 the house lay empty, and in 1889 Sir Sidney gave the house and grounds to the London County Council 'for the enjoyment of Londoners' and as 'a garden for the gardenless'. The 29 acres (11.7ha) of land became a public park and the house was restored in 1893 and served for 70 years as a park tearoom and park-keepers' flats. During the course of further renovation in 1963, a fire destroyed the roof and much of the interior. After 15 years lying derelict the local community established the Lauderdale House Society, which now runs the house as an arts and education centre (see website), with an excellent café.

Separately managed by Camden Council, Waterlow Park – returned to its former glory after extensive restoration in 2005 – is one of a select group of parks awarded Green Flag status and one of London's best-kept secrets (we hadn't heard of it before researching this book).

> Nestled on a hillside to the south of Highgate Village, Waterlow Park has some of the best cityscape views in London, but retains an incredible sense of peace and serenity.

Within its expansive acreage you'll find a potpourri of formal terraced gardens (one of Britain's earliest examples); three historic ponds fed by natural springs; tree-lined walkways and mature shrub beds; herbaceous borders and ornamental bedding; and verdant expanses of lawn on which to play, relax or have a picnic. The park also boasts six tennis courts, a natural children's play area and an ever-changing events programme.

66 *One of London's best-kept secrets* **99**

Address: 12-13 New Wharf Rd, N1 9RT (020-7713 0836, www. canalmuseum.org.uk).

Opening hours: **Tue-Sun, 10am to 4.30pm (7.30pm on the first Thu of each month). Closed Mon except for bank holidays.**

Cost: **£4 adults, £3 concessions, £2 children, £10 families.**

Transport: **King's Cross tube.**

LONDON CANAL MUSEUM

The London Canal Museum tells the absorbing story of the capital's canals from their early days as vital trade routes – long before motorised vehicles and motorways – through years of decline and abandonment, to their resurrection as today's corridors of leisure and urban greenery for boats, walkers and cyclists.

The museum opened in 1992 in a former Victorian ice warehouse, constructed around 1863 by Carlo Gatti (a famous ice-cream maker) to house ice imported from Norway by ship and canal barge. The museum features two floors of exhibits, including half a narrow boat, the *Coronis*, which allows you to experience the cramped conditions in which boatmen and their families lived; there are also some fascinating recordings, displays and photographs of a way of life, now long gone.

Outside, in Battlebridge Basin, is moored the museum's own tug, *Bantam IV* (plus private narrowboats), while upstairs is a detailed history of how the canals developed and were

> **From the River Thames at Limehouse to Paddington, the nine-mile Regent's Canal is one of London's best-kept secrets, largely hidden behind high-rise buildings.**

engineered, fascinating archival film footage on a continuous loop, and a mechanical model lock. Further exhibits explain the role of lock keepers, reservoirs and horses, the backbone of the early canal network. The museum also contains a copy of a drawing by Leonardo da Vinci, inventor of the mitre gate that's still used today in most of the world's locks. As an added bonus, there are two preserved ice wells under the building, one of which can be viewed from the public area.

The museum tells the story of the building of Regent's (London) Canal – built to link the Grand Junction Canal's Paddington Arm (which opened in 1801) with the Thames at Limehouse – in texts, pictures and archive film from the '20s to '40s. The 'Big Map' provides an excellent overview of the scope of London's waterways and offers a detailed historical survey of the capital's canals and other navigations, including canals that were built and closed, those that were planned but never built, and those that survive today.

Visitors to the museum can take a short tunnel trip on a narrow boat through Islington Tunnel to Regent's Canal (on selected summer Sundays – see website), or go the whole hog and take an enchanting trip back in time from Camden to picturesque Little Venice (see page 211) in west London, meandering through the rich urban landscape of yesteryear.

❝ *The fascinating history of London's waterways* **❞**

Address: St John's Gate, St John's Ln, EC1M 4DA (020-7324 4005, www.museumstjohn.org.uk and www.sja.org.uk).

Opening hours: Mon-Sat, 10am to 5pm. Closed Sun and bank holidays. Tours of the 16th-century gatehouse and 12th-century crypt at 11am and 2.30pm on Tue, Fri and Sat.

Cost: Free. Tours suggested 'donation' £5 (£4 concessions).

Transport: Farringdon tube.

MUSEUM OF THE ORDER OF ST JOHN

The Museum of the Order of St John tells the unique and fascinating story of the Order of the Hospital of St John of Jerusalem, founded after the first Crusade captured Jerusalem in 1099. It occupies two sites in Clerkenwell: St John's Gate (1504), the entrance to the former Priory of the Knights of St John, and the Priory Church of St John, Clerkenwell, with its surviving 12th-century crypt. The Museum's diverse collections explore all aspects of the Order's history and include rare illuminated manuscripts (such as the Rhodes Missal of 1504), armour, weapons, paintings, coins, furnishings, ceramics, silverware and textiles, plus historic first-aid equipment and memorabilia from St John's role in the two world wars.

The story spans over 900 years and includes many key events and people. Beginning with the Crusades, and continuing through revolts and revolutions, war and peace, it traverses the centuries and shows how warrior monks set out from the priory in Clerkenwell to fight for the faith and tend the sick.

> **Men, money and supplies were sent from the priory to hospitals – including one founded to care for sick pilgrims in 11th-century Jerusalem – on the great medieval pilgrim routes.**

The Order originally consisted of a group of Knights; men from noble European families who took vows of poverty, chastity, obedience and care of the sick. Later it took on a military role and took control of Crusader castles. When Palestine was recaptured by Muslim forces in 1291, the Order moved briefly to Cyprus and then, in 1309, to Rhodes. When the Turkish Sultan, Suleiman the Magnificent, conquered the island in 1522, the Order moved to Malta. After a famous siege by Suleiman in 1565, which the Knights and the Maltese people survived, a new capital city, Valetta, was built. The Order's ships patrolled the Mediterranean and remained on Malta until 1798, when the island was lost to Napoleon.

The original Roman Catholic Order still has its headquarters in Rome, its full title being 'The Sovereign Military Hospitaller Order of St John of Jerusalem, of Rhodes and of Malta.' It remains a sovereign entity in international law and is engaged in international charity work. St John has maintained its caring role to this day, working worldwide on numerous humanitarian projects. Victorian pioneers began a first-aid movement that spread around the globe and continues today with St John Ambulance and the St John Eye Hospital in Jerusalem.

❝ *An absorbing 900-year odyssey* **❞**

Address: Bulls Cross, Enfield, EN2 9HG (08456-770600, www.visitleevalley.org.uk/en/content/cms/nature/gardens-heritage/myddelton-house-gardens).

Opening hours: Mon-Fri, 10am to 5pm (or dusk if earlier). See the website for exact dates and opening times. A range of guided tours are offered.

Cost: Free. Guided walks from £3 to £6 (see website).

Transport: Best reached by car from the M25, junction 25.

MYDDELTON HOUSE GARDENS

Myddelton House was built by Henry Carrington Bowles (1763-1830) around 1818, replacing an earlier Elizabethan property, Bowling Green House. It was built in the then fashionable Suffolk white brick and named Myddelton House in honour of Sir Hugh Myddelton (1560-1631), an engineering genius who created the New River to supply London with fresh water, a section of which bisected the garden from 1613 until 1968.

When Bowles died in 1830 the house passed to his son (also Henry Bowles), who bequeathed it in 1852 to his nephew, Henry Carrington Bowles Treacher. He assumed the name Bowles in order to inherit the estate, thus becoming Henry Carrington Bowles Bowles! The garden was created by Henry's youngest son, E. A. (Edward Augustus or 'Gussie') Bowles (1865-1954), a renowned botanist, author, artist and Fellow of the Royal Horticultural Society – and one of the great gardeners of the 20th century. He originally trained for the church, but family tragedies caused him to change course, and he remained at Myddelton House and developed the remarkable garden as a self-taught horticulturist. He became an expert on many plants, particularly snowdrops and crocuses, which earned him the soubriquet 'The Crocus King'.

Bowles never married and kept the house just as it was in his childhood. On his death, the house and gardens passed to the Royal Free Hospital School of Medicine and the London School of Pharmacy, which grew a range of medicinal plants there. In 1967, the property was bought by the Lee Valley Regional Park Authority as its headquarters.

Myddelton House Gardens – recently restored to their former glory – cover an area of 6 acres (2.4ha) and offer an impressive range of flora and fauna.

> Secreted away near Enfield, this wonderful garden was neglected and forgotten for 30 years, hidden under layers of ivy and bramble.

Within the Gardens are the national collection of award-winning bearded irises and 'special' areas which include the Lunatic Asylum (home to unusual plants), Tom Tiddler's Ground, Tulip Terrace, Alpine Meadow, Arboretum and the Kitchen Garden (created in 2002). The Gardens also contain a beautiful Carp pond, a Victorian conservatory, a rock garden, plus a number of historical artefacts collected by Bowles, including pieces from the original St Paul's Cathedral and the Enfield Market Cross.

The beautiful restored gardens contain a small visitor centre and tea room, and are an enchanting place to visit at any time of year.

❝ *An enchanting master gardener's garden* ❞

Address: BAPS Shri Swaminarayan Mandir, 105-119 Brentfield Rd, Neasden, NW10 8LD (020-8965 2651, http://londonmandir.baps.org).

Opening hours: Daily, 9am to 6pm. An exhibition 'Understanding Hinduism' and video explains how the temple was built and its significance, as well as telling the history of Hinduism.

Cost: Free. Exhibition, £2 adults, £1.50 seniors and children.

Transport: Neasden, Stonebridge Pk or Wembley Pk tube.

NEASDEN TEMPLE

Included by *Reader's Digest* in its list of 'the Seventy Wonders of the Modern World', this is one of London's unsung treasures, partly due to its location in an unglamorous part of northwest London. But its striking size, intricate design and warm, smiling worshippers make it well worth the trip (it attracts over 500,000 visitors a year).

Its full name is BAPS Shri Swaminarayan Mandir, London (popularly known as the Neasden Temple), a place of worship or prayer for Hindus following a tradition dating back many millennia. The *murtis* and rituals of *arti* and worship in the mandir form the very core in elevating the soul to the pinnacle of God-realisation. Swaminarayan mandirs worldwide fulfil the lofty concept of the Hindu tradition of mandirs.

The website states that it's 'Europe's first traditional Hindu temple' and it's also said to be the largest of its kind outside India, 70ft high, covering 1.5 acres and topped by several pinnacles and five domes. The assembly hall can accommodate 5,000 people.

It was built according to the principles of ancient Indian Shilpashastras using traditional methods and materials. Its construction took just two years and included some 3,000 tons of the finest Bulgarian limestone and 2,000 tons of Italian Carrara marble, which was hand-carved in India into 26,300 pieces by 1,526 craftsmen and shipped to Britain for assembly. The website describes the temple as 'a masterpiece of Indian stonework and craftsmanship, replete with its towering white pinnacles, smooth domes and intricate marble pillars, all based on ancient Vedic principles of art and architecture'.

As it's a religious building, there are guidelines for visitors that should be observed, including no shorts or skirts above the knee; shoes must be removed before entering (so wear your best socks!); no photography inside the temple; mobile phones must be switched off and silence maintained; and those aged under 17 must be accompanied by an adult. A full list of guidelines is provided on the website.

As well as the monumental exterior, you can wander through the incredibly decorative, carving-encrusted interior, and there's a souvenir shop and one of London's best Indian vegetarian restaurants (Shayona). Perhaps the most striking impression you'll be left with is the warm welcome provided by the friendly, tranquil worshippers at this intriguing temple.

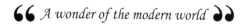

66 *A wonder of the modern world* **99**

AT A GLANCE

Address: Canonbury Grove, N1 (020-7527 2000, www.islington.gov.uk – see parks and green spaces).

Opening hours: **Daily, 8am to dusk.**

Cost: **Free.**

Transport: **Highbury & Islington tube or Essex Rd rail.**

NEW RIVER WALK

New River Walk – neither new nor a river! – is a delightful public park of 3.48 acres (1.4ha) in Islington that's part of the New River Path and a tranquil oasis for wildlife. The New River was an aqueduct commissioned in 1613 by Sir Hugh Myddleton (1560-1631) – whose statue stands at the southern tip of Islington Green – to bring water from the River Lee in Hertfordshire to central London. The aqueduct still supplies water today, accounting for some 8 per cent of London's consumption, although it now terminates at Stoke Newington.

The New River Path is 28mi (45km) long, following the course of the New River from Hertford to Islington, linking the inner city to the open countryside. It was developed between

> The narrow pathway winds intriguingly over pretty bridges, while benches are strategically placed for rest stops and to enjoy the views.

1991 and 2003 at a cost of over £2m, in a partnership that included Thames Water, Groundwork, the New River Action Group and others. Wherever possible, the route follows the historic water channel, as well as some straightened and piped sections between the New River's starting point near Hertford to its original end in Islington. The route is waymarked throughout its length by signs displaying the NR Path logo.

The section of the New River Path that comprises the New River Walk runs between Islington and Canonbury. The park follows the New River as it runs above ground between St Pauls Road and Canonbury Road in Islington. The charming linear park is landscaped along the river and is around 4mi (7km) in length, exploring some of Islington's many and varied squares and garden spaces. Much of the route is along service paths on private land running beside the watercourse, while other sections follow public rights of way – the 'heritage' section south of Stoke Newington uses paths through parks and along streets.

The park is a haven for wildlife and is landscaped with native English plants and specimen trees, including swamp cypress, dawn redwood and weeping willows; signboards provide information about the local flora and fauna. The river teems with life and you're likely to encounter ducks, coots and moorhens, plus – if you're lucky – rarer species such as sparrowhawks, grey wagtails, firecrests and grey herons.

A popular walk is from Canonbury Square to Newington Green, where you can enjoy lunch in one of the area's many excellent eateries.

❝ *A magical, secret watery 'park' in Islington* **❞**

ST CHRISTOPHER'S CHAPEL, GOSH

St Christopher's Chapel (Grade II listed) – dedicated to St Christopher as the Patron Saint of children – at the Great Ormond Street Hospital (GOSH) is a stunningly decorative building, and the most sumptuous hospital chapel in the country.

Great Ormond Street Hospital for children was created in response to the shocking mortality rate in the mid-19th century, which meant that only half of all babies born into poverty would celebrate their first birthday. Desperate to save children's lives in the capital, Dr George West campaigned for a specialist hospital to be built. In 1852, he got his wish and with ten beds, two physicians and five nurses, GOSH was born.

Built in the High Victorian style, the stunning Chapel interior – in elaborate Franco-Italianate design – may remind you of Augustus Pugin's work, which isn't surprising as it was designed by Edward Middleton Barry (1830-1880), third son of Sir Charles Barry, who along with Pugin, designed the Houses of Parliament. Completed in 1875, the Chapel is dedicated to the memory of Caroline, wife of William Henry Barry (eldest son of Sir Charles Barry) who donated £40,000 to build the Chapel and provided a stipend for the chaplain.

The Chapel is small, with just four rows of seats on either side of the main aisle, with a dramatic altar at the end. The beautiful terrazzo floor is by the Italian mosaicist Antonio Salviati, said to be modelled on St Mark's, Venice. The stained glass depicts the nativity, the childhood of Christ and biblical scenes connected with children, above which is a series of angels holding tablets inscribed with the Christian virtues.

> **The Chapel's small size adds to the intimate atmosphere and makes the stunning decoration less intimidating than it might otherwise be.**

When the old GOSH was replaced by a new hospital in the '90s, there was no question of demolishing the Chapel, which was 'simply' moved! A concrete cast was laid under the Chapel, supported by jacks, and the whole building was placed in a giant waterproof 'box' and moved by sliding it along a purpose-built runway, pushed by hydraulic ram-jacks; a world first and an amazing feat of engineering. Restored to its former splendour, the Chapel was officially reopened by Diana, Princess of Wales, on Valentine's Day 1994.

A moving Chapel (in more ways than one) and a magical place that's well worth a visit.

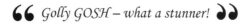

66 *Golly GOSH – what a stunner!* **99**

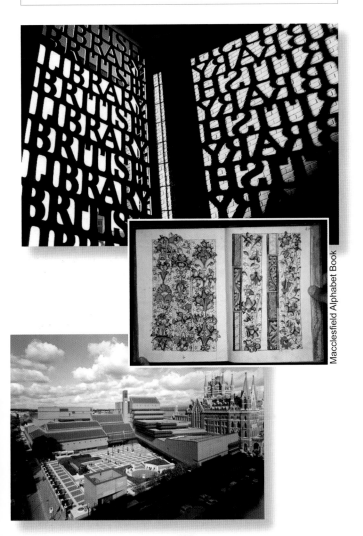

Macclesfield Alphabet Book

SIR JOHN RITBLAT GALLERY

The Sir John Ritblat Gallery – sub-titled 'Treasures of the British Library' – is named after a major donor who also provided £1m for the library's display cabinets, and is a permanent display of some of the world's rarest and most precious manuscripts and books. It contains over 200 beautiful and fascinating items, including sacred texts from the world's religions, documents that made and recorded history, landmarks of printing, masterpieces of illumination, major advances in science and map-making, and great works of literature and music.

Discover some of the world's most exciting and significant books and documents, from the *Lindisfarne Gospels* (698AD), with their wonderful illustrations, to the *Gutenberg Bible* (1455), the first book printed in Europe. From the genius of Leonardo da Vinci's sketchbooks to the earliest versions of some of the greatest

> A room off the main gallery houses the 'Turning the Pages' system, where you can scan selected books on a computer terminal, such as the *Lindisfarne Gospels*, the *Sforza Hours* – one of the finest surviving Renaissance manuscripts – the *Diamond Sutra* and da Vinci's notebook, as if you were actually turning the books' pages.

works of English literature, including Shakespeare's *First Folio* (1623), Jane Austen's *History of England* (1791) and Lewis Carroll's *Alice in Wonderland* (1865). Also on display is the *Diamond Sutra*, the world's earliest dated printed book, made with carved wood blocks in 868AD, the only surviving copy of the epic poem *Beowulf*, thought to date from the 10th or 11th century, and the Earl of Essex's death warrant (1601) signed by Elizabeth I.

Among the most important documents on display is the *Magna Carta* – considered by many historians to be the greatest constitutional document of all time – which King John was compelled to sign by his feudal barons in 1215, accepting that no 'freeman' (in the sense of non-serf) could be punished except through the law of the land – a right which still exists today.

The gallery also includes musical scores by the likes of Bach, Handel and Mozart, Beethoven's tuning fork, and scribbled lyrics of Lennon and McCartney, such as *A Hard Day's Night*, written on a sheet of stationery picturing a cartoon train. Also in the British Library are the National Sound Archive – where you can hear recordings of Florence Nightingale (1890) and James Joyce reading from *Ulysses* (1924) – and the Humanities Reading Room.

 See the Magna Carta and Shakespeare's First Folio

Address: **13 Lincoln's Inn Fields, WC2A 3BP (020-7405 2107, www. soane.org).**

Opening hours: **Tue-Sat, 10am to 5pm; closed Sun-Mon and bank holidays. Special candlelit evenings (6-9pm) on the first Tue of each month (no advance booking, so expect long queues from around 5pm). Tours (1hr) Tue and Thu-Sat at noon (can be booked online). Also free tours (30 mins) of Soane's private apartments on selected days.**

Cost: **Free, £10 for tours.**

Transport: **Holborn tube.**

he Riva degli Schiavoni, Canaletto

SIR JOHN SOANE'S MUSEUM

Sir John Soane (1753-1837) was a bricklayer's son who became one of Britain's greatest, most innovative architects, noted for his designs of the Bank of England (see page 69 for the Bank's Museum) and the Dulwich Picture Gallery (see page 279). The museum is housed in his former home, which he designed both to live in and to house his antiquities and works of art (he was a great collector). Soane believed in the 'poetry of architecture' and the house is an embodiment of his experiments and ideas about how light and space should work.

The building has a distinctive, striking front, with a projecting first-floor loggia, Coade Stone statues and Gothic pedestals. Internally, Soane used top-lighting – sometimes with coloured glass – and lots of mirrors to produce an atmospherically lit environment.

He amassed a huge collection of interesting objects and artworks, so many that he had to be creative to house it all, including having panels hung with paintings lining the walls that can be pulled out like leaves or which unfold from the walls. At one stage, Soane and his family lived in just two small rooms, so great was the collection! It's now a happy sort of ordered chaos and deserves to be better known.

Exhibits include Roman cremation urns, a human skeleton, the Egyptian sarcophagus of Seti I, the marble tomb of Soane's favourite dog and pieces from the classical, medieval, renaissance and Oriental periods, including furniture, timepieces, stained glass, drawings, paintings, sculptures, jewellery and architectural models; there's also a library. Paintings include significant works by Canaletto, Piranesi, Reynolds, Turner and Hogarth, including all eight of Hogarth's *Rake's Progress* series.

The museum was established in Soane's own lifetime by a private Act of Parliament in 1833, which took effect on Soane's death in 1837. The Act required that the house be kept 'as nearly as possible' as it was when he died, and that's largely been the case. Soane fell out with his two sons, hence his decision to bequeath his property as a museum.

❝ *Delightful eclectic 'clutter' of a great architect* **❞**

Address: 183 Euston Rd, Camden, NW1 2BE (020-7611 2222, www. wellcomecollection.org).

Opening hours: Tue-Wed and Fri-Sat, 10am to 6pm; Thu 10am to 10pm; Sun 11am to 6pm. Closed over Christmas and New Year (see website for dates). Library closed on Sun.

Cost: Free.

Transport: Euston Sq tube or Euston rail.

WELLCOME COLLECTION

This is one of London's most original and interesting but lesser-known museums, housed in an impressive, sleek building. It's an unusual collection of medical artefacts and works of art, which 'explore ideas about the connections between medicine, life and art in the past, present and future'. The website dubs it a 'free destination for the incurably curious' and is a useful mirror for the collection, being detailed, interactive (including audio and video presentations), visually interesting, current (including a blog) and full of nuggets of obscure information.

The museum charts the development of medicine through the ages and across many cultures, and explores the impact of medicine on our lives, through a mixture of galleries, events and a library. The Wellcome Library contains over two million items, including 750,000 books and a large collection of manuscripts, some 6,000 of which are in Sanskrit; it's open to the public but you're required to register on your first visit, and you need to become a member to use it fully (see website for details).

The collection is named after Sir Henry Wellcome (1853-1936), an American-British pharmaceutical entrepreneur, philanthropist, pharmacist and collector, whose will created the Wellcome Trust, one of the world's largest medical charities (it spends over £600m annually, largely on biomedical research and the medical humanities – the Wellcome Collection is part of the Trust). He was also a keen collector of medical artefacts and amassed over a million items. The Wellcome Collection displays a modest number of these and there are some bizarre items, including used guillotine blades, Napoleon's toothbrush, ivory carvings of pregnant women, shrunken heads, royal hair, ancient sex aids, a DNA sequencing robot and a Picasso drawing.

The Wellcome Collection has three areas: upstairs is an exhibition drawn from Sir Henry's finds, while next door is 'Medicine Now' which has some striking art on medical themes, including a postcard wall where visitors are encouraged to contribute drawings; downstairs there's a series of temporary exhibitions, many of which are excellent, often challenging and provocative – past exhibitions have included shows about skin decoration; sleep and dreaming; the relationship between madness and art; the history of human drug use and our attitudes to it; and the hidden past of 26 skeletons found in sites around London. There's also a café, bookshop, conference facilities and a members' club.

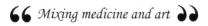

❝ Mixing medicine and art ❞

AT A GLANCE

Address: Lloyd Park, Forest Rd, Walthamstow E17 4PP (020-8496 4390, www.walthamforest.gov.uk/william-morris and www.friendsofthewmg.org.uk).

Opening hours: Wed-Sun, 10am to 5pm.

Cost: Free.

Transport: Walthamstow Central tube.

William Morris

WILLIAM MORRIS GALLERY

The William Morris Gallery is delightfully housed in a substantial (Grade II* listed) Georgian dwelling – the Morris' family home from 1848 to 1856 – set in Lloyd Park in Walthamstow. Morris, who was born in Walthamstow, lived here with his widowed mother and his eight brothers and sisters, from the age of 14 to 22. It's the only public gallery devoted to William Morris (1834-1896) – artist, designer, writer, socialist, conservationist, and father of the Arts and Crafts Movement – and is home to an internationally important collection, illustrating his life, achievements and influence.

The house is a superb example of Georgian domestic architecture dating from around 1744. Records indicate that there was a house on the site – or perhaps on the moated 'island' to the rear of the present house – as far back as the 15th century. The existing house was variously known as The Winns or Water House, the latter deriving from the ornamental moat at the rear of the house.

A map of 1758 shows the building with its original east and west wings, but without the two semi-circular bays on the south front which were added some thirty or forty years later. Today, only the west wing of the original building remains, the east wing having been demolished in the early 1900s. (A recent development created an extension on the site of the former east wing, restoring the symmetry of the building.) One of the finest exterior features is the Corinthian-style porch, its fluted columns and elaborately carved capitals executed in timber, with rosettes used as decorative motifs on the canopy soffit.

> The house and grounds were purchased in 1856 by the publisher Edward Lloyd (1815-1890), whose family donated them to the people of Walthamstow; Lloyd Park – renamed in Edward Lloyd's memory – opened in July 1900.

The William Morris Gallery was opened in 1950 by the Prime Minister, Clement Attlee, and illustrates Morris' life, work and influence. It includes printed, woven and embroidered fabrics, rugs, carpets, wallpapers, furniture, stained glass and painted tiles, designed by Morris and others who together established the firm of Morris, Marshall, Faulkner & Company in 1861.

The Gallery has undergone major redevelopment in the last few years – at a cost of over £5m – and re-opened in 2012 with innovative new displays and hands-on exhibits, a new tea room, a shop, a dedicated learning space, and an exciting programme of temporary exhibitions, activities and events for all ages.

 Shrine to the 19th century's most influential designer

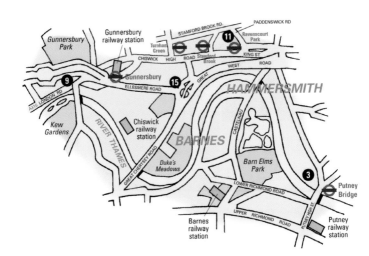

CHAPTER 5

WEST LONDON

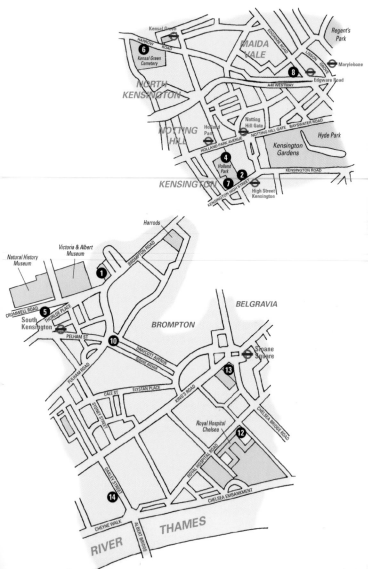

Address: Brompton Rd, SW7 2RP (020-7808 0900, www. bromptonoratory.com).

Opening hours: **Daily, 6am to 8pm. Tours can be arranged (see website).**

Cost: **Free.**

Transport: **S Kensington tube.**

BROMPTON/LONDON ORATORY

The Church of the Immaculate Heart of Mary – popularly known as the Brompton/London Oratory – is a stunning Roman Catholic church on Brompton Road next to the Victoria and Albert Museum. It's the church of a community of priests (lay brothers) called 'The Congregation of the Oratory of St Philip Neri' or Oratorians. Neri (1515-1595) founded his congregation in Rome, which spread worldwide and now numbers around 70 'houses' (including Birmingham and Oxford in the UK) with some 500 priests.

The Oratory was designed by Herbert Gribble (1847-1894, who won a design competition at the age of just 28), and the unabashed Italian style and ebullient design are entirely

> As impressive as the exterior is, it's the extraordinary interior – where Italian influence is at its greatest – that takes the breath away.

intentional. Construction commenced in 1878 and it was consecrated in 1884, although the remarkable dome, designed by George Sherrin (1843-1909) in neo-Baroque style, wasn't completed until 1896. The result is a church that's unique in Britain, particularly in its use of decorative colour and structure.

The Oratory is the second-largest Catholic church in London, with a nave wider than that of St Paul's Cathedral (exceeded in Britain only by Westminster Abbey and York Minster). Until the opening of Westminster Cathedral in 1903, the London Oratory was the venue for all great Catholic occasions in London.

Much of the interior decoration is of 20th-century provenance and isn't as Gribble intended; the lavishly-gilded nave and dome mosaics are the work of Comandatore Formilli in 1927-32. Although the dome is striking, it's the pulpit that really catches the eye; this baroque wonder is alive with flowing lines and extravagant decoration, rarely seen in British churches. There's also a beautiful altarpiece by Rex Whistler (1905-1944) in St Wilfrid's Chapel.

The Oratory is primarily 19th century, but it contains a number of much older elements, including the figures of the 12 apostles in the nave, which were carved for Siena cathedral in 1680; the altar and reredos in the Lady Chapel are also from the late 17th century. Taken as a whole, the Brompton Oratory is an extraordinary architectural monument, made even more remarkable by the fact that such extravagant Italian style is so rare in Britain.

The church is also noted for the excellence of its liturgical and musical traditions, and is graced by no less than three renowned choirs (see website for information).

❝ *An impressively ornate Italianate church* **❞**

Address: 18 Stafford Ter, W8 7BH (020-7602 3316, www.rbkc.gov.uk/subsites/museums/18staffordterrace.aspx).

Opening hours: **Visits by guided tour (90 mins) only, from mid-Sep to mid-Jun. Conventional tours on Wed, Sat and Sun at 11.15am and Wed at 2.15pm. Costumed tours (led by a costumed actor) on Sat-Sun at 1pm, 2.15pm and 3.30pm. Private group tours for 12-30 people can also be arranged. Closed in summer, Dec 25-26th and Jan 1st.**

Cost: **£8 adults, £6 concessions, £3 children under 16, under 5s free. Booking essential.**

Transport: **High St Kensington tube.**

Linley Sambourne - self portrait

18 STAFFORD TERRACE/LINLEY SAMBOURNE HOUSE

Behind the shops of Kensington High Street lies 18 Stafford Terrace (which is also known as Linley Sambourne House, after Edward Linley Sambourne), another of central London's hidden gems. It's a unique, beautifully preserved late Victorian (1874) townhouse, classical Italianate in style, with most of its original décor and furnishings. While preserved Victorian exteriors aren't uncommon, it's rare to have an almost-original interior.

Sambourne was a photographer, book illustrator and the chief political cartoonist of the (now defunct) satirical magazine *Punch*, and an ancestor of the Earl of Snowdon, who married Queen Elizabeth II's sister, Princess Margaret. Their son, Viscount Linley, is 16th in line to the throne. Appropriately, given the shared name, he runs a successful furniture design and manufacturing business.

Sambourne and his family lived at 18 Stafford Terrace until his death in 1910. After the death of his wife (Marion) in 1914 the house was inherited by their son Roy, who preserved it largely unchanged (including the furniture and decoration) until his death in 1946. It then passed to his sister Maud (grandmother of the future Earl of Snowdon, who took Linley as his subsidiary title) and then to her daughter Anne, Countess of Rosse. In 1957, Lady Rosse proposed the foundation of The Victorian Society and continued the preservation of the house largely as it had been in Linley Sambourne's days.

The house was originally decorated by the Sambourne family, following the then-fashionable aesthetic principles, with William Morris wallpapers, heavy velvet curtains, exotic Turkish carpets, stained glass windows, ebonised wardrobes and a wealth of Chinese ornaments. However, it developed from this and became an even more varied and interesting interior, an attractive jumble.

The notable collection of Chinese export porcelain, from the 17th to 19th centuries – including blue and white and enamelled wares (famille rose, famille verte and Chinese Imari) – is displayed throughout the house. Other highlights include English tin-glazed wares, Whitefriars glass lampshades and miscellaneous glass vessels. There are also a number of Sambourne's cartoons, drawings and sketches on display.

The property paints a vivid picture of intellectual, late-Victorian tastes and lifestyle, and the tour give you a sense of stepping back into the past and what it was like to be a member of the Sambourne family.

 An original late Victorian townhouse and its contents

Address: Bishop's Ave, Fulham, SW6 6EA (020-7736 3233, www.fulhampalace.org).

Opening hours: Palace: summer, Mon-Thu 12.30-4.30pm, Sun and bank holidays 12-5pm; winter, Mon-Thu 12.30-3.30pm, Sun and bank holidays 12-4pm. Walled garden: summer, 10.15am to 4.15pm; winter, 10.15am to 3.45pm. Botanical gardens: daily, dawn to dusk. Regular tours and garden walks (both 2pm) are available for £5 per person (no booking, see website for dates). Private group history and garden tours (minimum 10 people) can be arranged for £8 per person.

Cost: Entrance to the palace and grounds is free. Tours £5-8.

Transport: Putney Br tube or Putney rail.

FULHAM PALACE

Fulham Palace is a well-kept local secret; an unexpected, tree-enclosed haven in west London, with lovely gardens in a tranquil, Thameside location. It's one of London's oldest and most historically significant buildings, yet strangely little known outside the local area.

The palace was the country home of the Bishops of London for over 900 years, and excavations in recent years revealed several former large-scale buildings and evidence of settlements dating back to Roman and Neolithic times. The land is recorded as belonging to the Bishop of London in 700AD, and the palace was their country house from at least the 11th century and their main residence from the 18th century until 1975. Today it's owned by the Church Commissioners and leased to Hammersmith and Fulham Council and the Fulham Palace Trust.

Much of the surviving palace building dates from 1495 and is Grade I listed. It encompasses a variety of different building styles and ages, while the extensive gardens (the grounds used to extend to over 30 acres, but only 12 remain) contain a range of international plant species, some dating from the 18th century. The gardens were famous and home to a number of the country's botanical firsts, although their fortunes vacillated as some bishops weren't interested in them. The palace used to have England's longest moat (infilled in 1924), which enjoyed direct access to the Thames.

The gardens are now an ideal picnic spot, with lawns, unusual tree species (including black American walnut, cork and Virginian oak) and an 18th-century walled herb garden with an orchard and a wisteria-draped pergola. There are also regular displays of sculpture and other art works in the gardens. Part of the palace grounds were converted into allotments during World War II, which have remained in use ever since allowing local people to grow their own vegetables, fruit and flowers.

Although the palace has its own chapel, the gardens adjoin the churchyard of the neighbouring parish church, All Saints Church, where several former bishops are buried.

Fulham Palace also has a shop, a museum, a contemporary art gallery and a café, which overlooks the grounds. The museum collection includes paintings, archaeology and artefacts, as well as the palace itself, as demonstrated by the 1:50 scale model of the building. The collection is displayed in two palace rooms which have been restored to their original Georgian splendour. The palace is said to be haunted by the ghosts of Protestant heretics, who were 'persecuted' there.

 A medieval bishop's palace by the river

Address: Ilchester Pl, W8 (www.rbkc.gov.uk/leisureandlibraries/parksandgardens/yourlocalpark/hollandpark.aspx).

Opening hours: Daily, 7.30am to dusk.

Cost: Free.

Transport: Kensington High St or Notting Hill tube.

HOLLAND PARK & KYOTO GARDEN

Holland Park (the area) is an affluent, fashionable part of west London, dotted with large Victorian townhouses and upmarket restaurants and shops. It's one of the capital's most expensive residential districts and therefore an appropriate location for arguably London's most peaceful and romantic park. Yet it's a park that's either unknown or ignored by many who aren't local residents.

At a mere 54 acres (22ha), Holland Park is one of the capital's smallest public parks, but has plenty to offer: beautiful views, gardens, sports areas, peacocks, an ecology centre, some of the city's best children's play facilities, a café, large areas of woodland and a Japanese (Kyoto) garden. The park is also a renowned picnic spot, with plenty of secluded hideaways in a variety of environments.

Holland Park was formerly the grounds of Cope Castle, a large Jacobean mansion dating from the early 17th century, built for Sir Walter Cope, James I's Chancellor. It was one of the area's first great houses, later renamed Holland House, but it was almost destroyed during a ten-hour bombing raid in 1940; one wing remains, part of which is the London Holland Park youth hostel, possibly the capital's most attractive. In the summer, opera performances are staged by Opera Holland Park (www.operahollandpark.com) under a temporary canopy, with the remains of Holland House as a backdrop.

The park is roughly divided into three areas: the northern half is semi-wild woodland, in which the sounds of the city all but disappear; the central part – around the remains of Holland House – is more formal, with a number of garden areas; while the southern part is used for sport.

The highlight of Holland Park for many people is the beautiful Kyoto Garden, a Japanese garden donated by the Chamber of Commerce in Kyoto in 1991 to celebrate the Japan Festival which was held in London in 1992. Refurbished in 2001, the garden is immaculately kept and widely regarded to be one of London's most tranquil places. It has a lovely pond, with stepping stones, and a 15ft waterfall. It's surrounded by elegant plantings of Japanese shrubs and trees, which are at their best in spring and autumn, offering an ever-changing variety of vivid colours.

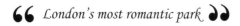

❝ *London's most romantic park* **❞**

INSTITUT FRANÇAIS DU ROYAUME-UNI

The Institut français du Royaume-Uni (French Cultural Institute in the UK) is the official French government centre for language and culture in the UK, occupying a handsome Art Deco building in Kensington containing a cinema/theatre, library, bistro and reception rooms. The Institut was founded in 1910 by Marie d'Orliac, who was eager to introduce Londoners to French writers, thinkers and artists, and is now a worldwide organisation with over 150 centres.

The Institut occupied a number of buildings before its current home was commissioned from French architect Patrice Bonnet (1879-1964) and inaugurated by President Albert Lebrun and HRH Princess Mary on 21st March 1939. Inside, a sweeping staircase leads from the foyer area to the first floor, decorated by the famous Rodin statue *L'Age d'Airain* and a tapestry by Sonia Delaunay. The building's distinctive red-brick exterior is decorated with columns incised with delicate lattice work, and with brickwork and beige ceramic plaques depicting the Graces of Minerva, the goddess of intelligence.

During its 100-year history many great names have passed through the doors, including Jean Renoir, Eugène Ionesco, Catherine Deneuve and Michel Tournier. The Institut exists to promote French language and culture and encourage cross-cultural exchange, which is reflected in the programme of talks and films, with speakers from both sides of the Channel meeting regularly in discussion, and screenings of films from around the world. The Institut's wine-tasting sessions provide a valuable insight into this vital part of French culture.

Some 7,000 students enrol annually on courses at the Institut's Language Centre, which offers traditional language courses, business

> **The Institut has an inexpensive French restaurant – Le Bistrot – and bar open for breakfast, lunch and dinner.**

French and courses on different aspects of French culture and current affairs. The centre also has a media lending library (*La Médiathèque*) containing 50,000 books, DVDs and CDs. A window onto contemporary France, it contains the largest free-access collection of French material in the UK, including feature films, documentaries, music, poetry, novels, comic books and children's books.

The public cinema, *Ciné lumière*, has 240 seats, and is one of the UK's best repertory cinemas, screening a mix of French, European and world feature films and documentaries. It shows both classics and new releases, and regularly hosts special events such as premières, retrospectives and themed seasons.

❝ *A taste of La Bonne Vie in Kensington* ❞

Address: **Harrow Rd, W10 4RA (020-8969 0152, www. kensalgreencemetery.com and www.kensalgreen.co.uk/documents/ kg_tours.html).**

Opening hours: **Apr-Sep: Mon-Sat, 9am to 6pm, Sun 10am to 6pm. Oct-Mar: Mon-Sat, 9am to 5pm, Sun 10am to 5pm. Bank holidays, including Christmas Day, 10am to 1pm.**

Cost: **Free to wander around on your own; £7 'donation' (£5 concessions) for two-hour guided tour, Sun 2pm, Mar-Oct and first and third Sun of the month Nov-Feb.**

Transport: **Kensal Grn tube/rail.**

KENSAL GREEN CEMETERY

Kensal Green is an undistinguished, slightly shabby part of northwest London, but it plays host to one of the capital's most beautiful (if ramshackle) cemeteries. The access point to the cemetery is unpromising, being from the traffic-choked Harrow Road, with its plethora of fast-food joints and second-hand shops. But enter and it's like being in the countryside, full of mature shrubs and trees, which help make the cemetery one of London's richest and most important wildlife habitats.

Kensal Green opened in 1833, making it London's oldest public burial ground. It's one of the so-called 'Magnificent Seven', the other six being Abney Park (see page 147), Brompton, Highgate, Nunhead (see page 297), Tower Hamlets (see page 135) and West Norwood. It's the largest and most opulent of these Victorian cemeteries, containing around 250,000 bodies. It has a heady mix of architectural styles, with graves from the 1700s to the 1990s, often sited close together with little apparent order or pattern to its layout. There are a number of Grade I and II listed buildings and tombs, and the whole cemetery is Grade II listed. It's an interesting blend of Georgian splendour, Victorian decadence, 19th-century Gothic and modern styles.

There are two ways to visit: on a two-hour guided tour (see box opposite) or by exploring it yourself. Wear stout shoes or boots, as the terrain is uneven and often muddy. Vast tracts of the cemetery are nature and wildlife reserves, hence their overgrown state. The eastern end of the cemetery has a butterfly and bee garden, home to plants designed to attract them such as bergamot, hyssop, rosemary and sage. The cemetery is a place where it pays just to wander, while getting slightly lost and stumbling across a plethora of visual and architectural treats.

Near the cemetery's chapel are Georgian catacombs in the form of a colonnade, crumbling but atmospheric and well worth visiting. Kensal Green has a number of famous 'residents' you might wish to seek out, including the Brunel family of engineers, in a surprisingly understated tomb in a quiet corner of the cemetery. It's also the last resting place of the children of George III, authors Wilkie Collins and Anthony Trollope, and playwright Terence Rattigan.

 One of London's most atmospheric cemeteries

LONDON COUNTY COUNCIL

Lord
LEIGHTON
1830-1896
Painter
lived and
died here

Lord Leighton

LEIGHTON HOUSE MUSEUM

This unjustly obscure museum on the edge of Holland Park occupies the former home of painter and sculptor Frederic, Lord Leighton (1830-1896). It's one of the 19th century's most remarkable buildings – from the outside it's elegant rather than striking, but it contains one of London's most original interiors.

Leighton was associated with the Pre-Raphaelite Brotherhood (although he later looked to contrast with them) and his work depicted biblical, classical and historical subjects. He's most famous for his painting *Flaming June* and has the dubious distinction of being the bearer of the shortest-lived peerage in history: he died the day after the patent created him Baron Leighton and, as he was unmarried, his Barony expired with him.

The first part of the house was designed in 1864 by George Aitchison and resembles an Italianate villa. It's of red Suffolk brick with Caen Stone dressings in a restrained classical style. Subsequently, the building was extended over 30 years by Aitchison, to create a private art palace for Leighton. The house's centrepiece is a remarkable two-storey Arab Hall, designed to display Leighton's priceless collection of over 1,000 Islamic tiles, dating from the 13th to 17th centuries, collected during his trips to the Middle East.

The interior of this pseudo-Islamic court provides a stunning impression of the Orient, including a dome and a fountain. It has featured as a set in a number of films and television programmes, including *Brazil*, *Nicholas Nickleby* and *Spooks*, and in music videos for *Golden Brown* by The Stranglers and *Gold* by Spandau Ballet. These song titles give an indication of how opulent the interior is throughout the house, with gilded ceilings, peacock blue tiles, red walls, intricate black woodwork and much more. It has been described as one of London's most bizarre and magical interiors.

With all this architectural and decorative finery it would be easy to overlook the permanent collection. That would be a pity, as there are works by various members of the Pre-Raphaelite Brotherhood, including Edward Burne-Jones, John Everett Millais and George Frederick Watts, as well as 81 oil paintings by Leighton himself and a number of his sketches, watercolours, prints and personal documents and mementos. On the first floor is Leighton's huge, beautifully lit artist's studio, with its apse, dome and great north window.

66 *An opulent Islamic court in London* **99**

Address: Maida Vale, W2 1TH (https://canalrivertrust.org.uk/directory/3000/little-venice).

Opening hours: Unrestricted access.

Cost: Free.

Transport: Warwick Ave tube.

LITTLE VENICE

London isn't all about grand sights and blockbuster destinations. Certain areas – often survivors from a time when the city was a collection of villages and suburbs – simply warrant wandering around to soak up the atmosphere and marvel that such a large, hectic city has so many havens of elegance and tranquillity, sometimes close to the centre. One such area is Little Venice.

The term is employed rather loosely – particularly by estate agents – but it's generally used to describe an area of around a square mile in London's Maida Vale district. Technically speaking, it's the area at the point where the Paddington arm of the Grand Union Canal meets the Regents Canal. But the term – which was apparently coined by local resident and poet Robert Browning, who compared the area with Venice, although the name didn't come into general use until after the Second World War – has come to encompass the whole part of the south of Maida Vale.

It's one of the most exclusive residential areas of central London, noted for being an oasis on or near some of London's canals. Paddington Basin (one of Europe's largest regeneration schemes and a rival to London's Docklands) is only a short walk away. Yet Little Venice is an unexpected haven of calm and beauty, comprising around ten tree-lined streets of lovely 17th-century white stucco houses, with shops on Formosa Street and Clifton Gardens. The area has easy access to Oxford Street, the West End, Paddington Station and even Heathrow airport; no wonder it has become so fashionable and expensive.

The canal is lined with weeping willows and flanked by graceful stucco Regency mansions, many designed by the noted architect John Nash. Houseboats in bright red, dark green and navy blue dot the canal (Richard Branson used to live in one). Some have window boxes bursting with flowers, while others are adorned with elaborate nameplates. Ducks, geese and herons drift languidly by on the canal, which has Browning's Island at its centre, named after the poet who lived nearby.

This tranquil waterside area feels a long way from the surrounding hub of central London and brings to mind the words of the Water Rat in Kenneth Grahame's book *The Wind in the Willows*: 'There is nothing – absolutely nothing – half so much worth doing as simply messing about in boats'. It's a lovely spot for a walk along the towpath (2.5 miles to Camden Lock), while Little Venice itself boasts the Puppet Theatre Barge, the Cascade Floating Art Gallery, and many attractive cafés, pubs and restaurants.

 London's tranquil watery retreat

Address: Green Dragon Ln, Brentford, TW8 0EN (020-8568 4757, www. waterandsteam.org.uk).

Opening hours: Daily, 11am to 4pm. Groups by appointment.

Cost: £11.50 adults, £10 concessions, £5 children (5-15), plus a range of family tickets. Free entry on selected days in Jan-Feb, but no steam.

Transport: Kew Bridge rail or Gunnersbury tube.

LONDON MUSEUM OF WATER & STEAM

The London Museum of Water & Steam (previously the Kew Bridge Steam Museum) is a unique museum of water supply, housing a magnificent collection of steam engines and diesel-powered water pumping machines. Although this may not immediately set the pulse racing, it's a fascinating museum which allows visitors to experience how London's water supply evolved over the last 2,000 years, from Roman times to the present day.

It's housed within Georgian and Italianate buildings in the former Kew Bridge Pumping Station, opened in 1838 by the Grand Junction Waterworks Company. The station supplied west Londoners with water for over 100 years, closing in 1944. The Metropolitan Water Board decided not to scrap the resident steam pumping engines and set them aside to form the basis of a museum display, which eventually opened in 1975, two years after the formation of the Kew Bridge Engines Trust. Today, it's an internationally-recognised museum of steam pumping engines and the most important historic site of the water supply industry in Britain.

The museum houses the world's largest collection of Cornish beam engines (developed in Cornwall, although the name also refers to the engine's operating cycle), including the largest working beam engine, the spectacular Grand Junction 90 Engine, used to pump water for 98 years. It has a cylinder diameter of 90 inches, is over 40ft (12m) high and weighs some 250 tons. In 2008, the museum completed the restoration of its Bull Engine (built in 1856), which is one of only four known examples in the world, and the only engine in its original location and still operating. The steam pumping engines are run most weekends and on bank holiday Mondays, the rotative engines usually operate for three weeks each month, while the Cornish steam engines are run once a month during 'Giants of Steam' weekends (see website).

The museum is also home to London's only operating steam railway. The 2ft (610mm) narrow gauge railway is operated by volunteers and in 2009 saw the debut of the museum's new Wren class locomotive, 'Thomas Wicksteed', following the departure of the previous 'Cloister' engine. The line runs for 400 yards (366m) around the Kew Bridge site, with passenger trains operating on Sundays during the summer, on bank holiday Mondays and other 'special' days. The museum has a café, garden (where you can have a picnic) and a car park for 20 cars.

66 *Steam, glorious steam!* **99**

Address: 81 Fulham Rd, SW3 6RD (Bibendum Restaurant, 020-7581 5817, www.bibendum.co.uk/the-building.html).

Opening hours: Restaurant: Mon-Fri, noon to 2.30pm, Sat-Sun 12.30 to 3pm, evenings 7-11pm daily (10.30pm Sun). Reservations necessary. Oyster bar: Mon-Sat, noon to 11pm, Sun noon to 10.30pm (no reservations). Crustacea stall: Tue-Sat, 9am to 5pm.

Cost: Free – apart from a drink or meal!

Transport: S Kensington tube.

MICHELIN HOUSE

Michelin House was built as the permanent UK headquarters and tyre depot of the Michelin Tyre Company Ltd. and opened on 20th January 1911. Designed by one of Michelin's employees, François Espinasse (1880-1925), the original building had three large stained-glass windows based on Michelin adverts of the time, featuring the Michelin Man. At street level, there are a number of decorative ceramic tiles (which wrap around the front of the building) of famous racing cars which used Michelin tyres. One of the Michelin company's other passions is maps, which are represented by etchings of the streets of Paris on some of the first floor windows.

Walking into the reception area of the building, you're greeted by a mosaic on the floor showing Bibendum (the corpulent 'Michelin Man') holding aloft a glass of nuts, bolts and other hazards

> Its exuberant, stylistic, individualism has variously been described as Art Nouveau, proto-Art Deco, Secessionist Functionalism and geometrical Classicism.

proclaiming *Nunc Est Bibendum* – Latin for 'now is the time to drink'. The reception area features more decorative tiles around the walls, while two glass cupolas, which look like piles of tyres, frame either side of the front of the building.

Michelin House is known for its decorative design, but it's also an early example of reinforced concrete construction. It was designed and built at the end of the Art Nouveau period, which is apparent in the decorative metalwork above the tyre-fitting bays, the tangling plants around the tyre motifs and the mosaic in the entrance hall. However, it's very like an Art Deco building, the popular style of the '30s, with its strong advertising images, albeit one 20 years ahead of its time.

Michelin vacated the building in 1985, when it was purchased by the late publisher Paul Hamlyn (1926-2001) and restaurateur and retailer Sir Terence Conran (b 1931). The pair had shared a love of the building for many years and embarked on a major redevelopment, which included restoring many of its original features (unfortunately the original stained-glass windows were removed for 'safety' and lost during WWII). The new development contains offices, a Conran shop, and the Bibendum Restaurant & Oyster Bar – which opened in August 1987. The Oyster Bar is on the ground floor, along with a more informal bistro-café. The restaurant is well worth a visit to behold this amazing building – and the food's excellent too!

❝ *A flamboyant Art Nouveau/Art Deco delight* ❞

Address: Ravenscourt Ave, W6 0TH (020-8753 4103, www.lbhf.gov.uk > parks and open spaces and www.ravenscourtpark.com).

Opening hours: Daily, 7.30am to sunset, e.g. 10pm (summer) and 4.30pm (winter).

Cost: Free.

Transport: Ravenscourt Pk tube.

RAVENSCOURT PARK

Ravenscourt Park is a beautiful 32-acre (13ha) public park and garden established in 1888 and designed by J. J. Sexby on land surrounding Ravenscourt House. The origins of Ravenscourt Park lie in the medieval manor and estate of Palingswick (or Paddenswick) Manor, first recorded in the 12th century. By the 13th century the manor house was a mansion surrounded by a moat fed by Stamford Brook. Edward III's mistress, Alice Perrers, lived in the manor during the 14th century. The house was rebuilt in 1650 and in 1747 was sold to Thomas Corbett who named it Ravenscourt, probably derived from the raven in his coat of arms, which was itself a pun on his name, as *corbeau* is French for *raven*.

In 1812, the house and estate were purchased by their last private owner, George Scott, a builder and philanthropist who developed nearby St Peter's Square. Scott employed leading landscape architect Humphry Repton to design the gardens, and encouraged the building of houses along their edges. In 1887, the Scott family sold the estate to a developer, but it was then purchased by the Metropolitan Board of Works (later the London County Council), which established a public park in 1888, now owned and managed by the borough of Hammersmith and Fulham. Ravenscourt House was demolished after being severely damaged during WWII; only the stable block remains, which is now the park's café.

The park combines attractive landscaping and a range of wildlife habitats, and is a Green Flag award winner. Its crowning glory is the magical, scented walled garden, secreted in the northeast corner of the park. Originally the kitchen garden of

> **The park offers a wide range of leisure facilities, including tennis and basketball courts, bowling and putting greens, multiple play areas and a tea-house. Annual events include a spectacular bonfire night, Carter's Steam Fair and an alfresco opera season.**

the house, it's laid out in a traditional Victorian symmetrical design with rose beds and rose arches, and exotic herbaceous beds featuring yuccas, giant poppies, irises and gunnera. It's bordered below the wall with shrubs, while scented plants such as lavender and honeysuckle make it a real treat for the nose as well as the eyes. The garden is a wonderful, Zen-like retreat, with benches and bowers. A park for all seasons and for everyone to enjoy.

 A lovely park with a secret garden

Address: Royal Hospital Rd, Chelsea, SW3 4SR (020-7881 5298, www. chelsea-pensioners.co.uk).

Opening hours: Courtyards and chapel: Mon-Sat, 10am to noon and 2-4pm. Great Hall: Mon-Sat, 11am to noon and 2-4pm. Museum: Mon-Fri, 10am to 4pm. Note that the grounds are closed in May for the Chelsea Flower Show (see www.rhs.org.uk/shows-events/rhs-chelsea-flower-show for dates).

Cost: Entry is free for individuals and small groups (fewer than 10 people). Larger groups must book a tour (020-7881 5516), Mon-Fri at 10am and 1.30pm. Tours (1½ hrs), £10 adults (£7 children under 16) for small groups (min. 4 people) and £8 adults (£4 children) for larger groups (min. 15 people).

Transport: Sloane Sq tube.

ROYAL HOSPITAL CHELSEA

The Royal Hospital Chelsea is set back from the embankment on the north shore of the Thames and, as a result, is often overlooked. That's a pity, as this beautiful, redbrick, Grade I listed building is regarded as London's second-loveliest façade on the Thames (after much-visited Greenwich). The grounds are also attractive and have been the site of the Chelsea Flower Show since 1913, the ultimate international event in the gardening calendar and a premier fixture on the London social scene, very much somewhere to see and be seen.

There are few institutions in the United Kingdom with an unbroken three centuries of service and none of them is so close to the heart of the nation as 'The Men in Scarlet', the Chelsea Pensioners, and their home, the Royal Hospital Chelsea. The hospital was founded by Charles II and was intended for the 'succour and relief of veterans broken by age and war', a purpose which it still serves in the 21st century. (It has been suggested that Charles was persuaded to build a hospital for veterans by his mistress, Nell Gwynn, whose father had been made destitute by the Civil War.)

The hospital was designed by Sir Christopher Wren and by the time of Charles II's death (1685) the main hall and chapel of the Hospital had been completed (the first patients included those injured at the Battle of Sedgemoor). The work was completed in 1692 and by the end of March that year the full capacity of 476 former soldiers (pensioners) were in residence.

The Royal Hospital Chelsea was built around three courtyards, the centre one opening to the south, the side ones to the east and west. The building remains almost unchanged except for minor alterations by Robert Adam between 1765 and 1782, and the stables, which were added by Sir John Soane in 1814. The hospital is thus the work of three of Britain's finest architects. Even the stable block is regarded as an architectural gem, one of Soane's finest exteriors, although it's little known or recognised by the general public.

Today, the hospital is still home to around 400 pensioners, who receive board, lodging, nursing care and a distinctive uniform. However, much of the site is open to visitors: the Great Hall, Octagon, chapel and courtyards. There's also a small museum dedicated to the hospital's history. The site of the 18th-century pleasure gardens, Ranelagh Gardens, now forms part of the grounds and is also open to the public.

66 *Old soldiers' home on the Thames* **99**

Address: Sydney St, SW3 6NH (020- 7351 7365, www.chelseaparish. org).

Opening hours: Mon-Sat, 9am to 5pm.

Cost: Free.

Transport: S Kensington or Sloane Sq tube.

ST LUKE'S CHURCH & GARDEN

St Luke's (Grade I listed, with Grade II listed gardens) was built in 1824 to cater to an increasing congregation in Chelsea which had out-grown its parish church (now Chelsea Old Church). Designed by John Savage (1799-1852), it's built of Bath stone with flying buttresses and Gothic perpendicular towers along the nave and to the east end. It was one of the first Neo-Gothic churches built in London, with a 60ft (18.3m) high nave, the tallest of any parish church in London. Savage was one of the foremost authorities on medieval architecture, and the church has a grandeur of conception and great attention to detail. The interior was laid out in the traditional 18th-century manner of a preaching house, with an enormous pulpit, pews everywhere and a diminutive altar, although it was redesigned in the late 19th century to become substantially what you see today.

> The church has associations with many famous people, not least Charles Dickens, who married Catherine Hogarth here in 1836 (the wedding took place two days after the publication of the first part of *The Pickwick Papers*).

The stunning east window, designed by Hugh Easton in honour of The Trinity and The Church, was installed in 1959 to replace one destroyed during WWII, while the painting behind the altar depicts the deposition of Christ from the cross and is by James Northcote (1746-1831), a noted portrait painter. The two large sculptures (Stephen Cox, 1997) on either side of the altar represent Adam and Eve at the fall of man in the Garden of Eden, bowing their heads in shame for their disobedience to God.

St Luke's has a fine organ built by John Compton in 1932 (incorporating some parts from the original 1824 organ), which served as the prototype for organs at Broadcasting House and Downside Abbey; the church is also noted for the excellence of its choirs (both St Luke's and Christ Church). It has a ring of ten bells in the tower, which were cast at Whitechapel when the church was built.

The large burial ground which surrounded the church was converted into a public garden in 1881, with the gravestones forming a boundary wall. Today the delightful gardens are famous for their beautiful flower beds and lovely trees (visit in spring when they're in blossom), and a welcome retreat from the teeming streets. The garden also has a children's playground and a games area. The church also has a café (9am to 5pm).

“ *A lovely church with a charming garden* **”**

Address: 24 Cheyne Row, Chelsea, SW3 5HL (020-7352 7087, www.nationaltrust.org.uk/carlyles-house).

Opening hours: Mar-Oct (see website for exact dates), Wed-Sun, 11am to 4.30pm. Also open on bank holiday Mon.

Cost: £5.10 adults, £2.60 children, £12.80 family.

Transport: Sloane Sq tube.

Thomas Carlyle

THOMAS CARLYLE'S HOUSE

This beautiful Queen Anne house is an atmospheric, interesting, well-preserved example of what life was like in a middle class, creative Victorian home, and remains much as it would have been in 1895. The building itself is older, a typical Georgian terraced house (built in 1708), set in Cheyne Row – one of London's best preserved early 18th-century streets – in Chelsea, one of its richest and ritziest districts.

In a part of London noted for its writers and other artistic types, this is the former home of Thomas and Jane Carlyle, a literary celebrity couple of their day. Native Scots, they moved to London in the 1830s and to Cheyne Row in 1834. Jane died in 1866, but Thomas remained here until his death in 1881 (he apparently died in the Drawing Room). For the following 14 years it was rented out, but remained largely untouched. In May 1895 the house was purchased and the Carlyle's House Memorial Trust created to administer it. In 1936 it was transferred to the National Trust, which retains control.

Thomas Carlyle was one of the Victorian era's greatest writers, said to have inspired Dickens, although he's little read nowadays, which perhaps explains why his house often fails to register on people's radar. He was a historian, philosopher and satirist, and his wife was a woman of letters, as well as a renowned hostess and story-teller. They had many famous friends and their home became a magnet for a wide circle of artists, philosophers, scientists and writers.

The Carlyles had a notably stormy marriage; a mixture of affection, anger and jealousy, and they weren't universally admired. Some regarded them as thinking too highly of themselves and Thomas was said to have a tendency to be rather gloomy. However, they made an appealing home, and their devotees have tracked down many of the Carlyles' original possessions, giving the house an authentic feel.

The attractive furniture, pictures, books, etc., paint a vivid picture of their domestic and work lives, and there's also a small walled garden – planted with flowers and shrubs that the Carlyles enjoyed – as indicated in their correspondence. Thomas was famously obsessed with noise: he hated it and found it difficult to work with any distractions. As a result, he tried to sound-proof his study, but was only partly successful, as visitors can discover for themselves.

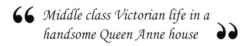

Middle class Victorian life in a handsome Queen Anne house

Address: Hogarth Ln, Great West Road, W4 2QN (020-8994 6757, www. hounslow.info/arts/hogarthshouse/index.htm).

Opening hours: **Tue-Sun, noon to 5pm. Closed Mon (except for bank holidays), 25-26th Dec, Good Fri and Easter Sun.**

Cost: **Free.**

Transport: **Turnham Grn tube or 190 bus to Hogarth Roundabout.**

William Hogarth (self-portrait)

Marriage à-la-mode: 1. The Marriage Settlement
(National Gallery)

WILLIAM HOGARTH'S HOUSE

Hogarth's House (Grade I listed) is the former country home of the famous 18th-century English painter, engraver and satirist William Hogarth (1697-1764), where he lived (with his wife, wife's cousin, mother-in-law and sister!) from 1749 until his death in 1764. It provided a quiet summer retreat from the bustle of city life around Hogarth's main house and studio, in what is now Leicester Square.

The house was built between 1713 and 1717 in the corner of an orchard belonging to the Downes family. Its first occupant was the Rev George Andreas Ruperti, the pastor of St Mary's Lutheran church in the Savoy. Hogarth purchased it from Ruperti's son in 1749 and extended it in 1750, and his widow added a single-storey extension in 1769.

Hogarth was born near Smithfield Market in London, where his childhood was blighted by his father's imprisonment for debt. He was apprenticed to a silver engraver, which gave him skills that helped him produce prints and teach himself to paint. Hogarth hated injustice, snobbery and pretension, and deplored the degradation suffered by the poor. One of his best-known images, *Gin Lane*, has come to represent the worst aspects of slum life in 18th-century London. Hogarth was a shrewd businessman and sold his prints at relatively modest prices, thus reaching a much wider audience than the few who could afford his paintings.

Hogarth's House was opened to the public in 1904 by a local landowner and Hogarth enthusiast,

> After visiting the house, why not take a few minutes to visit Hogarth's tomb in the graveyard of nearby St Nicholas' church.

Lieutenant-Colonel Robert William Shipway (1841-1925), who gave the house to Middlesex County Council in 1907. The house was damaged in 1941 during WWII, but was repaired and reopened in 1951. It was restored again for the Hogarth Tercentenary in 1997 and closed again for refurbishment in September 2008, during which it was badly damaged by fire in August 2009, which led to the house remaining closed until November 2011.

Two floors of the house are now open to the public and include the most extensive collection of Hogarth's prints on permanent public display. The panelled rooms also house some replica pieces of 18th-century furniture. An exhibition documents Hogarth's life and work with copies of his best-known series of engravings, including *The Harlot's Progress*, *A Rake's Progress* and *Marriage à-la-mode*. The house has an attractive walled garden containing a 300-year-old mulberry tree.

 Summer retreat of Britain's greatest satirical artist

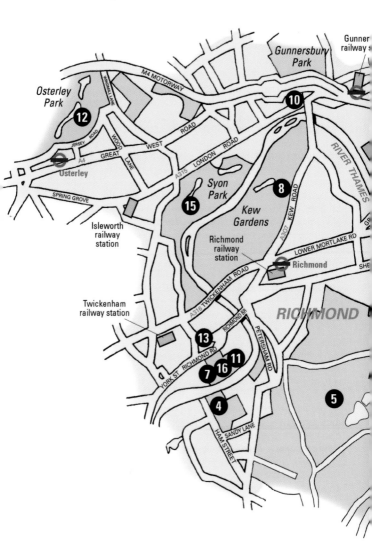

SOUTHWEST LONDON

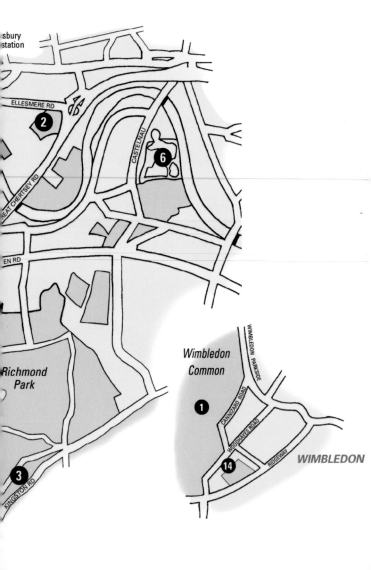

Address: **West Side Common, Wimbledon, SW19 4UE (020-8879 1464, www.cannizaropark.com and www.cannizarohouse.com).**

Opening hours: **Daily, 8am to dusk.**

Cost: **Free.**

Transport: **Wimbledon tube/rail.**

CANNIZARO PARK

The lovely Cannizaro Park is a Grade II* listed park of 35 acres (14ha) on the edge of Wimbledon Common, although it sounds as if it should be in Rome. It was a private garden for some 300 years, opened to the public as a park in 1949, and combines great natural beauty with a unique collection of rare and exquisite trees and shrubs, including sassafrass, camellia, rhododendron and other ericaceous plants. It's also noted for its rich wildlife.

It has a large variety of green areas, from expansive lawns to small intimate spaces such as the herb and tennis court gardens, and lovely leisurely walks through the woodlands. Formal areas have been developed, with a sunken garden next to the park's hotel

The park has a long history of staging arts and musical events (including the Wimbledon Cannizaro Festival in summer), and contains a variety of sculptures, including a statue of Diana and the fawn, and a fountain in the driveway.

and an Italian Garden near its pond, expressing the changing face of garden design through the years.

Warren House – now Cannizaro House – was built in the early 1700s, when the kitchen garden served the tables of some of its most famous residents and guests, from its 18th-century heyday to the last private owners in the '40s (the house is now a hotel). The name Cannizaro dates back to 1832 when Count St Antonio leased the house. He later succeeded to the dukedom of Cannizzaro in Sicily and left England to live with his mistress in Milan, but his long-suffering wife, Sophia, prided herself on the title of Duchess of Cannizzaro. When she died in 1841, the estate was recorded under her name, and apart from the spelling change, has stuck ever since.

With the exception of Viscount Melville (1742-1811), who planted Lady Jane's Wood in 1793, the greatest private contributors to today's park were Mr and Mrs E. Kenneth Wilson who lived there from 1920 to 1947. Their daughter, Hilary, married the 5th Earle of Munster in 1928 and 20 years later (after her parents died) sold the estate to Wimbledon corporation for £40,000.

The park's timeless appeal is a joy at any time – thanks to the tireless efforts of the Friends of Cannizaro Park – and is particularly special in spring when the rhododendrons, azaleas and magnolias are in bloom. Or visit in autumn, when the birch, maple and horse chestnut trees are equally colourful and spectacular.

66 *One of London's most beautiful 'secret' parks* 99

AT A GLANCE

Address: Burlington Ln, Chiswick, W4 2QN (020-8742 3905, www.chgt. org.uk).

Opening hours: House: Apr-Oct, Sun-Wed and bank holidays, 10am to 6pm; Nov-Mar closed to visitors (although open in Mar for the Camellia Festival – see website). Conservatory: daily, 10am to 4pm. Gardens: daily, 7am to dusk. Café: daily from 8.30am (closing time varies).

Cost: Gardens: Free. House: £6.10 adults, £5.50 concessions, £3.70 children (5-15), £15.90 family, under 5s free.

Transport: Turnham Grn tube or Chiswick rail.

CHISWICK HOUSE & GARDENS

Nestled unexpectedly in affluent, mock-Tudor Chiswick suburbia is a glorious piece of Palladian Italy, with plenty of surrounding green space in which to walk, picnic, let off steam and become happily lost. Chiswick House was completed in 1729, the vision of the third Earl of Burlington, who'd been inspired by the architecture he saw during his 'grand tours' of Italy. It's one of England's finest examples of neo-Palladian design, i.e. modelled on the architecture of ancient Rome and 16th-century Italy.

It wasn't built as a private residence so much as a showcase for art and a venue for entertaining; the Earl played host to the luminaries of the day, including Alexander Pope and Handel. The design of the house echoes that of classical temples and is the result of a collaboration between the Earl and the architect William Kent.

There's much to see in the house, including eight beautiful landscape views of Chiswick by the 18th-century Dutch artist Pieter Andreas Rysbrack (they can also be seen on the website); The Chiswick Tables, which are some of the best examples of English neo-Palladian furniture; The Blue Velvet Room Ceiling, an ornate blue and gold representation of the goddess of architecture; statues of the architects Palladio and Inigo Jones; two porphyry urns; the Coffered Dome in the Upper Tribunal; carvings of the pagan god The Green Man in the fireplaces of the Green Velvet Room; beautiful, half-moon apses in the Gallery; a splendid lead sphinx and much more.

The gardens are also full of interest and are of historical significance: they were the birthplace of the English Landscape movement, i.e. a style of sweeping elegance which replaced the previous formality. They offer grand vistas and hidden pathways, dazzling flower displays and architectural treats. There's also a 19th-century conservatory (famous for its large collection of camellias, the largest in the Western world and celebrated in a Festival in Feb-Mar), a Classic Bridge, cricket pitch, lake, Italian garden, statues, walled gardens and much more. The gardens were recently restored (at a cost of £12m), in one of the largest and most ambitious garden regeneration projects ever undertaken in Britain.

The café, designed by Caruso St John, was named RIBA London Building of the Year in 2011; one of London's best park cafés, it serves delicious sandwiches, soups and the best of modern British cooking.

66 *Palladian Italy comes to Chiswick* **99**

Address: 67 Kingston Vale, Kingston-upon-Thames, SW15 3RN (020-8417 5515, www.dorichhousemuseum.org.uk).

Opening hours: Monthly open days (see website), 11am to 4pm, with guided tours at 11.30am and 2.30pm (booking advisable). Private curator's tours and school visits are also available (020-8417 5519).

Cost: Admission: £4 adults, £3 concessions, children under 16 free. Private tours (min. 10 people) £9 per head.

Transport: Kingston or Putney rail then 85 bus, or by car.

Dora Gordine

DORICH HOUSE MUSEUM

Dorich House was the studio, gallery and home of the sculptor Dora Gordine (1895-1991) and her husband the Hon. Richard Hare (1907-1966), a Professor of Russian Literature. Built in 1936 and restored by Kingston University in 1994, Dorich House is a fine example of Art Deco design, its severe exterior concealing the warmth of the interiors where Richard and Dora lived and worked. The couple left the house and its collections in trust for the education and enjoyment of the British public, and the newly restored building was opened in 1996 and became a museum in 2004.

Dora Gordine was hailed in 1938 as 'possibly the finest woman sculptor in the world' and she remained a major presence in European sculpture until the late '60s. Trained in Tallinn and Paris during the '20s, Gordine achieved critical acclaim in 1926 with the bronze *Head of a Chinese Philosopher* (on display at Dorich House) exhibited at the Salon des Tuileries in Paris. She settled in Kingston in 1936 and remained at Dorich House until her death in 1991.

> **The two studios, gallery and top floor apartment were designed by Gordine in 1935-6; you may recognise her stylish and artistic interiors, which have been used as sets for films, videos and TV programmes.**

Richard Gilbert Hare was the second son of the 4th Earl of Listowel. Educated at Oxford, the Sorbonne and Berlin University, he developed a lifelong interest in the study and collection of Russian art and culture. Following a brief career in the Foreign Office, he spent the war working for the Anglo-Soviet Relations Division of the Ministry of Information, before becoming a Professor of Russian Literature at the School of Slavonic and East European Studies, University of London. He died suddenly from a heart attack in 1966.

The Museum houses the world's largest collection of Gordine's bronzes and plaster sculptures, as well as many of her paintings and drawings, spanning her early years in Paris in the '20s to her last works created at Dorich House in the '60s and '70s. Hare's Russian art collection includes icons, paintings, ceramics, glassware, metalwork, folk art and furniture, dating from the early 18th century to the early 20th century. All are displayed in the unique surroundings of this studio home, described as 'one of Kingston's hidden treasures'.

A masterful treasure trove of a collection, well worth a trip to the suburbs.

❝ *A delightful house and stunning collection* ❞

Address: Ham St, Ham, Richmond, TW10 7RS (020-8940 1950, www. nationaltrust.org.uk/ham-house).

Opening hours: **House: daily, Apr-Oct, noon to 4pm, below stairs 10.30am to 4.30pm (see website for exact dates and opening times). Garden, shop and café, usually 10am to 5pm.**

Cost: **Entry to the House and Garden: £11 (incl. gift aid) adults, £5.50 children, £27.50 family. Garden only: £4.50 (incl. gift aid) adults, £2.25 children, £11.25 family. National Trust members free.**

Transport: **Richmond tube/rail or Twickenham rail.**

HAM HOUSE

Perhaps better known than its neighbours, Marble Hill House (see page 243) and Strawberry Hill, but still unjustly ignored by many, Ham House is an unusually complete 17th-century survivor on the Thames, rich in atmosphere and history. It's owned by the National Trust and is one of London's architectural and garden gems, but often overlooked, despite being only a short journey from central London. The name Ham comes from an old English word for 'a place in the bend in the river'.

Ham House was built in 1610 for Sir Thomas Vavasour, Knight Marshal to James I, and was extended and refurbished as a palatial villa under the ownership of Lord and Lady Dysart. It was mainly the vision of Lady Dysart, Elizabeth Murray, who's variously described as ambitious, beautiful, greedy and sharp-witted. She was also a renowned political schemer, involved with the restoration of the monarchy after the Civil War.

The Lady must also have been a fine time manager, as she and the Lord produced 11 children! Her hold on the house is said to continue to this day: her ghost and that of her dog still walk the corridors of what's reputed to be a very haunted property.

Ham House has rooms of sumptuous splendour, including walls hung with tapestries, rich fabrics and rococo mirrors. Meticulous restoration has created an atmosphere redolent of its original splendour. There are spectacular collections of furniture, textiles and paintings, while Ham has a notable collection of Coade Stone statues (Coade is a hard ceramic, which is cast and fired, named after its inventor Eleanor Coade); the statue 'River God' outside the front of the house is one of the largest pieces of Coade ever produced. (Eleanor took the secret for making Coade stone to her grave.)

One of the most remarkable survivors at the house is the 17th-century formal garden. Most were replaced in the following two centuries by then-fashionable natural garden landscapes, but these have been little changed for over 300 years and include Britain's oldest orangery and a lovely, trellised cherry garden.

❝ *Haunted 17th-century splendour on the Thames* **❞**

AT A GLANCE

Address: Richmond Pk, Richmond TW10 5HS (0300-061 2200, www. royalparks.org.uk/parks/richmond-park/richmond-park-attractions/ isabella-plantation).

Opening hours: From 7.30am to 4pm (see website for seasonal closing times).

Cost: Free.

Transport: Richmond tube/rail or 85 bus from Putney tube or by car to Broomfield Hill car park.

ISABELLA PLANTATION, RICHMOND PARK

The Isabella Plantation in Richmond Park is a 42-acre (17ha) ornamental woodland garden – south of Pen Ponds – packed with exotic plants and designed to be interesting all year round. The name is thought to derive from the old English word 'isabel', in use from the 15th century, meaning 'greyish-yellow' – the colour of the soil in this part of the park. In the 17th century the area was known as The Sleyt, a name usually used for boggy ground or an open space between woods or banks, but by 1771 it was called the Isabella Slade. In 1831, Lord Sidmouth, the park deputy ranger, renamed it the Isabella Plantation; he fenced it in to protect the plants from the park's deer and planted oak, beech and sweet chestnut trees.

Today's garden of clearings, ponds and streams was established from the '50s onwards and is largely the work of George Thomson, the park superintendent from 1951-1971. Along with his head gardener, Wally Miller, he removed *Rhododendron ponticum* from large areas and replaced it with other rhododendron species. They established evergreen Kurume Azaleas around the Still Pond and planted other exotic shrub and tree species. The gardens have two ponds, the Still Pond and Peg's Pond, and a small stream flows through it, colonised by ferns, water plantains and brook lime. The Bog Garden was refurbished in 2000.

Today, the Plantation is a popular part of Richmond Park – at least among those in the know! It contains different species that flower in different seasons, making it a garden for all seasons. In spring there are camellias, magnolias, daffodils and bluebells, while the azaleas and

> **The Plantation has 15 known varieties of deciduous azalea, and houses the national collection of 50 Kurume Azaleas – introduced to the West in around 1920 by the plant collector Ernest Wilson – as well as 50 different species of rhododendron and 120 hybrids.**

rhododendrons flower in late April. These are followed by Japanese irises and day lilies in summer and then by Guelder rose, rowan and spindle trees in the autumn, when the Acer trees are also a riot of colour. During the winter months there are early camellias and rhododendron, as well as mahonia, winter-flowering heathers and stinking hellebore.

The Isabella Plantation is also home to an abundance of wildlife and a joy at any time of the year.

❝ *A magical garden for all seasons* **❞**

LONDON WETLAND CENTRE

Situated in the elegant, upmarket west London enclave of Barnes, this is off the usual tourist beat for most visitors to the capital, which is a pity because there's nothing quite like it in any other major city; an amazing and unexpectedly large wildlife habitat near the centre of the metropolis. Without wishing to oversell it, this must be one of London's wonders, despite being one of the least 'London-like' attractions. As *The Times* said of the Centre 'when you enter, you leave London behind'.

The London Wetland Centre extends to over 100 acres (42ha) on land formerly occupied by several small reservoirs, which were converted into a wide range of wetland features and habitats, including grassland, mudflats and reed beds. This incredibly rich wetland reserve is managed by the Wildfowl and Wetlands Trust (which runs a total of nine sites in the UK) and is recognised as a Site of Special Scientific Interest.

The Centre is probably Europe's best urban wildlife viewing area and is an important site, not just for birds (over 180 species, including many that aren't found elsewhere in London) but also for bats, other small mammals, insects and amphibians. It's a haven for hundreds of species, but there are a handful of 'stars' that many visitors are particularly excited to spot. In the summer months these include the gregarious lapwing and the undeniably cute water vole, while the winter months bring significant numbers of snipe, bittern and other migrating birds to the reserve.

The London Wetland Centre is a notably user-friendly environment, where you're loaned binoculars for your visit and small fishing nets are provided for children, with the facility to examine catches later. Free guided walks are organised with experts or you can just wander off on your own and stroll along the walkways among the lakes, pools, meadows and reed beds. The reserve also features a heated viewing observatory, a bat house, hides where you can get up close to the wildlife, and an adventure area and interactive discovery centre for children.

There's also a regular programme of children's activities at weekends and during holiday periods (see the website for details), and an impressive visitor centre, with a gift shop, café and a cinema showing a short documentary about wetlands.

We will leave the last words to the esteemed wildlife film-maker and television presenter Sir David Attenborough: 'The London Wetland Centre is the ideal model for how mankind and the natural world may live side by side in the 21st century'. Praise indeed!

❝ *Wildlife haven in the city* ❞

MARBLE HILL HOUSE

Marble Hill House is a beautiful Palladian villa on the north bank of the Thames, the last complete survivor of the lovely villas and gardens that bordered the Thames between Richmond and Hampton Court in the 18th century. It's little known – despite its proximity to the much-visited Hampton Court Palace – but fine enough to be included in the journalist Sir Simon Jenkins's book, *England's Thousand Best Houses*. The house is now owned by English Heritage.

It was built between 1724 and 1729 for Henrietta Howard, Countess of Suffolk, King George ll's mistress (built when he was still Prince of Wales), by the architect Roger Morris, who collaborated with Henry Herbert, Earl of Pembroke (one of the 'architect earls'). In 1723, the Prince had given the Countess £11,500 (around £1.7m today) to furnish her with a retreat from crowded, insalubrious 18th-century London. It was set in 66 acres of glorious riverside parkland, the Marble Hill Park.

The house was built to a compact design, with tightly controlled elevations, which became influential and a standard model for villas in southern England and much further afield, including plantation houses in the American colonies. Its grand interiors have been beautifully restored and conjure up the atmosphere of fashionable Georgian life better than almost anywhere else in Britain.

The Great Room has five architectural *capricci* by the Italian painter Giovanni Paolo Pannini and ornate gilded decoration, while the dining parlour has hand-painted Chinese wallpaper. The house also contains a collection of early Georgian furniture and some fine paintings, as well as the Lazenby Bequest Chinoiserie collection.

The gardens of Marble Hill House are linked to Ham House (see page 237) on the opposite southern bank of the river by Hammerton's Ferry (www.hammertonsferry.com), a pedestrian and cycle ferry service across the Thames. It's one of only four remaining ferry routes in London that hasn't been replaced by a bridge or tunnel, operating at weekends and on weekdays from March to October (£1 adults, 50p children under 16 and bikes, buggies and dogs free).

❝ *A home fit for a king's mistress* **❞**

Address: Royal Botanic Gardens, Kew, TW9 3AB (020-8332 3622, www. kew.org/visit-kew-gardens/explore/attractions/marianne-north-gallery).

Opening hours: Daily, 9.30 or 10am until between 4.15pm (winter) and 6.30 or 7.30pm (summer); see website for exact times.

Cost: Adults £15, concessions £14, children (under 17) free when accompanied by an adult. Includes admission to most Royal Botanic Gardens' buildings and attractions.

Transport: Kew Gardens tube.

Marianne North

MARIANNE NORTH GALLERY

The beautifully restored and refurbished Marianne North Gallery at Kew Gardens – opened in 1882 and the only permanent solo exhibition by a female artist in Britain – is an experience not to be missed.

Marianne North (1830-1890), naturalist and botanical artist, was a remarkable Victorian woman who travelled the globe to satisfy her passion for recording the world's flora with her paint brush. Although she had no formal training in illustration and was rather unconventional in her methods, North had a natural artistic talent and was very prolific. In 1871, at the age of 40, she began her astonishing series of trips around the world. She was inspired by earlier travels with her father, Frederick North MP, and the exotic plant collections she saw at Kew. Her political connections served her well, providing her with letters of introduction to ambassadors, viceroys, rajahs, governors and ministers throughout the world. In the UK, North also had many supporters, including Edward Lear, Charles Darwin and Sir Joseph Hooker, then Director of Kew.

Between 1871 and 1885, North visited America, Canada, Jamaica, Brazil, Tenerife, Japan, Singapore, Sarawak, Java, Sri Lanka, India, Australia, New Zealand, South Africa, the Seychelles and Chile. Often she would stay away for long periods. In India she visited a number of regions over a period of almost 18 months, while in Brazil she spent 13 months travelling into the interior, making long and arduous journeys across rough terrain during which she completed over 100 paintings. Today her paintings from her travels provide an important historical record.

> In 2008-09, the gallery building was restored with a £1.8m Heritage Lottery Fund grant and support from donors. The paintings were also restored and conserved.

After exhibiting her paintings in a London gallery in 1879, North had the idea of showing them at Kew. She wrote to Sir Joseph Hooker offering to build a gallery if he would agree to display her life's work in it. The Gallery was designed by James Ferguson, the architectural historian, in a mixture of classical and colonial styles. After a visit to Australia and New Zealand, North spent a year arranging her paintings inside the building, which opened to the public in 1882. The Gallery contains 833 paintings – depicting over 900 plant species – all completed in 13 years of world travel.

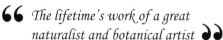

The lifetime's work of a great naturalist and botanical artist

Address: **Morden Hall Rd, Morden, SM4 5JD (020-8545 6850, www. nationaltrust.org.uk/main/w-mordenhallpark-2).**

Opening hours: **Park, daily from dawn to dusk. Car park, café, rose garden, craft shop and garden centre, 8 or 9am to 6pm.**

Cost: **Free.**

Transport: **Morden tube.**

MORDEN HALL PARK

Morden Hall Park, owned by the National Trust, covers over 125 acres (50ha) of parkland in what was once rural Surrey. This tranquil former deer park is one of the few remaining estates that used to line the River Wandle during its industrial heyday, and contains Morden Hall itself (currently let), a stable yard (now restored and containing interactive exhibitions), the pretty Morden Cottage situated in the rose garden, and many old farm buildings, some of which house a garden centre and a city farm. Visitors can still see the conserved (original) waterwheel that, until 1922, turned the massive millstones used to crush tobacco into fine powder. Today the Snuff Mill – one of the original Grade II listed mills – is used as an education centre.

> **The beautiful rose garden was originally laid out by Gilliat Edward Hatfeild in 1922 and contains some 2,000 roses, including 25 varieties of florabunda roses displayed across 38 flowerbeds. Visit between May and September to enjoy the rich aroma of the roses in full bloom.**

The estate land was originally owned by Westminster Abbey and there's evidence of an earlier manor house, although the current Morden Hall dates from the 1770s. The Hall was home to the Garth family for generations and was a school for young gentlemen in around 1840, until being sold in the 1870s by Sir Richard Garth QC (1820-1903) to a tobacco merchant, Gilliat Hatfeild (1827-1906). Hatfeild's son, Gilliat Edward Hatfeild (1864-1941), left the core of the estate (including the Hall) to the National Trust.

Morden Hall Park sits on the flood plain of the beautiful River Wandle and consists of three main habitats: meadowland, marshland and woodland. Water lies at the heart of the park, with the river, mill ponds and a lake. The lush wetlands, riverbanks and islands provide an ideal habitat for a variety of plants, animals, insects and abundant birdlife, including wildfowl, heron and kingfishers. There's an ornamental avenue of lime and horse-chestnut trees, and a mulberry tree thought to have been planted by Huguenots in the 18th century; the park also contains native trees such as oak, beech, ash, birch, and some lovely riverside willows and alders, including one of the oldest yews in England.

The walled kitchen garden once employed 14 gardeners and is now home to the Riverside Café and National Trust shop. There's also a demonstration kitchen garden.

A much-loved rural idyll well worth a visit.

66 *Watery green oasis in the heart of suburbia* **99**

Address: **399 High St, Brentford, TW8 0DU (020-8560 8108, www.
musicalmuseum.co.uk).**

Opening hours: **Fri-Sun, 11am to 5pm, including most bank holiday
Mon. Guided tours at 11.30am, 1.30pm and 3.30pm. Group tours by
appointment.**

Cost: **£10 adults, £7.50 concessions, £4 children (5-16), under 5s free,
£25 families (2 adults and 3 children).**

Transport: **Kew Bridge rail and 10-minute walk.**

MUSICAL MUSEUM

The Musical Museum is unique and contains one of the world's largest collections of automated musical instruments. It was founded in 1963 by the late Frank Holland MBE (1910-89), who was passionate in his belief that self-playing musical instruments should be preserved and not be lost to future generations. Holland was a pioneer in this field and firmly believed that collections of musical instruments should be heard as well as seen. His collection eventually consumed all the space in his flat and in 1963 was moved to a redundant church, St George's in Brentford, where it remained until 2008 before moving to the new purpose-built Museum you see today (with a café overlooking the river).

Today, it's hard to imagine a world without iPods, let alone one with no CDs, Walkmans, ghetto blasters, jukeboxes or stereos, where music can accompany you wherever you go and is accessible at the touch of a button. However, less than 100 years ago most people had never even heard an orchestra, concert pianist or opera singer, and the only way to enjoy recorded music was through an automatic musical machine, such as a wind-up musical box or a self-playing piano.

From the tiny clockwork musical box (first made in the late 18th century) to the self-playing 'Mighty Wurlitzer' concert organ, the collection embraces an impressive and comprehensive array of sophisticated reproducing pianos,

> **The concert hall offers a range of musical entertainment, spanning organ recitals, concerts, cabaret, classical music and light opera, with performers from throughout the UK and overseas (see website for information).**

pianolas, cranky barrel organs, orchestrions, orchestrelles, residence organs and violin players. The Museum is also home to the world's largest collection (30,000!) of historic musical rolls and an extensive archive of related material. The ground floor galleries display instruments once found in the large houses of the wealthy and in more humble dwellings and cafés, while the street setting reproduces shop windows with displays of musical toys and street instruments, where you can experience the actions and sounds of self-playing instruments.

Upstairs is a concert hall seating 230, complete with a stage and, of course, an orchestra pit from which the Wurlitzer organ console (formerly resident at the Regal Cinema, Kingston) rises to entertain you, just as it did in the cinema in the '30s.

A unique collection and musical experience for all the family.

66 *A magical musical mystery tour* **99**

Address: Riverside, Twickenham, TW1 3DJ (020-8831 6000, www. richmond.gov.uk/orleans_house_gallery).

Opening hours: Tue-Sun, 10am to 5pm. Café: Tue-Sun, 9.30am to 5.30pm. Hours may vary in winter (see website). Closed 24-27th December and 31st December to 2nd January.

Cost: Free.

Transport: St Margaret's rail.

Louis Phillipe I, Duc d'Orleans

ORLEANS HOUSE GALLERY

The Orleans House Gallery is one of south London's finest small galleries, located within woodland overlooking the Thames. It opened in 1972 and is home to the London borough of Richmond's art collection, one of the most outstanding fine art collections in London outside the city's national collections, comprising some 3,200 paintings, drawings, photographs, prints and objects dating from the early 18th century to the present day. The collection contains oil paintings, watercolours, drawings and prints by many notable artists, including Peter Tillemans (1684-1734), Samuel Scott (c1702-1772), Jean-Baptiste-Camille Corot (1796-1875), and Eric Fraser (1902-1983).

The original Thames-side house was built in 1710 for James Johnston (1655-1737), Joint Secretary of State for Scotland under William III, by John James (1672-1746). In stark contrast to the rather plain house, the ornate baroque Octagon Room – designed by the renowned architect James Gibbs (1682-1754) – was built as a garden pavilion in around 1720 for lavish entertainment (Queen Caroline, the wife of George II, dined there in 1729).

Orleans House has a rich and vibrant history and takes its name from its most famous resident, Louis Phillipe I, Duc d'Orleans (1773-1850), who lived here from 1815 to 1817 during his exile from Napoleonic France (and who became King of the French from 1830 to 1848). Most of the house was demolished in 1926 but the Octagon and two wings were saved by the Hon. Mrs Nellie Ionides (1883-1962), who bequeathed the riverside property and 500 portraits and local topographical landscapes to Richmond borough to create a public gallery.

The gallery has a reputation for its innovative exhibitions and hosts five a year in the main gallery, ranging from historical exhibitions of works from the permanent collection to contemporary exhibitions of paintings, photographs, crafts

> **The simple exterior belies the stunning baroque interior, decorated by the renowned Swiss stuccatori Guiseppe Artari and Giovanni Bagutti, who also decorated St Martin-in-the-Fields church in central London.**

and ceramics. Each exhibition features a changing themed display of works ('In Focus') from the permanent collection. The nearby Stables Gallery (opened in 1994) is housed in the evocative 19th-century stable buildings, and shows work by up-and-coming, avant-garde artists, local artists, and community groups and organisations.

 A superb little-known gallery in a delightful setting

Address: Jersey Rd, Isleworth, TW7 4RB (020-8232 5050, www. nationaltrust.org.uk/osterley-park).

Opening hours: Park: daily, 7am to 6pm. Gardens: 10am to 5pm. House: usually Wed-Sun from 11am to 5pm. See website for exact opening dates and times.

Cost: House and garden: £11 (incl. gift aid) adults, £5.50 children, £27.50 families. Garden only: £4.80 adults, £2.40 children, £12 family. Car park: £5. National Trust members free. Park and grounds free to all.

Transport: Osterley tube or Isleworth rail.

Sir Thomas Gresham

OSTERLEY PARK & HOUSE

Osterley House is a large, striking, National Trust-owned Tudor mansion set in gardens, park and farmland. It's one of London's last surviving country estates, once dubbed 'the palace of palaces'. The property is an original Tudor (1576) redbrick house of square design with four towers, built for Sir Thomas Gresham, an Elizabethan tycoon (who, among other things, was financial adviser to Queen Elizabeth I). It was not only somewhere for him to relax away from the city, but also a source of income. The land was fertile and well-watered, ideal for wheat, and he also established one of England's first paper mills here (only the stable block survives).

The property was remodelled by the fashionable architect and designer Robert Adam for the (wealthy banking) Child family between 1760 and 1780. His vast entrance portico is particularly notable, an expression of classical refinement. The stunning interiors are one of the most complete surviving examples of Adam's work, with beautiful plasterwork, splendid carpets and fine furniture, all designed by Adam specifically for Osterley Park House. However, by the beginning of the 19th century, Osterley was no longer a main residence and, apart from a few brief periods of occupation, would never be again.

Today, the rooms are an ornate visual treat and you can explore the house with a handheld audio-visual guide, which helps to bring it to life. It remains much as it was in the mid-18th century, and the interesting 'below stairs' area allows you to imagine what it was like to be a servant here.

The house is set in 357 acres of gardens and parkland, one of west London's largest open spaces. However, it isn't the most tranquil, as the M4 motorway cuts across the middle of it and you can hear aircraft arriving and departing from nearby Heathrow airport. Nevertheless, there's some lovely planting, notably in the Pleasure Gardens (where the floral displays are at their best between June and September) and a fine collection of trees.

Beginning in the 1760s, the process of landscaping Osterley Park saw the ponds and streams integrated to form three long lakes – the Garden, Middle and North Lakes – which today are important wildfowl habitats. In the late 18th century the park's main attraction was its menagerie by the North Lake, which contained a host of rare and unusual birds. Substantial tree-planting over the centuries include the introduction of cedars and a collection of oak trees, which include an impressive cork oak, a Japanese Daimyo oak, Hungarian oaks and North American red oaks.

 Vast Tudor palace and estate near Heathrow

Address: 40 Sandycoombe Rd, Twickenham, TW1 2LR (www. turnerintwickenham.org.uk).

Opening hours: First Sat of the month, 2-4.30pm, Apr-Oct, and by arrangement for groups at other times (info@turnerintwickenham.org. uk).

Cost: £4.

Transport: St Margaret's rail and bus. Street parking is limited and there's no parking on site.

JMW Turner

SANDYCOMBE LODGE

Sandycombe Lodge is a lovely Regency villa, the former home of Britain's greatest landscape artist, JMW (Joseph Mallord William) Turner (1775-1851). Supported by his father – a barber and wig maker – at the age of 14 Turner studied at the Royal Academy and by the age of 20 had established his own studio. In 1785, his sister Mary was taken seriously ill and died in 1786, after which his mother's mental health began to deteriorate; she died in a mental institution in 1804. The tragedies drew Turner and his father closer together and they shared a home for many years until his father's death in 1829. Turner never married but had two children by Sarah Danby in 1801 and 1811. In 1802, at the age of 27, Turner became a member of the Royal Academy.

In 1807, Turner purchased a plot of land near the Thames at Twickenham, then a fashionable riverside town. Here he built a villa – Solus

> **The combination of important artistic associations and an unusual architectural history, make this modest villa a building of great importance.**

Lodge, changing its name after a year to Sandycombe Lodge – to his own design with advice from his friend Sir John Soane, the leading architect of the day. It's a rare example of a house designed and built by a great artist for his own use; examples of sketches and ideas for the house can be found in Turner's notebooks. The external appearance of the house has been altered by the addition of second floors to the original side wings but the interior layout remains, and provides an insight into the character of its owner, being modest and unassuming.

Turner created a large pond covered in waterlilies in the grounds and kept a small boat moored nearby. He sold the house in 1826. The artist's original garden has long since gone, but miraculously the house has survived to this day. In the '40s it was purchased by the late Professor Harold Livermore (and his wife Ann), who lived here until his death in 2010, when he bequeathed the house to the nation, together with a collection of material about the artist.

Sandycombe Lodge is currently in a 'pre-conservation' state, and Turner's House Trust is seeking funding for its conservation, after which it will be open on a regular basis. The Friends of Turner's House run various events to support the Trust.

 Former home of Britain's greatest landscape artist

Address: 3-4 Woodhayes Rd, Wimbledon, SW19 4RJ (020-8946 7643, www.southsidehouse.com).

Opening hours: Guided tours (1hr 15mins), Wed, Sat, Sun and bank holidays, 2pm, 3pm and 4pm, from Easter Sat to the last Sun of Sep. The house is closed for Wimbledon tennis fortnight and during the winter.

Cost: £9 adults, £6 students, £15 families.

Transport: Wimbledon tube/rail, then a 93 bus to the Rose and Crown pub in Wimbledon Village and a ten-minute walk, or by car (but parking is difficult).

SOUTHSIDE HOUSE

Southside House is a 17th-century property situated (appropriately) on the south side of Wimbledon Common. It was built for Robert Pennington (who shared Charles II's exile in Holland), who commissioned Dutch architects to build the house, incorporating an existing farmhouse into the design. Two niches either side of the front door contain statues of *Plenty* and *Spring*, which are said to bear the likenesses of Pennington's wife and daughter.

Southside was later rebuilt in the William and Mary style; behind the long façade are the old rooms, still with much of the Pennington's original 17th-century furniture, and a superb collection of art and historical objects reflecting centuries of ownership. The house's 'musik' room was prepared for the entertainment of Frederick, Prince of Wales, who visited in 1750. Later visitors to the house included Sir William and Lady Emma Hamilton, together with Lord Nelson and Lord Byron.

The house passed through the Pennington-Mellor family, eventually coming into the possession of Malcolm Munthe (1910-1995), the son of Hilda Pennington-Mellor (1882-1967) and Axel Munthe (1857-1949), author of *The Story of St Michele*. During WWII Southside House was damaged, and Malcolm Munthe spent much of his later life restoring it. The house survived a fire on 28th November 2010, which caused considerable damage, and after being repaired was officially opened on 9th November 2011.

The gardens are a delightful hotchpotch of wilderness, order, woodland, secret pathways, classical follies and water, which combine to create a garden full of surprises. They're open under the National Gardens Scheme during the spring and visitors taking house tours are welcome to wander and explore. Arts and performance events are also staged here. Most of the gardening is organic, which encourages wildlife, with regular visitors including great tits, blue tits, hedge sparrows, green and bull finches, blackbirds, thrushes, lesser spotted woodpeckers, tawny owls and jays.

Described by connoisseurs as an unforgettable experience, Southside House provides an enchantingly eccentric backdrop to the lives and loves of generations of the Pennington-Mellor-Munthe families. Maintained in traditional style without intrusive refurbishment and crammed with centuries of family possessions, it offers a wealth of fascinating family stories. It hosts tour groups – including special candlelit tours followed by drinks and a buffet supper – and cultural events such as lectures, concerts and literary discussions.

 An eccentric William & Mary-style family home

Address: Estate Office, Syon Park, Brentford, TW8 8JF (020-8560 0882, www.syonpark.co.uk).

Opening hours: House: mid-Mar to end Oct (see website for dates) on Wed, Thu, Sun and bank holiday Mon (also Good Fri and Easter Sat), 11am to 5pm. Gardens: 10.30am to 5pm in summer, weekends only in winter.

Cost: House, gardens and Great Conservatory: £12 adults, £10.50 concessions, £5 children, £27 families. Gardens and Great Conservatory: £7 adults, £5.50 concessions, £3.50 children, £15 families.

Transport: Gunnersbury or Ealing Broadway tube then a 237 or 267 bus to Brent Lea bus stop, or E2 or E8 bus to Brentford.

SYON HOUSE & PARK

Although situated in less-than-glamorous Brentford, Syon House and its 200-acre (80ha) park are both Grade I listed. Indeed, they comprise one of England's finest estates and have a rich history. The name derives from Syon Abbey, a medieval monastery of the Bridgettine Order, founded nearby in 1415 by Henry V. It moved to the site now occupied by Syon House in 1431 and was dissolved in 1539, during the Dissolution of the Monasteries.

In 1594, Henry Percy, 9th Earl of Northumberland, acquired Syon House through his marriage to Dorothy Devereux, and the Percy family have lived there ever since. In 1750, Sir Hugh Smithson inherited the Percy estates through his wife, Elizabeth Seymour, and they revived the Percy name when Sir Hugh became Earl and then 1st Duke of Northumberland in 1766. In 1761, he commissioned architect and interior designer Robert Adam (1728-1792) and landscape designer Lancelot 'Capability' Brown (1716-1783) to redesign the house and estate. While Adam's architecture was inspired by classical Rome, Brown took the medieval deer park as his model.

Adam's plans for the interior of Syon House included a complete suite of rooms on the principal level, together with a rotunda in the main courtyard (not built). In the event, only five main rooms on the west, south and east sides of the House, from the Great Hall to the Long Gallery, were designed in the Neo-classical style. But Syon House is feted as Adam's early English masterpiece and is the finest surviving evidence of his revolutionary use of colour. Two rooms sum up Adam's genius: the grand scale and splendour of the Great Hall, which resembles the Imperial Rome of a Hollywood epic, and – in dramatic contrast – the richly-decorated Ante Room or Vestibule, with its riot of coloured marble – one of Adam's most ingenious and original designs.

Within the 200 acres of parkland there are 40 acres (16ha) of gardens and an ornamental lake, which are renowned for their extensive collection of over 200 species of rare trees. The crowning glory of the gardens is the Great Conservatory, designed by Charles Fowler (1792-1867) and completed in 1830, which was the first large-scale conservatory to be built from metal and glass. However, although the park and lake were designed by Capability Brown in 1760, today they have a 19th-century character.

Syon House remains the London home of the Duke of Northumberland and is the last surviving ducal residence complete with its country estate in Greater London. Worth every penny of the entrance fee.

 Robert Adam's masterpiece in a majestic setting

Address: Richmond Rd, Twickenham, TW1 3AA (08456-122 660, www.richmond.gov.uk > leisure and culture > parks and open spaces and www.yorkhousesociety.org.uk).

Opening hours: dawn to dusk. The York House Society organises regular garden tours (see website).

Cost: Free.

Transport: Twickenham rail.

YORK HOUSE GARDENS

York House (Grade II listed) is a fine 17th-century building with a fascinating history, set in beautiful grounds on the banks of the River Thames. The riverside gardens were commissioned by Sir Ratan Tata (1871-1918), a Parsee from Mumbai who purchased the house in 1906 from the Duc d'Orleans (after whom Orleans House is named – see page 249). Tata, whose family still runs one of the largest industrial companies in India, installed striking statues of naked female figures in the gardens.

The statues represent the Oceanides or sea nymphs of Greek mythology, and include two winged horses with a female charioteer in a shell chariot, plunging through the water at the top of a cascade and pool, while seven other figures are sitting on rocks or clambering up them.

The statues were brought to England to adorn Lea Park (now Witley Park) near Godalming, Surrey, by the financier Whitaker Wright, but were sold in 1904 after he was found guilty of fraud and committed suicide. The fin-de-siècle sculptures (Grade II listed) are carved in Italian white Carrara marble. The sculptor is unknown, although it's thought they came from the Roman studio of Orazio Andreoni at the turn of the 19th century. After decades of neglect, the statues were restored in 1988 thanks to Elizabeth Bell-Wright, who encouraged the York House Society and the Twickenham Society to save them.

York House Gardens comprise a diverse range of areas, including tennis courts, formal planting, amenity grass

> **Some of the statues are in highly unusual attitudes and can come as a great surprise to the unsuspecting visitor.**

and woodland. Around the recently restored cascades, planting has been designed to be in harmony with the statues, with greens, pinks and whites predominating. The aquatic planting in the pool has also been improved with additional water lilies, irises and arum lilies, while candelabra primulas have been extensively planted around the water's edge. Some unusual specimen trees and shrubs have also been added to enliven the landscaping, including several types of magnolia, cornus contraversa and tulip trees, and there's also a beautifully restored Japanese garden.

Although the house isn't officially open to the public – being the HQ of the London borough of Richmond (which purchased it in 1924 to use as offices) – it's a public building and parts of it are open on occasions (it can also be rented for weddings and other events).

66 *Splendid naked ladies in demure Twickenham* ****

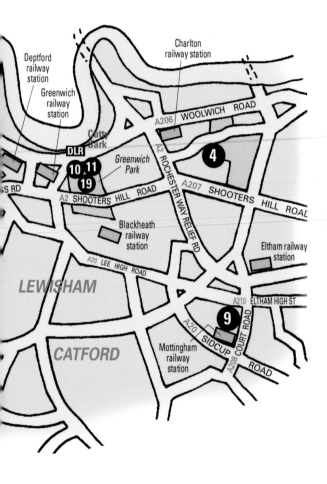

See next page for more maps & key

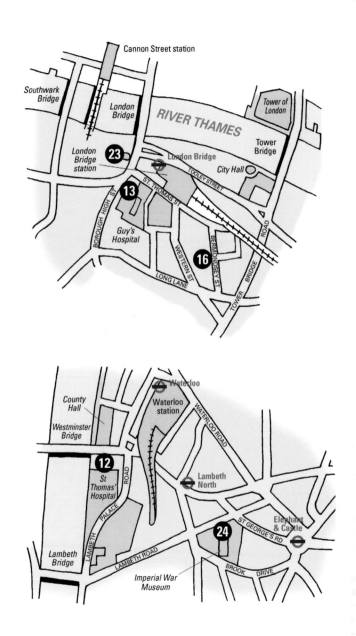

See previous page for more maps

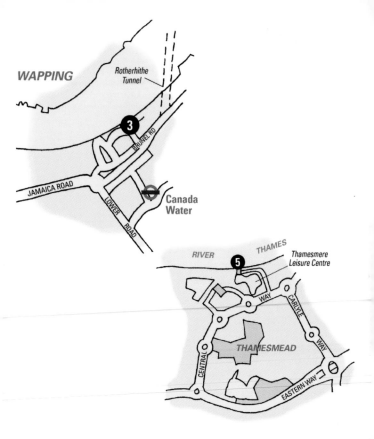

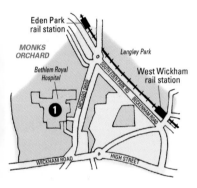

The Maze, William Kurelek

BETHLEM MUSEUM OF THE MIND

The Bethlem Museum of the Mind is the fascinating museum of the ancient Bethlem Royal Hospital – a psychiatric hospital variously known as St Mary Bethlehem, Bethlem Hospital, Bethlehem Hospital and Bedlam – now located in Beckenham. Although no longer based at its original location, Bethlem Royal Hospital is recognised as the world's first and oldest institution to specialise in mental illnesses.

Bethlem has been a part of London since 1247, first as a priory for the sisters and brethren of the Order of the Star of Bethlehem, from where the building took its name. Its first site was in Bishopsgate, where Liverpool Street station now stands. In 1337 it became a hospital which admitted some mentally ill patients from 1357, but it didn't become a dedicated psychiatric hospital until later.

Early 16th-century maps show Bethlem, next to Bishopsgate, as a courtyard with a few stone buildings, a church and a garden.

> In the 18th century people used to go to 'Bedlam' to stare at the lunatics. For a penny one could peer into their cells, view the freaks of the 'show of Bethlehem' and laugh at their antics.

Conditions were dreadful, with care amounting to little more than restraint, and the hospital became infamous for the brutal ill-treatment meted out to the mentally ill. In 1675, Bethlem moved to a magnificent new Baroque building in Moorfields designed by Robert Hooke, which provided better facilities and more spacious accommodation.

Eighteenth-century Bethlem was famously portrayed in a scene from William Hogarth's, *A Rake's Progress* (1735), the story of a rich merchant's son whose immoral living causes him to end up in Bethlem. In 1815, the hospital moved to St George's Fields, Southwark, to buildings designed by James Lewis (part of which is now the Imperial War Museum). Bethlem moved to its present site in 1930.

Since 1970, there has been a museum at Bethlem Royal Hospital that records the lives and experiences, and celebrates the achievements, of those with mental health problems. It includes items from the hospital's art collection, which specialises in work by artists who suffered from mental health problems, including former Bethlem patients William Kurelek, Richard Dadd, Vaslav Nijinsky and Louis Wain. Other notable exhibits include a pair of statues (see opposite) by Caius Gabriel Cibber, known as *Raving and Melancholy Madness*, from the gates of 17th-century Bethlehem Hospital, 18th- and 19th-century furniture and alms boxes, restraint devices and archive documents dating back to the 16th century.

 A unique and beguiling small museum

Address: Electric Ave, Pope's Rd and Brixton Station Rd SW9 (020-7926 2530, http://brixtonmarket.net and www.friendsofbrixtonmarket.org).

Opening hours: Electric Ave and Pope's Rd: Mon-Sat, 8am to 6pm (Wed 3pm); Brixton Village and Market Row: daily, 8am to 11.30pm (Mon 6pm); Brixton Station Rd Markets: Wed-Fri lunchtime (food corner), Fri-Sat market, 10am to 5pm, Sun farmers' market 10am to 2pm. Shops: daily, 8am to 7pm.

Cost: Free.

Transport: Brixton tube.

BRIXTON MARKET

Brixton Market is actually a number of markets, comprising a vibrant street market and covered market areas in the nearby arcades: Reliance Arcade, Market Row and Granville Arcade (the last now rebranded as 'Brixton Village'), packed with culinary treats. Nowadays, the market has expanded to cover several areas of Brixton, including Brixton Station Road.

The Market began life on Atlantic Road in the 1870s and subsequently spread to Brixton Road, which had a wide pathway. It became a popular attraction with working class shoppers, who were entertained by street musicians. Electric Avenue (made famous by Eddy Grant with his eponymous 1983 hit song), now part of the street market, was built in the 1880s and was one of the first streets in London to have electric light. Glazed iron canopies covered the footpath, although these were badly damaged during WWII and removed in the '80s.

The market comprises three areas (recently Grade II listed): the open-air Market Row (1928), which contains Electric Avenue, and two covered arcades – Reliance Arcade (1924) and Granville Arcade (1937). The three market arcades form an extensive network of stalls and are rare survivors, recently joined by a themed market or event each Saturday on Brixton Station Road, which also hosts a Sunday farmers' market (10am to 2pm).

After the huge wave of immigration in the '50s, the Market became an important focal point for the black community. It sells a wide range of foods and goods, but is best known for its African and Caribbean produce, including specialities such as flying fish, breadfruit and all manner of weird looking fresh meats, reflecting the diverse community of Brixton and the surrounding areas. The Market has a heaving, bustling atmosphere that you won't find elsewhere in London; whereas many markets are interesting to wander around and browse the wares on offer,

> **Brixton Market has a unique character, which distinguishes it from other London markets and shopping areas: a combination of history, interesting architecture, the variety of goods on sale and the cultural mix of Brixton, generally acknowledged as the symbolic 'soul of black Britain'.**

Brixton Market is a 'real' market offering a wide choice of world produce at modest prices with minimum frills. The Atlantic Road part of the market offers more in the way of clothes, leather goods, household linen and children's toys, rather than food.

❝ *London's most vibrant and colourful market* ❞

Address: Railway Ave, Rotherhithe, SE16 4LF (020-7231 3840, www.brunel-museum.org.uk).

Opening hours: Daily, 10am to 5pm (later for special events). Guided descents into the tunnel on Sat-Sun and Tue-Thu. There are also guided boat and walking tours (see website for information).

Cost: £3 adults, £1.50 concessions, under 16s free.

Transport: Canada Water tube, change for Rotherhithe rail (London Overground).

Isambard Kingdom Brunel

Sir Marc Isambard Brunel

BRUNEL MUSEUM

The Brunel Museum celebrates the life and work of three generations of the legendary Brunel engineering family: Sir Marc Isambard Brunel (1769-1849), his more famous son, Isambard Kingdom Brunel (1806-1859) – widely considered to be Britain's greatest engineer – and Isambard's second son, Henry Marc Brunel (1842-1903), also a civil engineer.

The museum is situated above the Thames Tunnel in the Brunel Engine House in Rotherhithe, designed by Sir Marc, part of the infrastructure of the Thames Tunnel which contained steam engines to pump water from the tunnel. A permanent exhibition tells the story of the construction and history of the tunnel, including display panels, models of the tunnel under construction, original artefacts and a video presentation.

Marc Isambard Brunel had a fascinating, if turbulent, life. Born in Normandy to a farming family, he became a naval cadet in 1786 and after returning to France during the French Revolution, unwisely predicted the demise of Robespierre and had to flee to New York. He took American citizenship in 1796 and was appointed chief engineer of the city of New York. In 1799 he sailed to England and soon after married Sophia Kingdom (an Englishwoman he had met in France in 1793).

Among his most notable inventions was the first automated production system in the world (for making ships' rigging pulley blocks), but he was later involved in a number of unprofitable projects. By 1821 he was deep in debt and was tried and committed to debtor's prison in Southwark, where he spent 88 days, only being released after the intervention of the Duke of Wellington. Marc Isambard Brunel's most famous project was the Thames Tunnel (1825-1843) – the first tunnel constructed beneath a navigable river. Originally designed for horse-drawn carriages, it was first used by trains in 1869 and is now part of the London Overground railway network, and is the oldest tunnel in the oldest metro system in the world.

Isambard Kingdom Brunel was even more famous than his father; he built dockyards and the fastest railway in the world, the 7ft broad gauge Great Western; constructed a series of steamships, including the first propeller-driven transatlantic steamship; and engineered numerous important bridges and tunnels. His designs revolutionised public transport and modern engineering.

This fascinating museum also has a riverside terrace and gardens, a café and a bookshop. Work started in 2015 on a new gallery and theatre.

❝ *Britain's 'first family' of engineers* **❞**

Address: Charlton Rd, Greenwich, SE7 8RE (020-8856 3951, http://charlton-house.org).

Opening hours: Gardens and exhibition area with information about the history of the house, Mon-Fri, 8.30am to 6pm. Mulberry tea rooms: Mon-Fri, 9am to 4pm. Charlton House is home to a public library and community centre and isn't open to the general public, except on certain days, such as during the Open House London weekend (www.openhouselondon.org.uk).

Cost: Free.

Transport: Charlton rail.

CHARLTON HOUSE

Charlton House is one of London's least-known architectural gems, a magnificent Jacobean mansion improbably situated in unfashionable Charlton. It commands an impressive site on a hill overlooking lawns and trees, at the heart of Charlton village, one of the few areas of southeast London to have kept its distinctive village features, including a parish church, part of the village green and the village main street.

Charlton House dominates the area as the community's original manor house, and if you stand outside it and gaze towards the village you get a distinct flavour of an earlier age and what life used to be like here (reason enough to visit). All this is within sight of the iconic modern skyscrapers of Canary Wharf across the river.

It's one of several English houses called Charlton House, but is the most prominent and regarded as London's best-preserved Jacobean house and one of England's finest examples of Jacobean domestic architecture. The Jacobean phase of architecture (1603-1625) forms a link between the expansive Tudor style and the tidy, geometrical style associated with Inigo Jones.

Charlton House was built between 1607 and 1612 from red brick with stone dressing, in an 'E'-plan layout. It was built for Sir Adam Newton (who's buried across the road in St Luke's Church), Dean of Durham and tutor to Prince Henry, son of James I and elder brother of the future Charles I. Prince Henry died the year the house was completed.

The architect is unknown, but is thought to be John Thorpe. The orangery (later a public lavatory, but no longer used) is possibly the work of Inigo Jones. Charlton House was acquired by Greenwich Council in 1925 and later converted into a public library and community centre. The house, stables, orangery and park are intact except for the house's north wing, which was destroyed in the Second World War and later rebuilt.

An ancient mulberry tree in the garden was apparently planted at the suggestion of James I in 1608, making it probably the oldest in England. He was keen to develop a silk industry, but his plans turned into something of a joke: he planted a large mulberry garden on the land where Buckingham Palace was later built, but the delightfully unpredictable English climate killed it off (and, embarrassingly, they were in any case the wrong type of mulberry for breeding silkworms!).

 London's best-preserved Jacobean mansion

Address: The Old Works, Crossness S.T.W., Belvedere Rd, Abbey Wood, SE2 9AQ (020-8311 3711, www.crossness.org.uk).

Opening hours: Restricted due to major restoration. Public Steaming days (10.30am to 4pm) on certain Sun from Apr-Oct (see website for dates).

Cost: £6 adults, £2 children (5-16), under 5s free.

Transport: Abbey Wood rail, then mini-bus service.

CROSSNESS PUMPING STATION

The Crossness Pumping Station (Grade I listed) was built by Sir Joseph William Bazalgette (1819-1891) and architect Charles Henry Driver (1832-1900) as part of Victorian London's main sewerage system, and officially opened by the Prince of Wales in April 1865. In the early 19th century, London's water supply and the Thames were heavily polluted with sewage, which resulted in several cholera outbreaks during which up to 20,000 people died annually.

Joseph Bazalgette was one of the most distinguished Victorian civil engineers, and after being employed on various railway projects he was appointed chief engineer of the Metropolitan Board of Works in 1855, having previously worked for the Metropolitan Commission of Sewers. Bazalgette built 83 miles (134km) of 'interceptory' sewers that prevented raw sewage from running into the Thames and took it to East London where it was pumped into the river with minimal effect on the population. This system involved four major pumping stations, at Abbey Mills (in the Lea Valley), Chelsea (close to today's Grosvenor Bridge), Deptford and Crossness on the Erith marshes.

> **It was the 'Great Stink' of 1858, when the Houses of Parliament became so smelly that members demanded action, that was the catalyst for the creation of the sewerage system we still have today.**

At Crossness Pumping Station the Beam Engine House was constructed in the Romanesque (Norman) style in gault (clay) brick, with considerable ornamentation, red brick arches and dog-tooth string courses. The interior features spectacular, colourful ornate Victorian wrought and cast ironwork and was described as 'a masterpiece of engineering – a Victorian cathedral of ironwork' by architectural expert Nikolaus Pevsner. It contains the four original pumping engines, which are possibly the largest remaining rotative beam engines in the world, with 52-ton flywheels and 47-ton beams. Although modern diesel engines were subsequently introduced, the old beam engines remained in service until work on a new sewerage treatment plant began in 1956.

The Crossness Engines Trust was created in 1987 to restore the installation, which is a unique part of Britain's industrial heritage and an outstanding example of Victorian engineering. The spectacular building, engines and pumps remain as a monument to Bazalgette's genius in solving London's problems: he was also responsible for the Thames Embankments; Battersea, Hammersmith and Putney Bridges; and many of London's other capital projects.

 A stunning Victorian engineering delight

Address: Old Palace Rd, Croydon CR0 1AX (01883-715393, www.friendsofoldpalace.org).

Opening hours: Open only for tours (2hrs) on certain days at 1.30pm in Apr, May and Oct (see website for information). Bookings are unnecessary except for groups of ten or more. Also open (free) during Open House London weekend (see www.londonopenhouse.org.uk).

Cost: £7 adults, £6 concessions/children.

Transport: Tramlink to Church St or E or W Croydon rail.

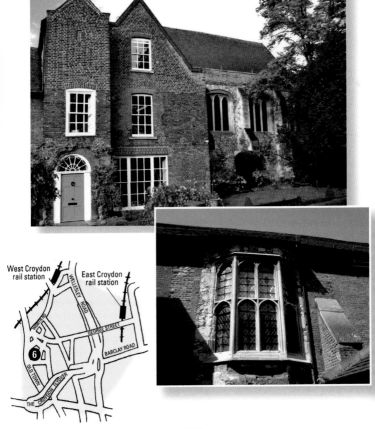

CROYDON (OLD) PALACE

Croydon Palace – now known as the Old Palace – is a spectacular surviving 15th-century palace that was the summer residence of the Archbishops of Canterbury for over 500 years. Nowadays the buildings comprise part of the Old Palace School, an independent girls' school of the Whitgift Foundation.

The manor of Croydon was connected with the Archbishop of Canterbury from at least the late Saxon period, and records of buildings date back to before 960. The palace as it now exists is a group of largely 15th- and 16th-century buildings. The 15th-century Great Hall – thought to have been installed by Archbishop Stafford (d 1452) – has a late 14th-century, two-storey porch and a vaulted ceiling to the lower chamber. The hall interior has a rich 16th-century timber roof and windows with interesting features such as the late Gothic interior porch. The hall was partially remodelled in the 17th century by Archbishops Laud and Juxon, who also rebuilt the chapel.

West of the hall are the state apartments, including the first-floor guard room, now the school library. This room is ascribed to Archbishop Arundel (Archbishop 1396-1414), and has an arch-braced roof with carved stone supports and an oriel window. Other rooms have later panelling and fireplaces. The chapel contains fine 17th-century stalls and an elaborate corner gallery (the altar rails are now in the guard room). The exterior of the whole palace is stone or red brick, with early stone windows or Georgian sash windows.

The relationship between Croydon and the Archbishops was of great importance, several of whom were local benefactors. Six are buried in Croydon Minster, neighbouring the Palace: John Whitgift, Edmund Grindal, Gilbert Sheldon, William Wake, John Potter and Thomas Herring.

> Archbishop Whitgift, who first called it a 'palace', liked Croydon for 'the sweetness of the place'. However, not everyone admired Croydon Palace; Henry III found the low-lying site 'rheumatick', a place where he could not stay 'without sickness', while Sir Francis Bacon thought it 'an obscure and darke place' surrounded by its dense woodland.

By the late 18th century, Croydon Palace had become dilapidated and uncomfortable and the local area was squalid. An Act of Parliament enabled it to be sold and Addington Palace (on the outskirts of Croydon) purchased (in 1807), which became the new Episcopal summer residence for much of the rest of the 19th century.

 A rare, surviving 15th-century Archbishop's palace

Address: Thicket Rd, SE20 8DT (20-8778 7148, http://cpdinosaurs.org/ visitthedinosaurs).

Opening hours: Dawn to dusk.

Cost: Free.

Transport: Crystal Palace rail.

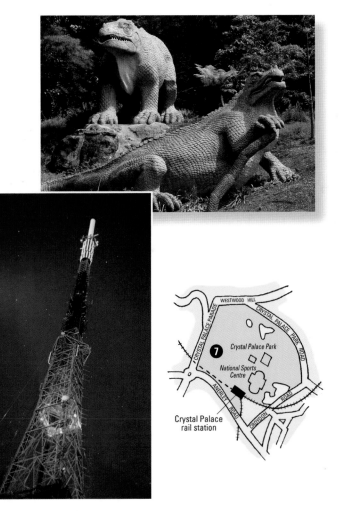

CRYSTAL PALACE PARK & DINOSAURS

Crystal Palace Park is a historic pleasure ground used for a variety of cultural and sporting events. It's run by the borough of Bromley and gets its name from the Crystal Palace, a cast-iron and glass building erected in Hyde Park to house the Great Exhibition of 1851. After the exhibition, the palace was reconstructed in 1854 in a modified and enlarged form in Penge Place estate at Sydenham Hill, which led to the local area being dubbed Crystal Palace – now named Crystal Palace Park. The Palace attracted visitors for over seven decades until being destroyed by fire in 1936 (two Sphinx statues survive).

The grounds that surrounded the Palace were extensively renovated and turned into a public park with ornamental gardens, replicas of statues and two man-made lakes. In 1852, Benjamin Waterhouse Hawkins (1807-1894) was commissioned to build the first ever life-sized models of extinct animals, which he did under the guidance of Sir Richard Owen (1804-1892) – who invented the word 'dinosaur' – a celebrated biologist and palaeontologist.

Unveiled in 1854, they were the first dinosaur sculptures (15 still exist) in the world, pre-dating the publication of Charles Darwin's *On the Origin of Species* by five years.

Their importance lies in being the first attempt to interpret what full-scale prehistoric animals would have looked like, based on the best scientific information available.

As further discoveries of dinosaurs were made, the models' reputation declined, and by 1895 experts looked on them with scorn and ridicule. Nevertheless, the dinosaurs (Grade I listed) continue to capture the imagination of both young and old, and were extensively restored in 2003, when the anatomical errors were retained to maintain authenticity with the Victorian originals.

The park once housed a football ground, which hosted the FA Cup final from 1895 to 1914, as well as staging London County Cricket games from 1900 to 1908 (WG Grace played here). The extensive grounds were also used in pre-war days for motorcycle and, after the '50s, car racing – known as the Crystal Palace circuit – which fell into disuse in 1973. The site is now home to the National Sports Centre, built in 1964, and also contains a boating lake, maze (the Tea Maze is London's largest), museum, pool with flamingos, children's playground, concert area, farm, café and the Crystal Palace TV transmitting station, the third-tallest structure in London (719ft/219m).

❝ *The Jurassic Park of south London* ❞

Address: Gallery Rd, Dulwich, SE21 7AD (020-8693 5254, www. dulwichpicturegallery.org.uk).

Opening hours: Tue-Fri, 10am to 5pm; Sat-Sun, 11am to 5pm; closed Mon except bank holidays. Closed 25-26th Dec and 1st Jan. Free guided tours of the permanent collection on Sat-Sun at 3pm.

Cost: £6 adults, £5 seniors, free for the unemployed, students and children under 18; prices vary for temporary exhibitions.

Transport: W Dulwich or N Dulwich rail.

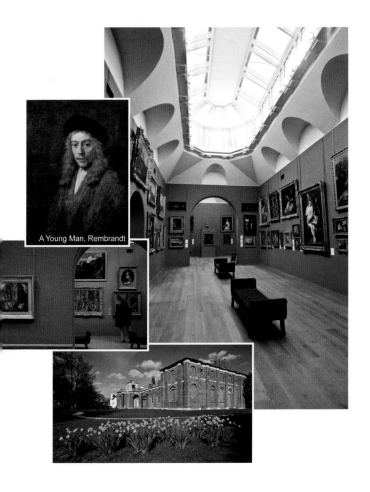

A Young Man, Rembrandt

DULWICH PICTURE GALLERY

The tranquil south London suburb of Dulwich is home to a quietly revolutionary art gallery. Built by Sir John Soane (a noted architect, most famous for designing the Bank of England and for his museum – see page 189) and opened in 1817, the Dulwich Picture Gallery was England's first purpose-built, public art gallery, and has proved highly influential on the way we view art.

The collection itself was mainly bequeathed by successful art dealers Francis Bourgeois and Noel Deschamps. They originally assembled it between 1790 and 1795 for the King of Poland, who intended to establish a national gallery in Warsaw. But when Poland was partitioned the plans were shelved and Bourgeois and Deschamps eventually left the collection to the British public, to be housed in a specially-built gallery. It's thought that Sir John Soane was chosen to design it as he was a friend of Bourgeois.

Soane's design, a series of simple interlinked rooms lit by natural light via overhead skylights, has been a major influence on the design of art galleries ever since. He cleverly designed the skylights to illuminate the paintings indirectly, to avoid damaging them with direct light. As the noted 20th-century architect Philip Johnson said, 'Soane has taught us how to display paintings'.

The building itself is beautiful – the world's most beautiful art gallery, according to some – an elegant study of abstract classicism, made from brick with Portland stone detailing. A modern extension, designed by Rick Mather, was built in 1999. The gallery is surrounded by tranquil gardens, mainly lawns, with a number of unusual trees, some over 200 years old. The gallery has a shop and café, and runs an extensive series of lectures and other educational events.

As for the collection itself, the gallery houses one of the world's most important collections of European old master paintings from the 17th and 18th centuries, including many of the highest quality. It's especially rich in French, Italian and Spanish Baroque paintings, and in British portraits from Tudor times to the 19th century. It includes works by Canaletto, Constable, Gainsborough, Hogarth, Landseer, Murillo, Poussin, Raphael, Rembrandt, Reynolds, Rubens and Van Dyck. You can search and display the works via the website.

The gallery regularly stages temporary exhibitions, which are often significant; these have included Canaletto in England, Paul Nash: The Elements, Norman Rockwell's America, and Twombly and Poussin – Arcadian Painters.

66 *Hidden treasures in south London* **99**

Address: Court Yd, Eltham, Greenwich, SE9 5QE (020-8294 2548), www.english-heritage.org.uk/visit/places/eltham-palace-and-gardens).

Opening hours: From around Apr-Sep (see website for exact dates), Mon-Thu, Sun and bank holidays, 10am to 6pm. Closed Fri-Sat. See website for 'winter' opening times.

Cost: £13 adults, £11.80 concessions, £7.80 children, £33.80 family (2 adults, 3 children).

Transport: Eltham or Mottingham rail.

ELTHAM PALACE

Eltham in suburban southeast London boasts a treat of a building that unexpectedly combines one of England's best Art Deco interiors with one of the few significant English medieval royal palaces with substantial remains – yet many people haven't even heard of Eltham Palace, let alone visited it. They might have seen it on screen, however, as it's a popular location with film and television directors.

Initially a moated manor house set in extensive parkland, the original palace was given to Edward II in 1305 and was a royal residence from the 14th to 16th centuries, including for Henry VIII in his younger days. It was eclipsed by the rebuilding of nearby Greenwich Palace – which was more easily accessible from the Thames – but hunting deer in its enclosed parks remained popular. These parks were almost stripped of trees and deer during the English Civil War (1642-1651), while the palace and its chapel were badly damaged.

The current building dates from the '30s, when Sir Stephen and Lady Courtauld were granted a lease. They restored the Great Hall, which boasts England's third-largest hammer-beam roof, gave it a minstrels' gallery, and transformed it into a sumptuous home with a striking interior in a variety of Art Deco styles. Among many notable features are Lady Courtauld's gold-plated mosaic bathroom and the stunning circular entrance hall, the work of the Swedish designer Rolf Engströmer, boasting an impressive glazed dome that floods it with light, elegant blackbean veneer and lush, figurative parquetry.

The red brick and Bath stone exterior is modelled on Wren's work at Hampton Court Palace, and parts of medieval buildings remain in and around the extensive gardens, as does a 15th-century bridge across the 14th-century moat (planted with lilies). The gardens are an added attraction – and ideal picnic spot – an important example of '30s garden design, and attractively dotted with medieval ruins and features.

The palace has a number of quirks, including three escape tunnels, which emerge in various parts of Eltham, under-floor heating, piped music and a centralised vacuum-cleaning system. As for the Courtaulds, they had a pet lemur (what else?), which apparently had free run of the house, as well as its own upstairs room, with a hatch leading downstairs. The Courtaulds departed in 1944 and the property passed to the Royal Army Educational Corps, who remained there until 1992. Eltham Palace was acquired by English Heritage in 1995, and major repairs and restoration of the interiors and gardens were completed four years later, along with the inevitable café and gift shop.

 Medieval palace meets Art Deco splendour

Address: 12 Crooms Hill, SE10 8ER (020-8305 1441, www. thefanmuseum.org.uk).

Opening hours: Tue-Sat, 11am to 5pm; bank holidays and Sun, noon to 5pm. Closed Mon. See website for exact dates.

Cost: £4 adults, £3 concessions and children (7 to 16), £10 families (2 adults, 2 children), under-7s free. National Trust members half price. Guided tours £5 per person.

Transport: Cutty Sark DLR or Greenwich rail.

FAN MUSEUM

The Fan Museum opened in 1991 and is the only museum in the world devoted entirely to fans and fan-making. It's housed in two Grade II* listed early Georgian houses built in 1721, which have been lovingly restored to retain their original character and elegance. An Orangery, faithful to the architecture of the period, has been added with a spectacular mural, overlooking a Japanese-style garden with a fan-shaped parterre, pond and stream – an oasis of tranquillity.

The stars of the collection are its wealth of rare and beautiful 18th- and 19th-century European fans. Fans from the collection and those on loan from other collections are displayed in changing themed exhibitions, presented in their historical, sociological and economic contexts. Visitors can enjoy the designs of these unique items which have served many purposes over the centuries: cooling and winnowing devices, ceremonial tools, fashionable accessories, status symbols, commemorative presents and advertising giveaways. There's a permanent educational display about fans, including their history, the materials used, the manufacturing process and the different kinds of fan.

> The museum's collection numbers over 4,000 fans, fan leaves and related ephemera, with the oldest fan dating from the 11th century. It's the world's most important collection of fans, with many extremely rare and exquisite examples, and some bizarre ones, such as a fan with a built-in ear trumpet, one that doubles as a bonnet and one with an in-built repair kit.

Few art forms combine functional, ceremonial and decorative uses as elegantly as the fan, and fewer still can match its diversity and history, stretching back to around 3,000BC. There's evidence that the Greeks, Etruscans and Romans all used fans as cooling and ceremonial devices, while Chinese literary sources associate the fan with ancient mythical and historical characters. Early fans were of the fixed type, and the folding fan doesn't appear either in the East or West until relatively late in its history. Today, in Europe, only in Spain is the fan part of everyday life, but it still has a place in many hot countries, particularly in the Far East and especially in Japan.

Fans can be designed and made to order by the museum for functions, presentations and commemorative occasions. The museum also has study and research facilities and a reference library, and holds fan-making workshops on the first Saturday of each month. There's also a conservation unit, gift shop and café in the Orangery (afternoon tea is served from 3pm on Tuesdays and Sundays).

66 *A fan-tastic breath of fresh air* **99**

Address: Royal Arsenal, Woolwich, SE18 6ST (020-8855 7755, www.firepower.org.uk).

Opening hours: Tue-Sat, 10am to 5pm. Also open on bank holidays and daily during local school holidays. Closed Sun-Mon.

Cost: £5.30 adults, £4.60 concessions, £2.50 children (5-15), £12.50 families (maximum 4), under 5s free.

Transport: Woolwich Arsenal DLR or rail.

FIREPOWER: ROYAL ARTILLERY MUSEUM

Firepower is one of the world's oldest military museums and tells the story of the Royal Regiment of Artillery (RA) and of the Royal Arsenal. However, it's much more than simply a regimental museum, as the RA has been involved in most British actions for over 200 years and over two million men and women have served in the regiment since its formation. The museum is located in some of the former buildings of the Royal Arsenal, which was Britain's principal ordnance manufacturing facility from the early 18th century until 1967.

The Royal Arsenal was one of the most important centres in the world for munitions manufacture and until recently was a well kept secret. Many of the guns and carriages on display were made in the Arsenal, making it a significant part of local heritage. Firepower tells the powerful and dramatic story of artillery, scientific discoveries made through warfare, and human stories of courage and endeavour. The 'ground shaking' Field of Fire audio-visual show puts you in the midst of battle, as shells whiz overhead and guns roar. The world class collection of artillery and associated weapons, uniforms, drawings, diaries and medals, bring together some 700 years of world artillery history.

The history of the RA goes back to 1716, when the first two permanent companies of artillery were formed at Woolwich. The use of artillery itself predates Roman times when slings, catapults and ballistas were used to project missiles. Later, longbows propelled arrows both as direct and indirect fire, e.g. to flush out the enemy.

> **The English first used guns in battle alongside longbows at Crécy in 1346. Since then the Army has used them in almost every war and campaign fought throughout the world, although it was almost 400 years before a permanent force of artillery was formed.**

The forerunner of Firepower was the Royal Military Repository, which was established on the Royal Arsenal site in May 1778 by Captain (later Lieutenant General Sir) William Congreve (d 1814). After a fire in 1802, the surviving artefacts were re-housed in the Old Royal Military Academy and in 1820 the main collection was moved to the Rotunda on Woolwich Common. The collection was relocated to Firepower in April 2001 and occupies buildings that were once part of the Royal Laboratory Department, which controlled the manufacture of ammunition.

When you need a break from loud noises, the museum has a tranquil licensed café and a shop.

66 *The guns that built an Empire* **99**

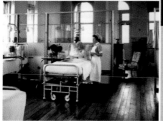

FLORENCE NIGHTINGALE MUSEUM

The Florence Nightingale Museum tells the engrossing story of the life of one of Britain's greatest heroines. From the slate she used as a child and her pet owl (Athena) to the Turkish lantern she used in the Crimean War, the collection spans the life of Florence Nightingale (1820-1910) and her nursing legacy.

> **It was in the Crimea that Florence was dubbed 'The Lady with the Lamp' after her habit of making rounds at night.**

Nightingale was born in Florence (after which she was named) on 12th May 1820, the daughter of wealthy landowner William Nightingale. At 17 she felt called by God to some unnamed great cause and despite her domineering mother's persistent attempts, refused to marry several worthy suitors. At the age of 25, Florence told her parents she wanted to become a nurse, to which they were totally opposed, as nursing was then associated with working class women. However, Florence persisted and in 1851, at the age of 31, her father relented and she travelled to Kaiserwerth (Germany) where she studied to become a nurse at the Institute of Protestant Deaconesses.

Two years later Florence was appointed resident lady superintendent of a hospital for invalid women in Harley Street, W1. The same year the Crimean War began, and there were soon reports describing the desperate lack of proper medical facilities and care for wounded soldiers at the front. In 1854, Florence led a team of 38 nurses who cared for thousands of soldiers during the war and helped save the British army from medical disaster.

She returned to England in 1856 and in 1860 established the Nightingale Training School for nurses at London's St Thomas' Hospital, now part of King's College. Once trained, nurses were sent to hospitals throughout Britain, where they introduced Nightingale's ideas and established nursing training. Her theories, published in *Notes on Nursing* (1860), were hugely influential and her concerns for sanitation, military health and hospital planning established practices which are still in use today.

Florence was also a visionary health reformer, a brilliant campaigner and the second most influential woman in Victorian Britain after Queen Victoria herself. Her ideas completely changed society's approach to nursing and her legacy remains strong to this day. The Nightingale Pledge taken by new nurses was named in her honour, and International Nurses Day is celebrated throughout the world on her birthday (12th May). She died on 13th August 1910, aged 90.

 The woman who 'invented' modern nursing

AT A GLANCE

Address: The George Inn Yard, 77 Borough High St, SE1 1NH (020-7407 2056, www.nationaltrust.org.uk/george-inn).

Opening hours: Daily, 11am to 11pm.

Cost: Free.

Transport: London Bridge tube/rail.

Samuel Johnson

THE GEORGE

Samuel Pepys

THE GEORGE INN

The George Inn is a pub near London Bridge on the south side of the Thames, dating from the late medieval period. It's Grade I listed and is tucked away in a cobbled courtyard just off Borough High Street. The George is one of London's only two surviving coaching inns and is the only one that's galleried. It's owned and leased to the current tenants by the National Trust.

The pub and its surrounds are steeped in history. The first map of Southwark (1543) shows it as the 'Gorge', and previously it was called the George and Dragon. Shakespeare was a visitor – the Globe Theatre was a short distance away – as was Charles Dickens; the pub is mentioned in *Little Dorrit*. Pepys and Johnson would also have drunk here. The George is located next to the White Hart, on a site where the inn was mentioned by Shakespeare in *Henry VI, Part 2* and by Dickens in *The Pickwick Papers*; its other neighbour is the site of the Tabard, an inn established in 1307, where (in 1388) Chaucer began work on *The Canterbury Tales*.

The George was rebuilt in 1676 after a fire that destroyed most of medieval Southwark. Later, the Great Northern Railway used it as a depot and pulled down two of its fronts to build a warehouse. As a result, just the south face remains. It's still a large inn, but much smaller than it was originally, when it was huge; only around a third survives.

Coaching inns were built around a courtyard so that coaches could enter and be unloaded in a sheltered, protected place. The ground floor would have been rooms for eating and drinking, with bedrooms above, entered by external galleries. In its heyday, the George would have received 70 or 80 coaches a week, and it was only one of Southwark's galleried inns, which were the bus and railway termini of their day. The City gates and London Bridge were locked at night, so there was a constant demand for accommodation from those arriving late.

The cosy, historic interior has an authentic atmosphere of yesteryear. The ground floor is divided into a series of bars. The Old Bar used to be a waiting room for coach passengers, while the Middle Bar was a coffee room (patronised by Dickens). The bedrooms were upstairs, in the galleried part of the building, which is now a restaurant. In summer, performances of Shakespeare's plays are staged in the inn yard.

66 *The local of Shakespeare and Dickens* 99

Address: Luxted Rd, Downe, BR6 7JT (01689-859119 or 0870-333 1181, www.english-heritage.org.uk/daysout/properties/home-of-charles-darwin-down-house).

Opening hours: Winter/spring (Nov-Mar), weekends, 10am to 4pm, Summer/autumn (Apr-Oct), open daily, including bank holidays (see website for times).

Cost: £10.60 adults, £9.50 concessions, £6.30 children, £27.50 families. English Heritage members free.

Transport: Bromley S rail and 146 bus.

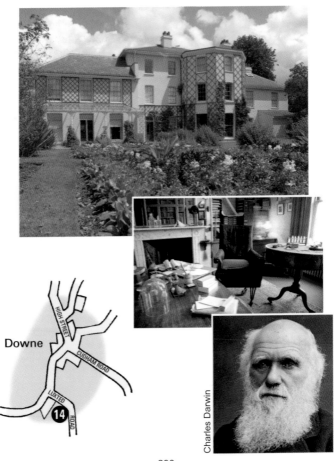

Charles Darwin

HOME OF CHARLES DARWIN (DOWN HOUSE)

Down House and its 18-acre (7.2ha) estate was the home of the renowned English naturalist Charles Darwin (1809-1882) and his family, from 1842 until his death 40 years later. Its history can be traced to 1651, when Thomas Manning sold a parcel of land to John Know the elder (for £345), who built the first house. The house passed through several hands and was rebuilt and enlarged in the 18th century by George Butler, a businessman and landowner, when it was called the Great House. In 1837, it was renovated under the supervision of Edward Cresy, a local architect, until being purchased by Charles Darwin in 1842 for £2,200.

When he moved to Down House with his young family, it was a plain and sturdy 18th-century block. Darwin made extensive alterations to the house and grounds, particularly during the first five years he lived there, extending and enlarging it with a new service wing. Darwin's wife, Emma, bore him ten children, of whom three died young, but the surviving five boys and two girls flourished at Down.

Situated in rural Kent (now the London borough of Bromley), the house offered the peace and privacy that Darwin needed to work on his revolutionary scientific theories. It was at Down (and its 'open-air laboratory') that he developed his landmark views on evolution by natural selection and wrote his groundbreaking work, *On the Origin of Species* (1859) – a book that shook the Victorian world and has influenced scientific thinking ever since.

After the death of Emma in 1896, the house was let on a series of short-term tenancies, except for the

> **The house and grounds were extensively restored by English Heritage to their 'original' state during Darwin's time and opened to the public in 1998.**

period 1907-1921 when it was a girls' school. It then languished empty for a number of years, until Sir Arthur Keith (1866-1955), curator of the Hunterian Museum (see page 169), encouraged the British Association for the Advancement of Science (BAAS) to preserve it as a national memorial to Darwin. Down House was maintained as a museum by the BAAS for 60 years, until in 1996 the house and its contents were purchased by English Heritage (ER) with support from the Wellcome Trust and Heritage Lottery Fund.

Today you can see Darwin's famous study and stroll through the extensive gardens that inspired the great scientist. A fascinating day out for all the family.

66 *Where Darwin's genius evolved*

Address: 100 London Rd, Forest Hill, SE23 3PQ (020-8699 1872, www.horniman.ac.uk).

Opening hours: Daily, 10.30am to 5.30pm, closed 24-26th Dec.
Gardens: Mon-Sat. 7.15am to sunset; Sun and bank holidays 8am to sunset; closed 25th Dec.

Cost: Free entry to museum and garden. Aquarium: £3.50 adults, £1.50 children (3-16), £7.50 families (2 adults, 3 children).

Transport: Forest Hill rail.

HORNIMAN MUSEUM

It's well worth journeying out to the southern suburbs to see this interesting and varied collection. It opened in 1901 in a lovely Arts and Crafts and Art Nouveau-style building designed by Charles Harrison Townsend, who was also responsible for the striking Whitechapel Art Gallery (see page 141). The museum was founded by the Victorian tea trader Frederick John Horniman to house his superb collection of cultural artefacts, ethnography, natural history and musical instruments, some collected personally on his travels (although he didn't leave Britain until he was 60), but most accumulated by his tea merchants.

The collection runs to 350,000 objects in total (over the past century, the museum has added significantly to the original bequest). The Horniman's exhibits aren't dusty or static, and the collection is constantly being extended, researched and brought into public view. The ethnography and music collections have designated status; i.e. are considered of great importance. The ethnography collection is the third most significant in the UK after the British Museum and the Pitt-Rivers Museum (Oxford). The earliest musical instrument dates from 1500BC (a pair of bone clappers in the form of human hands, made in Egypt).

The museum is noted for its large collection of stuffed animals and has one of London's oldest aquariums, noted for its unique design (there's a new, modern aquarium in the basement). There are also some interesting archaeological exhibits, from Africa, America, Asia, Europe and the Pacific, including much British prehistoric material, some of it from significant sites, e.g. Grimes Graves and Swanscombe. The detailed website contains comprehensive information about the various collections.

The Horniman is set in 16 acres of award-winning, beautifully maintained gardens, which include a Grade II listed conservatory, bandstand, animal enclosure, nature trail and an ornamental garden. A 20ft (6.1m) totem pole (dating from 1985) sits outside the museum's main entrance, and is one of the UK's few totem poles. There's also a grass-roofed 'Centre for Understanding the Environment' building, constructed from sustainable materials.

After visiting the museum, it's worth taking a stroll to Ringmore Rise, a road behind the museum, from where you can enjoy wonderful panoramic views of central London.

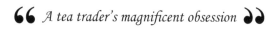

66 *A tea trader's magnificent obsession* **99**

Address: 62-66 Bermondsey St, SE1 3UD (020-7403 2800, www. londonglassblowing.co.uk).

Opening hours: Mon-Sat, 10am to 6pm. Classes (full day, Sat and Sun) are also offered (see website for information).

Cost: Free.

Transport: Borough or London Br tube.

Peter Layton

LONDON GLASSBLOWING STUDIO & GALLERY

The London Glassblowing Studio & Gallery was established by Peter Layton in 1976 in an old factory on the Thames at Rotherhithe, and was among the first hot-glass studios in Europe. Now situated (since 2009) on vibrant Bermondsey Street, opposite the Fashion and Textile Museum, the gallery offers a light, spacious area for the display of contemporary glass.

Peter Layton is one of the world's most famous and respected glassblowers who has done much to promote glassmaking as an art form. He has influenced and nurtured several of the UK's leading glassmakers and inspired many more internationally. Now in his late 70s (b 1937), Layton remains active and is regarded as the 'grand old man of glass'. Some glassmakers create technically brilliant pieces and follow a precise pattern, while others prefer to create more abstract works that are looser and evolve during the creative process. Layton's work falls firmly into the latter category – he's noted for his strong use of colour, organic forms and the sculptural quality of his larger pieces.

London Glassblowing is one of Europe's leading glassmaking workshops, renowned for its particular flair in the use of colour, form and texture. Layton operates his studio like a collective, where glassblowers are free to use the kilns to create their own work and develop their skills, as well as work on pieces that help to pay the vast energy bills. He has always put creativity before commercial needs, which is why his Gallery is an Aladdin's cave of unique and surprisingly affordable works of glass art, each signed by the artist. Much of the richly coloured glass art on sale is Layton's own work, which can also be found in museums, galleries and exhibitions across the UK, Europe and the US. The Studio also accepts commissions.

London Glassblowing offers one-day introductory classes in glassblowing under the guidance of a qualified glassmaker, designed to teach the basic techniques. The emphasis is on providing a hands-on experience and includes gathering the molten glass, blowing, shaping and forming.

Visitors experience the heat and magic of an ancient craft, while watching molten glass evolve into something of beauty and value. The Studio has a schedule of exhibitions throughout the year (see website for information).

❝ *The magical world of glassblowing* **❞**

Address: Linden Grove, SE15 3LP (020-7525 2000, www.southwark.gov.uk/info/461/a_to_z_of_parks/660/nunhead_cemetery and www.fonc.org.uk).

Opening hours: Apr-Sep, daily 8.30am to 7pm; Oct, daily 8.30am to 5pm; Nov-Feb, daily 8.30am to 4pm; Mar, daily 8.30am to 5pm (see website for exact dates). The Friends of Nunhead Cemetery (see website) organise tours (1½ to 2 hrs) on the last Sun of each month (2.15pm from the Linden Grove gates).

Cost: Free.

Transport: Nunhead rail.

NUNHEAD CEMETERY

Consecrated in 1840, Nunhead Cemetery is one of the 'magnificent seven' Victorian cemeteries built in a ring around London's outskirts. According to the Friends of Nunhead Cemetery it's 'perhaps the least known but most attractive of the great Victorian cemeteries of London'. Southwark Council regards it as 'one of Southwark's hidden treasures'.

The cemeteries were built in response to a massive surge in London's population in the first half of the 19th century, when it more than doubled, from 1m to 2.3m. The city's small parish churchyards quickly became dangerously overcrowded, with grim consequences: decaying corpses got into the water supply, causing a number of epidemics. As a result, seven large cemeteries were built between 1832 and 1841, the other six being Abney Park (see page 147), Brompton, Highgate, Kensal Green (see page 207), Tower Hamlets (see page 135) and West Norwood.

The new cemeteries appealed to the growing middle class, which was eager to distance itself from the working class and to demonstrate its status. Graves were regarded as a visible part of a family's property. Nunhead is the second-largest of the seven, covering 52 acres, with monumental entrance and lodges designed by James Bunstone Bunning.

Much of it's crumbling and wild – locals call it a nature reserve or wilderness – and it's certainly a tranquil place for a walk. Recent funding from the Heritage Lottery Fund and from Southwark Council is helping with its restoration, as are the efforts of the Friends of Nunhead Cemetery, but many people see Nunhead's wilderness element as fundamental to its appeal. Weathered gravestones and tumbling statuary peer through extravagant under- and overgrowth and weed-choked paths, and the cemetery is full of interesting contrasts, e.g. between some magnificent monuments in memory of the era's most prominent citizens and the modest, small headstones erected for common people, and between the formal, elegant avenue of tall lime trees and the many smaller pathways, some of which resemble country lanes.

The cemetery has also become an important haven for flora and fauna, and offers some great views over London. At its highest point it's around 200ft (60m) above sea level and commands vistas stretching from the towers of Canary Wharf westwards as far as the London Eye near the Houses of Parliament.

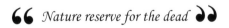

66 *Nature reserve for the dead* **99**

Address: Barge House St, SE1 9PH (www.coinstreet.org; Oxo Tower restaurant, www.harveynichols.com/oxo-tower-london).

Opening hours: Unrestricted access.

Cost: Free.

Transport: Southwark or Waterloo tube.

OXO TOWER & WHARF

The OXO Tower is a building (with a prominent tower) in Southwark on the south bank of the Thames. Originally constructed at the end of the 19th century as a power station for the Post Office, it was subsequently acquired by the Liebig Extract of Meat Company, manufacturers of OXO beef stock cubes, for conversion into a cold store. It was largely rebuilt to an Art Deco design by company architect Albert Moore between 1928 and 1929, and much of the original power station was demolished. Liebig wanted to include a tower featuring illuminated signs advertising the OXO name; when permission was refused the tower was built with four sets of three vertically-aligned windows, each of which was 'coincidentally' in the shapes of a circle, a cross and a circle spelling OXO!

By the '70s the building had fallen into disrepair and was largely derelict, and there were several proposals to demolish and develop it and the adjacent Coin Street site, which were met with strong local opposition. Permission for redevelopment was eventually granted, but the tower and 13-acre (5.3ha) site were purchased by the Greater London Council in1984 for £2.7m, who then sold it to the non-profit Coin Street Community Builders (CSCB) for just £750,000. In the '90s, the tower was refurbished to a award-winning design by Lifschutz Davidson as a mixed use development.

On its rooftop is the OXO Tower restaurant, bar and brasserie (operated by Harvey Nichols) and a free public viewing gallery (open daily). The residential area below consists of 78 flats on five floors for the Redwood Housing Co-operative. The ground, first and second floors are home to over 30 retail design studios, as well as specialist shops and the gallery@oxo, with a changing programme of exhibitions. A unique feature of the Wharf is its concentration of retail studios for contemporary designers, where you can watch artisans at work and buy a wide variety of original products including fashion, fine art, furniture, textiles, jewellery, ceramics and glass.

OXO Tower Wharf is situated on the riverside walkway, part of the Thames Path, a continuous riverside walk that passes in front of and below the building, and links it with other riverside attractions such as the Festival Hall, the National Theatre, the Tate Modern and the Globe Theatre.

The tower itself is a splendid sight – particularly at night when the OXO letters are lit up in red as a tribute to its creators – while the wharf is a shining example of what can be achieved with a derelict site.

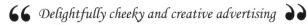 **66** *Delightfully cheeky and creative advertising* **99**

Address: Chesterfield Walk, Blackheath, SE10 8QX (0370-333 1181, www.english-heritage.org.uk/daysout/properties/rangers-house-the-wernher-collection).

Opening hours: Mar-Sep (see website for exact dates). Tours (1½hrs), Sun-Wed, 11am and 2pm. Booking recommended, particularly on Sundays. Closed Oct-Feb.

Cost: £7.20 adults, £6.50 concessions, £4.30 children (5-15), family £18.70. English heritage members free.

Transport: Blackheath rail.

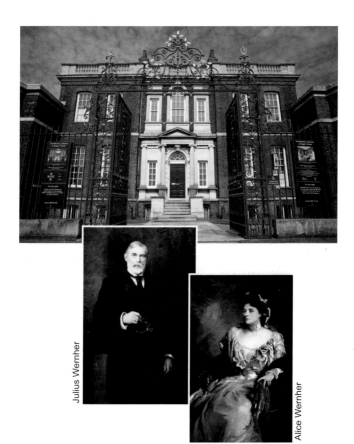

Julius Wernher

Alice Wernher

THE RANGER'S HOUSE & WERNHER COLLECTION

The Ranger's House is an elegant, medium-sized, red brick Georgian villa built in the Palladian style, adjacent to Greenwich Park. The house dates from the early 1700s, a graceful building with panelled interiors, now managed by English Heritage. It was first used as the official residence of the Ranger of Greenwich Park in 1816, when it was called Chesterfield House.

The building alone is worth visiting, but all the more so because since 2002 it has housed the Wernher Collection of works of art (jewels, paintings, porcelain, silver and more), collected in the late 19th and early 20th centuries by German-born railway engineer's son Sir Julius Wernher (1850-1912). He made his fortune mining diamonds in South Africa – the company he formed was later amalgamated with De Beers, and he left over £11m when he died – and had a lifelong passion for collecting.

It's an unusual collection, of international importance, one of the best private collections of art assembled by one person, including some of Europe's most spectacular jewellery. This makes it all the more surprising that it has such a low profile; in fact, few people seem to have heard of it.

Nearly 700 works of art are on display, spread over 12 rooms, including early religious paintings, Dutch Old Masters, tiny carved Gothic ivories, fine renaissance bronzes and silver treasures. They demonstrate the many skills of medieval craftsmen and the quality of renaissance decorative arts. There are paintings by Francesco Francia, John Hoppner, Filippino Lippi, Hans Memling, Gabriel Metsu, George Romney, Sir Joshua Reynolds and others. The largest part of the collection is a varied mix of decorative art, including renaissance jewellery, medieval art, Byzantine and renaissance ivories, tapestries, furniture, Sevres porcelain, woodcarving and statues.

Wernher lived at Bath House in Piccadilly, London (and Luton Hoo in Bedfordshire), and some of the rooms at the Ranger's House have been decorated and arranged in such a way as to reflect how the collection would have originally been displayed when it was at Bath House. It's a notably varied collection (for which the word – now a cliché – 'eclectic' seems to have been invented), with something to interest and delight most visitors.

❝ *An eclectic treasure trove in a Georgian setting* **❞**

Address: Red House Ln, Bexleyheath, Bexley DA6 8JF (020-8304 9878, www.nationaltrust.org.uk/red-house and www.friends-red-house.co.uk).

Opening hours: From around 20th Feb to 31st Oct, Wed-Sun and some Mon, 11am-5pm; 1st Nov to 22nd Dec (approximately), Fri-Sun, 11am-4.30pm. Closed most Mon, every Tue and for the whole of Jan. See website for exact dates and times. Admission by guided tour (booking recommended) only, except for 1.30pm.

Cost: £8 (incl. gift aid) adults, £4 children, £20 family. National Trust members free.

Transport: Bexleyheath rail.

Bexleyheath
rail station

CROOK LOG BROADWAY
ALBION RD
20
A2 EAST ROCHESTER WAY

William Morris

THE RED HOUSE

You sometimes have to travel for your pleasures, and that's the case, here. This important architectural gem and shrine for William Morris followers is situated in the borough of Bexley. It's bland commuterland, beyond the reach of London Underground (like much of southeast London), and is a 35-minute train ride from Charing Cross, plus a 15-minute stroll from Bexleyheath railway station. But the journey is surely worthwhile to see a building described by the Pre-Raphaelite painter Dante Gabriel Rossetti as 'more a poem than a house' and by the designer and artist Edward Burne-Jones as 'the beautifullest place on earth'.

It was designed by the architect Philip Webb and William Morris, founder of the Arts and Crafts movement, an international design movement inspired by the writings of the critic John Ruskin, which was influential in the late 19th and early 20th centuries. Morris and his family lived in the Red House for five years from 1860, only giving it up for financial reasons (he never returned).

The building is a significant landmark in English domestic architecture, and became a base for artists and craftsmen, being designed as both a home and an artists' workshop. It's regarded as an embodiment of the aesthetic principles that Morris upheld, and is a clever blend of the practical and the romantic, with Gothic and medieval influences.

The Red House is a large, elegant building, made of warm, red bricks and with substantial chimneys, a tall, steep tiled roof, diverse window styles and a beautiful stairway, making it striking both externally and internally. It retains plenty of Arts and Crafts features – original and restored – including furniture designed by William Morris and Philip Webb, and stained glass and paintings by Edward Burne-Jones (which might, perhaps, lead to accusations of bias regarding the earlier quotation).

The garden is also significant, intended to work in harmony with the building, or 'to clothe the house'. It was one of the first gardens to be designed as a series of rooms – extensions of the house – which were originally a herb garden, a vegetable garden, and two gardens of traditional British flowers and fruit trees.

The Red House is Grade I listed and was a private home until 2003, when it was acquired by the National Trust and subsequently opened to the public. Almost inevitably, it has a tea-room and gift shop.

66 *A William Morris masterpiece* **99**

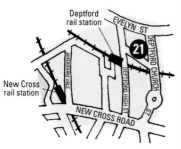

ST PAUL'S, DEPTFORD

St Paul's, Deptford (Grade I listed) is an exuberant 18th-century church and one of London's finest Baroque parish churches, designed by Thomas Archer (1668-1743) – the architect of St John's Smith Square – and built between 1712 and 1730. It was one of 50 churches that were planned by the New Church Commissioners, though only 12 were actually constructed. A pupil of Sir John Vanbrugh, Archer adopted a robust classical style inspired by Baroque churches in Rome. The plan form, in the shape of a Greek cross, is based on an ideal church plan prepared by Vanbrugh.

> Architectural expert Nikolaus Pevsner said that St Paul's 'came closer to Borromini and the Roman Baroque than any other English church of this date', an opinion echoed by Simon Jenkins (*England's Thousand Best Churches*) when he said, 'it's the kind of building foreigners can never credit to the English'.

The church is built of Portland stone and is almost square, raised on a crypt that is mostly above ground, thus requiring a flight of stairs to enter. The most unusual feature of the building is the circular tower with a steeple, around which is wrapped a semi-circular portico (believed to be copied from St Maria della Pace in Rome) of four giant Tuscan columns. The body of the church is roughly square in plan, with two additional side entrances in the middle of the walls, each approached by a grand staircase. The east wall has a projecting apse.

The interior is spectacular and theatrical, with two side aisles each separated by two giant Corinthian columns, which continue as attached columns on the other walls. There are side galleries supported by the giant columns, with an organ gallery above the entrance. The east window is in the form of a Venetian window following the curve of the apse, the latter being divided by small Tuscan columns. Four private pews, like Royal boxes, protrude from each corner on columns.

By the early '90s, the church and churchyard had fallen into disrepair and the north and south staircases to the podium were partially buried. In 1997, the Heritage Lottery Fund awarded the largest grant ever given to a parish church (just over £3m), which enabled the church to be restored. It was re-dedicated in a special service led by the Bishop of London on 1st October 2004.

❝ *An unexpected pearl in the heart of Deptford* **❞**

Address: 65 Peckham Rd, SE5 8UH (020-7703 6120, www.southlondongallery.org).

Opening hours: Tue-Sun, 11am to 6pm (Wed and the last Fri of the month until 9pm). Closed Mon.

Cost: Free.

Transport: Oval or Victoria tube, then 36 or 436 bus. Alight at Peckham Road/Southampton Way.

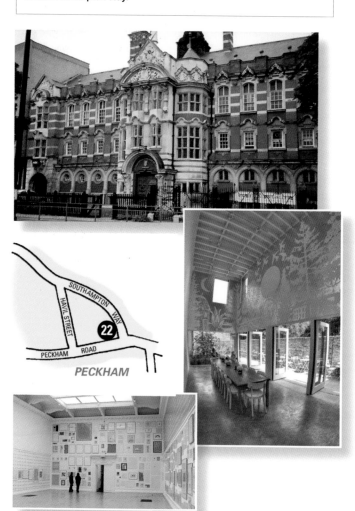

PECKHAM

SOUTH LONDON GALLERY

The South London Gallery (or SLG, as it's widely known) is a publicly-funded gallery of contemporary art in Camberwell. It was founded in 1891, when it was called the South London Fine Art Gallery. But the gallery's origins go back to the South London Working Men's College in Blackfriars Road in 1868, whose principal was the biologist Thomas Henry Huxley (1825-1895), the grandfather of *Brave New World* author Aldous Huxley. Leading artists such as Sir Frederic Leighton (President of the Royal Academy), Edward Burne-Jones and G. F. Watts supported the fledgling gallery, and Prime Minister William Ewart Gladstone was its first president, succeeded by Leighton in 1887.

During its formative years it moved to the site of a free library and continued to occupy various South London locations until moving to its current, purpose-built home constructed of Portland stone and hand-made pressed bricks, much favoured by the Arts and Crafts tradition of the time. The original marquetry floor (not on public display) was designed by Walter Crane and bears the inscription 'The source of art is in the life of a people.' In 1893, a lecture hall and library were added, funded by newspaper owner John Passmore Edwards (1823-1911) and officially opened by the Prince of Wales, but these were demolished after being badly damaged in WWII.

The gallery staged a changing programme of fine and applied arts' exhibitions and began to form a collection from works donated by artists and subscribers. It has grown over the gallery's lifetime and now includes works by modern British artists, a collection of over five hundred 20th-century prints and contemporary works relating to South London. Although the collection isn't on permanent display, it's a valuable resource for school projects, giving students hands-on experience of contemporary works of art.

The gallery's profile and visitor numbers have grown in recent decades as it began to stage exhibitions by internationally acclaimed artists such as Gilbert & George, Anselm Kiefer and Sherrie Levine, as well as younger artists such as Tracey Emin, Gavin Turk and Ann Sofi-Sidén. In 2010, the gallery opened additional buildings designed by 6a Architects to provide new small-scale galleries, an artists' flat, an excellent café, gardens, and an education and events studio on the footprint of the original lecture hall. The Matsudaira Wing, Clore Studio and Fox Garden opened to the public in 2010.

Today, the SLG has an international reputation for its programme of contemporary art exhibitions and live art events, with education projects for children, young people and adults.

 One of London's most elegant art spaces

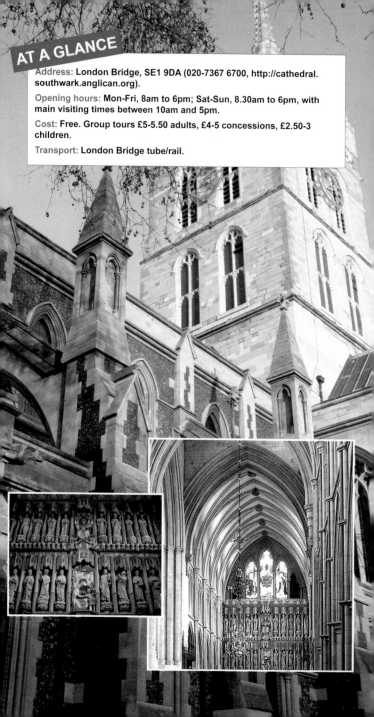

Address: London Bridge, SE1 9DA (020-7367 6700, http://cathedral.southwark.anglican.org).

Opening hours: Mon-Fri, 8am to 6pm; Sat-Sun, 8.30am to 6pm, with main visiting times between 10am and 5pm.

Cost: Free. Group tours £5-5.50 adults, £4-5 concessions, £2.50-3 children.

Transport: London Bridge tube/rail.

SOUTHWARK CATHEDRAL

Often unjustly overlooked in a much-visited part of London (the buzzy south bank of the Thames, near London Bridge and Borough Market), Southwark Cathedral is beautiful and historic. It has been a place of worship for over 1,000 years and is the mother church of the Anglican diocese of Southwark, but it has only been designated a cathedral since 1905.

The cathedral is strategically sited at the oldest crossing point of the tidal Thames, and has long been a place, not just of worship, but of hospitality and refuge. It continues to be a form of sanctuary in this secular age; its churchyard is a tranquil haven at the heart of London and a favourite lunch spot for visitors and the area's office workers.

There are claims that a convent was founded on the site in 606 and a monastery by St Swithun in the 9th century (but there's no proof of either), stories which were handed down by word of mouth and reported by the Elizabethan historian John Stow. Archaeological evidence, however, shows that the site was in use, long before any Christian building, by the Romans (who often built on top of earlier settlements, so its use is probably much older). Indeed, the cathedral's website refers – slightly disapprovingly? – to 'Roman pagan worship'. Despite this, parts of the old Roman paving can still be seen, having been incorporated into the floors of the north and south choir aisles.

The site's first official mention is in the *Domesday Book* of 1086, as the 'minster' of Southwark, but it's unlikely that this minster pre-dates the conversion of Wessex in the mid-7th century. The current building is mainly Gothic, dating from 1220 to 1420, making it London's first Gothic church. A Norman arch from the 12th century survives in the north aisle of the nave.

It isn't just the building that's beautiful and historic: the cathedral is also rich in internal interest, including an oak effigy of a knight dating from around 1275, and there's an 'archaeological chamber' within the cathedral which provides glimpses of the site's history, including a view of the gravelled surface of a Roman road that once ran through the area and of Saxon foundations of the early church.

The cathedral is a popular venue for concerts and recitals – check the website for the programme of events.

66 *London's first Gothic church* **99**

AT A GLANCE

Address: Geraldine Mary Harmsworth Park, St George's Rd, SE1 6ER
(www.tibet-foundation.org/page/peace_garden).

Opening hours: Summer, 8am to 9.30pm; winter, 8am to 4.30pm.

Cost: Free.

Transport: Lambeth N or Elephant & Castle tube.

THE TIBETAN PEACE GARDEN OPENED BY HIS HOLINESS THE DALAI LAMA 13 MAY 1999

Dalai Lama

TIBETAN PEACE GARDEN

The Tibetan Peace Garden – full name 'Tibetan Garden of Contemplation and Peace' or *Samten Kyil* – is a beautiful, tranquil garden situated in Geraldine Mary Harmsworth Park in Southwark. Hamish Horsley was the designer and sculptor of the Peace Garden, ably assisted by a team of skilled professionals. The Garden is a simple, poignant plea for peace, incongruously sited in the shadow of the Imperial War Museum – which very effectively records the history of modern warfare. The Garden was commissioned by the Tibet Foundation and opened and consecrated in 1999 by His Holiness the Dalai Lama; it honours one of his principal teachings: the need to create understanding between different cultures and to establish places of peace and harmony in the world.

The Garden also serves to create a greater awareness of Buddhist culture. At its heart is the Kalachakra Mandala, a symbol associated with world peace; here for the first time cast in bronze, it forms the central focus of the garden. Contemporary western sculptures – set on the north, south, east and west axis – represent the four elements of air, fire, earth and water (the open arena represents the fifth element, space). Around the Mandala are eight meditation seats representing the noble eightfold path: right view, thought, speech, action, livelihood, effort, mindfulness and concentration.

Near the Garden's entrance is the Language Pillar, containing a peace message for the new Millennium – in Tibetan, English, Chinese and Hindi – from His Holiness the Dalai Lama. The pillar

> **The Garden stands as a monument to the courage of the Tibetan people and their patient commitment to the path of non-violence and peace. It also reminds us that Tibet's culture is a treasure of our common heritage and how vital it is that it be kept alive.**

design is based on the Sho Pillar, a 9th-century treaty stone in Lhasa acknowledging the rights of both Tibet and China to coexist in peace. The three carved steps at the top of the pillar represent peace, understanding and love.

The inner gardens are planted with herbs and plants from Tibet and the Himalayan region, while the pergola is covered with climbing plants, including jasmine, honeysuckle and scented roses. The surrounding area is landscaped and planted with trees in a collaboration between the borough of Southwark and the local community.

A spiritual, uplifting garden where visitors can enjoy a few moments of peace and reflection.

❝ *A symbol of peace in a troubled world* ❞

London Sketchbook

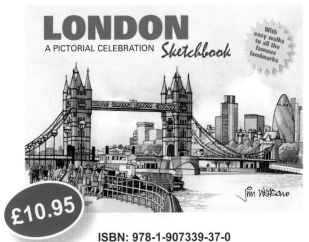

£10.95

ISBN: 978-1-907339-37-0

Jim Watson

A celebration of one of the world's great cities, London Sketchbook is a hardback packed with over 200 evocative watercolour illustrations of the author's favourite landmarks and sights. The illustrations are accompanied by historical footnotes, maps, walks, quirky facts and a gazetteer.

Also in this series:

Cornwall Sketchbook (ISBN: 9781909282780, £10.95)
Cotswold Sketchbook (ISBN: 9781907339108, £9.95)
Devon Sketchbook (ISBN: 9781909282704, £10.95)
Lake District Sketchbook (ISBN: 9781909282605, £10.95)
Yorkshire Sketchbook (ISBN: 9781909282773, £10.95)

see www.survivalbooks.net

INDEX

Living and Working in London

ISBN: 978-1-907339-50-9

6th edition, 336 pages

David Hampshire & Graeme Chesters

Living and Working in London, first published in 2000 and now in its 6th edition, is the most comprehensive book available about daily life – and essential reading for newcomers. What's it really like Living and Working in London? Not surprisingly there's a lot more to life than bobbies, beefeaters and busbys! This book is guaranteed to hasten your introduction to the London way of life, irrespective of whether you're planning to stay for a few months or indefinitely. Adjusting to day to day life in London just got a whole lot simpler!

£14.95

Where to Live in London

£15.95

ISBN: 978-1-907339-13-4, 464 pages

David Hampshire & Graeme Chesters

Essential reading for newcomers planning to live in London, containing detailed surveys of all 33 boroughs including property prices and rental costs, schools, health services, shopping, social services, crime rates, public transport, parking, leisure facilities, local taxes, places of worship and much more. Interest in living in London and investing in property in London has never been higher, both from Britons and foreigners.

see www.londons-secrets.com

London's Secrets

LONDON'S HIDDEN SECRETS VOL 2

ISBN: 978-1-907339-79-0

£10.95, 320 pages, colour

Graeme Chesters & David Hampshire

Hot on the heels of London's Hidden Secrets comes another volume of the city's largely undiscovered sights, many of which we were unable to include in the original book. In fact, the more research we did the more treasures we found, until eventually a second volume was inevitable.

Written by two experienced London writers, LHS 2 is for both those who already know the metropolis and newcomers wishing to learn more about its hidden and unusual charms.

LONDON'S SECRET WALKS

ISBN: 978-1-907339-51-6

£11.95, 320 pages, colour

Graeme Chesters

London is a great city for walking – whether for pleasure, exercise or simply to get from A to B. Despite the city's extensive public transport system, walking is also often the quickest and most enjoyable way to get around – at least in the centre – and it's also free and healthy!

Many attractions are off the beaten track, away from the major thoroughfares and public transport hubs. This favours walking as the best way to explore them, as does the fact that London is a visually interesting city with a wealth of stimulating sights in every 'nook and cranny'.

LONDON'S SECRET PLACES

ISBN: 978-1-907339-92-9

£10.95, 320 pages, colour

Graeme Chesters & David Hampshire

London is one of the world's leading tourist destinations with a wealth of world-class attractions: amazing museums and galleries, beautiful parks and gardens, stunning palaces and grand houses, and much, much more. These are covered in numerous excellent tourist guides and online, and need no introduction here. Not so well known are London's numerous smaller attractions, most of which are neglected by the throngs who descend upon the tourist-clogged major sights. What London's Secret Places does is seek out the city's lesser-known, but no less worthy, 'hidden' attractions.

also available as eBooks

LONDON'S SECRETS: MUSEUMS & GALLERIES

ISBN: 978-1-907339-96-7

£10.95, 320 pages, colour

Robbi Atilgan & David Hampshire

London is a treasure trove for museum fans and art lovers and one of the world's great art and cultural centres, with more popular museums and galleries than any other world city. The art scene is a lot like the city itself – diverse, vast, vibrant and in a constant state of flux – a cornucopia of traditional and cutting-edge, majestic and mundane, world-class and run-of-the-mill, bizarre and brilliant.

So, whether you're an art lover, culture vulture, history buff or just looking for something to entertain the family during the school holidays, you're bound to find inspiration in London. All you need is a comfortable pair of shoes, an open mind – and this book!

LONDON'S SECRETS: PUBS & BARS

ISBN: 978-1-907339-93-6

£10.95, 320 pages, colour

Graeme Chesters

British pubs and bars are world famous for their bonhomie, great atmosphere, good food and fine ales. Nowhere is this more so than in London, which has a plethora of watering holes of all shapes and sizes: classic historic boozers and trendy style bars; traditional riverside inns and luxurious cocktail bars; enticing wine bars and brew pubs; mouth-watering gastro pubs and brasseries; welcoming gay bars and raucous music venues. This book highlights over 250 of the best.

LONDON'S SECRETS: PARKS & GARDENS

ISBN: 978-1-907339-95-0

£10.95, 320 pages, colour

Robbi Atilgan & David Hampshire

London is one the world's greenest capital cities, with a wealth of places where you can relax and recharge your batteries. Britain is renowned for its parks and gardens, and nowhere has such beautiful and varied green spaces as London: magnificent royal parks, historic garden cemeteries, majestic ancient forests and woodlands, breathtaking formal country parks, expansive commons, charming small gardens, beautiful garden squares and enchanting 'secret' gardens. Not all are secrets, of course, but many of London's most beguiling green spaces are known only to insiders and locals.

see www.londons-secrets.com

A Year in London:
Two Things to Do Every Day of the Year

ISBN: 978-1-908282-69-1, 256 pages

David Hampshire

London offers a wealth of things to do, from exuberant festivals and exciting sports events to a plethora of fascinating museums and stunning galleries, from luxury and oddball shops to first-class restaurants and historic pubs, beautiful parks and gardens to pulsating nightlife and clubs. Whatever your interests and tastes, you'll find an abundance of things to enjoy – with a copy of this book you'll never be at a loss for something to do in one of the world's greatest cities.

£11.95

London's Secrets: Bizarre & Curious

ISBN: 978-1-908282-58-2, 320 pages

Graeme Chesters

London is a city with 2,000 years of history, over which it has accumulated a wealth of odd and strange buildings, monuments, statues, street trivia and museum exhibits, to name just a few examples. This book seeks out the city's most bizarre and curious sights and tells the often fascinating story behind them, from the Highgate vampire to the arrest of a dead man, a legal brothel and a former Texas embassy to Roman bikini bottoms and poetic manhole covers, from London's hanging gardens to a restaurant where you dine in the dark. This book is guaranteed to keep you amused and fascinated for hours.

£11.95

see www.londons-secrets.com

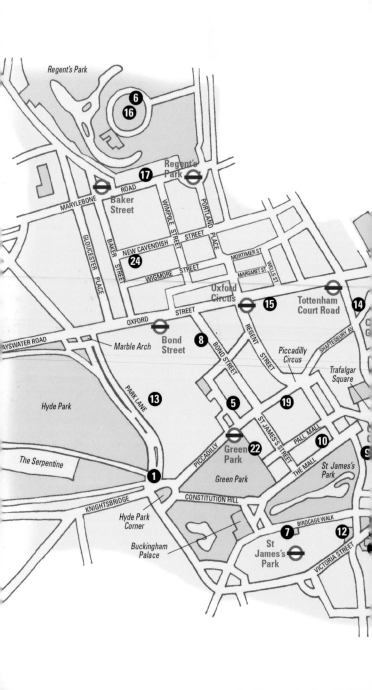